Writing and the Revolution
Venezuelan Metafiction
2004–2012

Liverpool Latin American Studies

Series Editor: Matthew Brown, University of Bristol
Emeritus Series Editor: Professor John Fisher

2 Habsburg Peru: Images, Imagination and Memory
  Peter T. Bradley and David Cahill

3 Knowledge and Learning in the Andes: Ethnographic Perspectives
  Henry Stobart and Rosaleen Howard (eds)

4 Bourbon Peru, 1750–1824
  John Fisher

5 Between Resistance and Adaptation: Indigenous Peoples and the Colonisation of the Chocó, 1510–1753
  Caroline A. Williams

6 Shining Path: Guerilla War in Peru's Northern Highlands, 1980–1997
  Lewis Taylor

7 South American Independence: Gender, Politics, Text
  Catherine Davies, Claire Brewster and Hilary Owen

8 Adventuring Through Spanish Colonies: Simón Bolívar, Foreign Mercenaries and the Birth of New Nations
  Matthew Brown

9 British Trade with Spanish America, 1763–1808
  Adrian J. Pearce

10 Colonial Tropes and Postcolonial Tricks: Rewriting the Tropics in the novela de la selva
   Lesley Wylie

11 Argentina's Partisan Past: Nationalism and the Politics of History
   Michael Goebel

12 The Reinvention of Mexico: National Ideology in a Neoliberal Era
   Gavin O'Toole

13 Armies, Politics and Revolution: Chile, 1808–1826
   Juan Luis Ossa Santa Cruz

14 Andean Truths: Transitional Justice, Ethnicity, and Cultural Production in Post-Shining Path Peru
   Anne Lambright

15 Positivism, Science, and 'The Scientists' in Porfirian Mexico: A Reappraisal
   Natalia Priego

16 Argentine Cinema and National Identity (1966–1976)
   Carolina Rocha

17 Decadent Modernity: Civilization and 'Latinidad' in Spanish America, 1880–1920
   Michela Coletta

18 Borges, Desire, and Sex
   Ariel de la Fuente

19 Contacts, Collisions and Relationships: Britons and Chileans in the Independence era, 1806–1831
   Andrés Baeza Ruz

Liverpool Latin American Studies, New Series 20

Writing and the Revolution
Venezuelan Metafiction
2004–2012

Katie Brown

LIVERPOOL UNIVERSITY PRESS

First published 2019 by
Liverpool University Press
4 Cambridge Street
Liverpool
L69 7ZU

Copyright © 2019 Katie Brown

The right of Katie Brown to be identified as the author of this book has been asserted by her in accordance with the Copyright, Design and Patents Act 1988.

All rights reserved. No part of this book may be reproduced, stored in a retrieval system, or transmitted, in any form or by any means, electronic, mechanical, photocopying, recording, or otherwise, without the prior written permission of the publisher.

British Library Cataloguing-in-Publication data
A British Library CIP record is available

ISBN 978 1 78694 219 7

Typeset by Carnegie Book Production, Lancaster
Printed and bound in Poland by BooksFactory.co.uk

Contents

Acknowledgements	vii
Introduction	1
1 Writing for the State	45
2 Writing and Distinction	61
3 Challenging the National Narrative	81
4 Making Literary Connections	105
5 Form and Popular Culture	127
6 Fiction and Reality	148
Conclusion	171
Bibliography	175
Index	195

Acknowledgements

This book was born of a love of the subjective, self-reflexive and provocative literature being produced by Venezuelans under the Bolivarian Revolution, and a frustration that this work has received neither the critical nor commercial attention that I believe it deserves. The biggest thank you must go to those authors included in this study and the many more besides who have kindly shared their work and their enthusiasm for literature with me.

This book would not have been possible without the support of Catherine Boyle and Matthew Brown, who so generously shared their knowledge about Latin America. Many thanks also to all the staff and students in the Department of Spanish, Portuguese and Latin American Studies at King's College London and the Department of Hispanic Portuguese and Latin American Studies at University of Bristol. For nurturing my budding love for Venezuelan literature, not to mention greatly shaping my theoretical approach to it, I am immensely grateful to Raquel Rivas Rojas. I am also deeply indebted to my 'bibliomula', José Rafael Pino, for smuggling books to me across the Atlantic.

Much of this book began life as conference presentations. I am very grateful to all the colleagues who asked questions or offered suggestions at these conferences for helping to shape my thinking, and to King's Graduate School, King's Faculty of Arts and Humanities, the Association of Hispanists of Great Britain and Ireland and the Latin American Studies Association for funding my attendance.

Introduction

Twenty-first-century Venezuelan literature is almost entirely absent from English language scholarship. This book is a small step towards rectifying this absence, presenting analysis of eight Venezuelan novels published between 2004 and 2012, in the context of the Bolivarian Revolution. While the Bolivarian Revolution began in 1999 and continues in power at the time of writing, these dates mark a key period in which concerns about the values and uses of literature were at the forefront of many novels, between the creation of the Minister for Culture (2004) and the last full year of Hugo Chávez's life (2012). The lack of studies of contemporary Venezuelan writing reflects the invisibility of Venezuelan literature from world literary space: limited international circulation, translations or recognition in literary prizes. Many contemporary writers and critics allude to the invisibility of Venezuelan literature abroad, such as Rubi Guerra (2007, 7), who highlighted the lack of knowledge of Venezuelan literature abroad in his introduction to *21 por XXI*, an anthology of twenty-first-century Venezuelan short stories. Venezuelan literature can be considered a minor literature following Deleuze and Guattari's (1975, 29) definition: 'Une littérature mineure n'est pas celle d'une langue mineure, plutôt celle qu'une minorité fait dans une langue majeure' [A minor literature isn't that of a minor language, but rather one made by a minority in a major language]. This is not a value judgement of the literature itself. Indeed, one of the aims of this book is to demonstrate the literary merit of the texts analysed. Instead, as I will demonstrate, a combination of factors, including the legacy of the Latin American 'Boom' and the relative economic and political stability of Venezuela in the 1960s to the 1990s, meant that Venezuelan literature has until recently been produced almost entirely within the Venezuelan state system. Consequently, it is unsurprising that the extensive changes in cultural policy introduced under President Hugo Chávez, as well as diverging ideas about the values attached to writing and the different uses thereof, are reflected in contemporary Venezuelan fiction. As such, analysis of contemporary Venezuela problematises the recent theories of 'global' (Hoyos, 2015) or 'post-national' (González, 2012; Robbins and González, 2014) Latin American literature which are based on studies of a handful of countries, revealing the enduring influence of national factors on literary production.

Literature from Argentina, Chile, Cuba, Colombia, Mexico and Peru has dominated Anglophone academic interest in recent years, leaving works from other countries in the margins. On the first page of his book on 'the global Latin American novel', for example, Héctor Hoyos (2015, 1) presents this, unproblematically, as 'novels by Chileans, Argentines, Colombians, Brazilians, and Mexicans'. The reasons for this are multiple. In *The World Republic of Letters* (2004), Pascale Casanova elucidates the disparity in prestige between literatures from different nations, and how this affects the visibility of authors from these countries. She argues that there are certain factors common to all 'small literatures' across the world, such as the distance from the world literary capitals like Paris, the lack of economic and political resources of the nation and historically high levels of illiteracy. Casanova also sheds light on the processes whereby elite gatekeepers, such as literary scholars, judge the worth of a nation's literature, forming, whether intentionally or not, canons based largely on economic and ideological factors. In the case of Latin America, Jean Franco (1994) cites both the impact of large publishing houses in Buenos Aires and Mexico and the pull of writers with 'celebrity status' (like Gabriel García Márquez, Carlos Fuentes, Jorge Luis Borges or Mario Vargas Llosa). Moreover, as textbooks such as *The Cambridge Companion to the Latin American Novel* (2005) illustrate, the legacy of the pre-Boom, Boom and post-Boom account of Latin American literary history still largely influences the choice of literature studied by Hispanists.

The power of the Boom is well-documented and self-evident; even those who know little else about Latin American literature can often name best-sellers like Gabriel García Márquez or Mario Vargas Llosa. While the Boom unquestionably produced some brilliant works, the phenomenon was not based on literary quality alone. As Jeremy Munday (2009) details, American philanthropists – sometimes with covert CIA funding – financed major efforts to translate and market Latin American literature, particularly via the Centre for Inter-American Relations, but the works selected for translation were those that projected an image of Latin America valued by domestic readers, one of the 'exotic' and 'magical'. As these books became best-sellers, publishers became increasingly interested in works that presented Latin America in this way, and to this day it is very common to see Latin American literature marketed and publicised in these terms. Indeed, Munday (2009, 55) calls the Boom 'an exercise in self-publicity and marketing which stifled other talents and styles for years afterwards'.

In a post about the absence of Venezuelan writing from the Boom, author Dayana Fraile (2012a) maintained that the Venezuelan literature of the 1960s and 1970s did not lack quality, but instead was too different to achieve success during the reign of the Boom:

¿Acaso pudo ser que Venezuela no encontrara lugar dentro del Boom porque sus escritores estaban ocupados con cosas más innovadoras? El temita de Latinoamérica exótica y el realismo mágico no podía cuajar en el escenario local. Se estaban explorando temas preeminentemente urbanos, de factura realista, muchas veces en constante diálogo con la contracultura.

[Could it be that Venezuela did not find a place within the Boom because its writers were occupied with other, more innovative things? The theme of exotic Latin America and magical realism could not fit in the local scene. Pre-eminently urban, realist themes were being explored, often in constant dialogue with counterculture.]

Evident in this statement is a hostility towards international publishers, critics and audiences who created a demand for literature which fit an exoticised view of Latin America and ignored other literary trends like the urban, counter-cultural works beginning to be produced in Venezuela in the 1960s and 1970s. There is certainly truth in this statement. Translator Suzanne Jill Levine (2005, 311), for example, argues that, at the time, 'readers were not looking for introspective or formally subversive or raw realist writing'. However, it is important to look back to the Venezuelan literary system of the 1960s to the 1990s for a more nuanced understanding of Venezuela's absence from international markets. As I will explore in the coming pages, because authors had the option to publish at home, funded by the state, they did not have to search for opportunities elsewhere in the way other Latin American authors did,[1] and could therefore remain insular. If we consider those authors posited as the leading voices of the Venezuelan literature of the 1960s and 1970s – Renato Rodríguez (Fraile, 2012a; 2012b), José Balza (Colmenares Gil, 2012), Guillermo Meneses and Salvador Garmendia (Gomes, 1997) – it is clear that their highly experimental works, influenced by the rapid urbanisation and modernisation of Caracas, were not written to appeal to mass international audiences. Another key structural factor to consider is that this was a period of 'democratic consolidation and apparent economic prosperity in Venezuela, in contrast to the rest of the region' (Gomes, 1997, 840). Because of this, exile was much less common among Venezuelans than other Latin Americans, and consequently Venezuelan literature 'was not publicised abroad by political émigrés interested in making their homeland known' (Gomes 1997, 840). Similarly, the lack of conflict in this period meant that Venezuela drew less international attention than its neighbours, whose dictatorships and guerrillas caught the attention of the media and the academy.

The consequences of Venezuela's absence from world literary space can be seen in terms of exports, translations and literary prizes. According to figures published by the Centro Regional para el Formento del Libro en América Latina y el Caribe [Regional Centre for the Development of the Book in Latin America and the Caribbean] (CERLALC, 2012, 3), in 2010,

---

[1] See José Donoso's account of how the lack of publishing opportunities in Chile forced him to publish abroad, in *Historia personal del Boom* (Donoso, 1972).

Venezuela made $700,000 from the export of books. Only Bolivia, Cuba, Honduras and Paraguay made less than Venezuela from exports. As a point of comparison, Peru had roughly the same population (*c*.30 million) and a much lower per capita gross domestic product ($3,801 compared with $6,010 for Venezuela), but it made $21.1 million from exporting books (CERLALC, 2012, 3). Of course, as well as differing levels of visibility in international markets, we must keep in mind that the Bolivarian government in Venezuela was far more interested in reaching a national audience than an international one and therefore did little to facilitate international distribution. Similarly, unlike in countries such as Mexico or Brazil, the Bolivarian government did not fund translations, compounding the international invisibility of Venezuelan literature. According to the databases of translations into English published each year compiled by Three Percent, based at the University of Rochester,[2] between 2008, when the database began, and 2012, only two Venezuelan texts were translated into English – Alberto Barrera Tyszka's *The Sickness* (2012) and *The Selected Works of José Antonio Ramos Sucre* (2012) – compared with 71 texts from Argentina and 46 from Mexico. Countries such as Ecuador, Paraguay, and much of Central America are equally absent from the list of translated works, but the relative size and wealth of Venezuela, compared with these countries, makes Venezuela's absence more notable. Casanova (2004, 135) describes translation as 'an act of consecration that gives [writers] access to literary visibility and existence'. She calls this process 'littérisation', maintaining that it is through being recognised as worthy of translation by the world literary gatekeepers that writing from peripheral literary nations becomes 'literature' (Casanova, 2004, 135). Another form of consecration from literary gatekeepers which Venezuelan literature has had relatively limited experience of is literary prizes. As Anadeli Bencomo (2007, 14) describes, when Alberto Barrera Tyszka won the Premio Herralde in 2006 for *La enfermedad*, his victory caused shock in a Venezuelan literary system not used to international recognition. Bencomo (2007, 14) adds that, while the prize was a cause for celebration, it also provided an opportunity for complaint about the marginalisation of Venezuela within Latin American literature. The lack of recognition of Venezuelan literature abroad has led, as writer and journalist Ana García Julio (2012) explained, to 'una autopercepción de que aún nos falta trabajar para alcanzar "las ligas mayors"' [a self-perception that we still need work to reach 'the big leagues']. Fraile (2012b) referred to this as the 'ugly duckling syndrome', which 'le deja a sus víctimas la desazón, el hastío y el firme propósito de leer más literatura argentina' [leaves its victims with anxiety, weariness and the firm intention to read more Argentine literature].

It is not only because of Venezuela's absence from world literary space that the Venezuelan case problematises the theories of 'global' or 'post-national'

---

[2] See www.rochester.edu/College/translation/threepercent/translation-database/.

Latin American literature, but also because of the undeniable presence of national social and political concerns in narrative produced during the Bolivarian Revolution. In putting forth his theory of 'the global Latin American novel', Héctor Hoyos (2015, 8) states, 'As a whole, Latin America is not particularly exceptionalist or isolationist. Why should its literature be?' Bolivarian Venezuela, however, is exceptionalist, with the government asserting that, in terms of culture, the national is necessary and sufficient. Moreover, the social, political and cultural changes which have taken place in Venezuela since Hugo Chávez came to power in 1999 have been so extensive that they are understandably a preoccupation for many writers. I do not wish to suggest that Venezuelan literature does not share many of the characteristics of 'global' or 'post-national' literature suggested by Hoyos (2015), Aníbal González (2012) and Timothy Robbins and José Eduardo González (2014). The awareness of 'increased proximity among distant cultures' (Hoyos, 2015, 27), 'the emergence of a global popular culture as a formative component of the Latin American subject' (Robbins and González, 2014, 6) and 'the realization that the discourse of the nation is unable to express each individual author's experiences' (Robbins and González, 2014, 12) are all notable features of the novels analysed in this book. However, the Venezuelan case is distinguished by the insistence of the Bolivarian government that writing should express the national and not be influenced by the foreign. Aníbal González (2012, 51) asserts that the reduction or even disappearance of national characters and landscapes in exchange for foreign ones is an increasingly common feature of Latin American literature. He adds:

> Aún cuando estos autores escriben acerca de un ambiente latinoamericano reconocible—ciudades como México, DF, o Santiago de Chile, por ejemplo—les preocupan menos las cuestiones de la identidad nacional o del 'color local' que el reto de representar situaciones humanas apasionantes con las cuales puedan relacionarse los lectores ajenos al ámbito latinoamericano e incluso ajenos a la lengua castellana. (González, 2012, 52)
>
> [Even when these authors write about a recognisable Latin American environment – cities such as Mexico City or Santiago de Chile, for example – they are less interested in questions of national identity or 'local colour' than in the challenge of representing gripping human situations with which readers foreign to Latin America and even to the Spanish language can relate.]

However, as I will demonstrate throughout this book, the authors studied here cannot simply ignore questions of national identity in the context of extreme nationalism. The Venezuelan novels I analyse question the discourse of the Venezuelan nation-state, but to do this they must think about what it means to be Venezuelan and about contemporary Venezuelan politics. Even books set in far-flung countries, such as Eduardo Sánchez Rugeles's *Transilvania unplugged* (2011a), or in a Utopia, such as *Todas las lunas* by Gisela Kozak

Rovero (2013), reflect on the situation in Venezuela. Indeed, in the final essay in the collection about post-national Latin American literature edited by Aníbal González, Miguel Gomes (2012) counters that, in Venezuela, the nation remains an indispensable factor for many writers. He maintains that the heroic myths of *chavismo* and the insistence on patriotic origins as a sign of collective identity created an anxiety which authors attempt to deal with through their fiction. This does not mean that the authors are unaffected by globalisation, but rather that they have to reconcile their experience of globalisation with the official insistence on national belonging.

Literature and politics

To understand contemporary Venezuelan literature, it is imperative to understand Bolivarian cultural policy. At the same time, the official approach to reading and writing is an instructive example of how the Bolivarian Revolution functioned on a wider scale. Ana Afanador et al. (2011, 6) maintain that research into cultural policies is necessary given that the government spoke of using culture as a tool to achieve political objectives. Chávez himself famously stated that a Revolution without culture 'es como lanzar un cohete sin combustible' [is like launching a rocket without fuel] (Ministerio de Comunicación e Información, 2005). While Venezuelan scholars including Gisela Kozak Rovero (2007b; 2008; 2015a), Manuel Silva-Ferrer (2014), Ana Afanador et al. (2011), and Emilia Bermúdez and Natalia Sánchez (2009 and 2013) have written instructive analyses of Bolivarian cultural policy, the wealth of academic studies of Hugo Chávez and/or his Bolivarian Revolution that have been produced in the United States and the United Kingdom in recent years either discuss culture only in terms of popular culture (editors Smilde and Hellinger's 2011 *Venezuela's Bolivarian Democracy*, for example, contains chapters on the *telenovela*, community radio, community television and protest poetry) or include a passing mention of the publishing industry (Kozloff, 2008, 98, for example). Analyses of Bolivarian policies have appeared as part of larger, international studies, such as discussion of Misión Cultura's storytelling workshops in Sujatha Fernandes's *Curated Stories: The Uses and Misuses of Storytelling* (2017). None of these works, however, has explored the effect of Bolivarian cultural policy – including state literary institutions, laws and statements by officials relating to literature and literary production – on literature by Venezuelans. Close literary analysis is at the heart of this book, as it is, above all, through the content and form of their fiction that writers comment on and challenge Bolivarian cultural policy.

Although those who criticise Bolivarian cultural policy are assumed to be opposed to the government politically – and many indeed are – this is not necessarily best understood as a question of political beliefs, but rather of a deep-seated ideological battle about the nature of literature which has its roots far beyond Venezuela and long before Chávez came to power. Should literature be 'autonomous'? And, if so, autonomous from what? Does autonomy mean literature as a separate field from politics? How has the politicisation of literature under the Bolivarian Revolution changed the way that writers view the relationship between literature and politics? To begin to answer these questions, it is useful to trace briefly the historical line of the confluence of politics and literature in Venezuela.

Raquel Rivas Rojas (2011, 6) notes that one of the most entrenched values in Venezuelan literary tradition has been the creation of stories designed to inculcate a sense of belonging to the country within readers. In the nineteenth century, the foremost Venezuelan thinkers, such as Andrés Bello, Simón Rodríguez, Francisco de Miranda and Simón Bolívar, considered their writing as 'pragmatic involvement in creating a country' (Gomes, 1997, 838). In their shadow, literature was rarely considered as separate from politics in the post-Independence period (Gomes, 1997, 838). As the Venezuelan nation-state tried to solidify and modernise in line with other nation-states throughout the nineteenth century and into the twentieth century, writing retained its role in the construction of national identity. Bermúdez and Sánchez (2009, 543) maintain that the primary purpose of cultural production in this period was to create a national consciousness to counteract the segregation that was standing in the way of the national political project.

Despite these efforts, high illiteracy rates persisted, still at 80 per cent in 1930 (Silva-Ferrer, 2014, 53). Nonetheless, in the late 1920s and early 1930s, 'foundational fiction' (Sommer, 1991) depicting national reality emerged in Venezuela. This period was arguably a high point of Venezuelan literary production, in so far as the works of Rómulo Gallegos remain the most celebrated, studied and commercially successful examples of Venezuelan fiction to date. Gallegos embodied the conjunction of literature and politics. His masterpiece, *Doña Bárbara* (1929), aimed to unite the country with its narrative of a civilised city lawyer returning to his father's land in Apure, taming the barbarous titular character and rescuing the degraded Marisela, while Gallegos himself was elected president of the Republic in 1948, ruling for nine months until he was overthrown by a military coup, leading to the dictatorship of Marcos Pérez Jiménez (1948–58). The political control of culture during the Pérez Jiménez dictatorship is analysed astutely by Raquel Rivas Rojas in *Narrar en dictadura: renovación estética y fábulas de identidad en la Venezuela perezjimenista* [Narrating under Dictatorship: Aesthetic Renovation and Identity Fables in the Venezuela of Pérez Jiménez] (2010). Rivas Rojas (2010, 11, 25) explains that literature had a didactic and foundational aspect under Pérez Jiménez, designed to inculcate a specific sense of Venezuelan national identity among readers, based on the folklorisation of popular cultures. Certain authors, she adds, did not feel comfortable with this official view of literature as a nation-building tool and tried to subvert it through their writing. Arturo Uslar Pietri and Ramón Díaz Sánchez revised official history and collective memory in their novels, and Antonio Arráiz and Manuel Otero Silva parodied the preceding tradition, while Andrés Mariño Palacio and Guillermo Meneses opted for a total formal rupture (Rivas Rojas, 2010).

The 40 years following the fall of the Pérez Jiménez dictatorship became known as the 'Punto Fijo' period, after a pact signed between the Unión Republicana Democrática [Republican Democratic Union], Acción Democrática [Democratic Action] and COPEI [Independent Political Electoral Organization Committee] to guarantee relative democratic stability. In practice, the pact led to the latter two parties alternating power for most of the period. Punto Fijo was also a time of economic stability and prosperity, with average GDP growth of 5 per cent between 1958 and 1980, thanks mainly to unprecedented oil revenue (Smilde, 2011, 3). The success of the state-run petrol industry during this period financed a paternalist state determined to manage and protect Venezuela's real and symbolic wealth (Bencomo, 2006, 763). Despite *chavista* Minister for Culture Francisco Sesto's claims that the state during 'Punto Fijo' was nothing more than a 'telecujero' [cash machine], only handing out money (Wisotzki, 2006, 21, 17), Anadeli Bencomo (2006, 763–765) points to the interventionist attitude of the Punto Fijo state, which led to it playing a leading role in Venezuelan culture.[3] The principal instances of this state involvement in literature were the creation of the Rómulo Gallegos literary prize (1964), the formation of the Instituto Nacional de Cultura y Bellas Artes [National Institute of Culture and Fine Art] (INCIBA, 1966), the foundation of Monte Ávila and Biblioteca Ayacucho publishing houses (1968 and 1974 respectively) and the replacement of INCIBA with the Consejo Nacional de la Cultura [National Council for Culture] (CONAC, 1975). While Punto Fijo is often referred to as one continuous period in which state financing of culture prevailed, Ana Teresa Torres (1999, 55–56) breaks the period into three distinct eras, which chart the evolution of attitudes towards how and why literature should be created. She argues that the first decade, 1958–1968, was marked by a populist state defending the rights of the dominant bourgeoisie, sparking an armed struggle between the state and revolutionaries, reflected in a literature of violence. The following 15 years, 1968–1983, are then characterised, according to Torres, by the defeat of the revolutionary movement. Torres describes how the 'policy of pacification' undertaken by Acción Democrática president Raúl Leoni Otero (1964–1969) was continued by his COPEI counterpart president Rafael Caldera Rodríguez (1969–1974), initiating a political neutralisation of intellectuals through high spending on culture. Finally, Torres asserts, the period from 1983 onwards is defined by the external debt crisis, which sparked a turn towards neo-liberalism, reflected in an abundant and varied literary production.

With the end of dictatorship in 1958, literary reactions to Pérez Jiménez became more common as writers were finally free to criticise the repressive regime openly. Salvador Garmendia (2006, 594), one of the leading voices

---

3 See Silva-Ferrer, 2014 for an in-depth analysis of how oil wealth allowed the state to create and fund institutions responsible for practically all aspects of culture in Venezuela during this period.

of Venezuelan experimental fiction in the 1960s and 1970s, describes the optimism with which authors of his generation greeted the fall of Pérez Jiménez:

> Nos prometimos a nosotros mismos y de muchas maneras, todas inocentes, lo ratificamos al mundo, que aquel tendrá que ser el último acto de ilegalidad, corrupción y oprobio que soportaríamos los venezolanos.

> [We promised ourselves and, in many ways, all of them innocent, we confirmed to the world, that this would be the last act of unlawfulness, corruption and shame we Venezuelans would stand for.]

This backlash against the dictatorship led to massive support for revolutionary movements among writers. María Carmen Porras (2006, 626) underlines how the generation of the 1960s was referred to as the cultural Left, while Luis Britto García (1999, 40) suggests that the 1970s were marked by a fight against imperialism. In this period, political and ideological reactions to the old regime translated into art and literature (Rama, 1982, 174). The centrality of political commitment to literary production in Venezuela at that time is made clear in Garmendia's (2006, 597) assertion that identification with leftist movements became the way to be accepted and respected as a writer. In the early 1960s, Garmendia and other writers in his circle could not imagine literary creation that was not inspired by strong political passions and would only recognise someone as a real writer if his or her political behaviour matched these expectations. This is one of the reasons given for Venezuela's absence from the Boom; at the time, authors such as Garmendia were responding to specific, national political circumstances, not writing for an international market. This politicised view of literature is remarkably similar to that held by the Bolivarian government, for which they are criticised by new generations of writers who demand space for the individuality and aestheticism rejected by Garmendia and his generation. What happened to produce such a dramatic turnaround?

As Bencomo (2006, 765) describes, during Punto Fijo, Acción Democrática instigated a project to institutionalise a modern and democratic identity for Venezuela. Paradoxically, as a result of this drive to preserve democracy, López Ortega (1999, 75) claims that expressing criticism became more difficult and less common. Evident here are competing definitions of 'democracy': while for intellectuals such as López Ortega democracy meant the freedom to criticise the dominant power and to support whichever political current they chose, democracy for Acción Democrática and COPEI meant the preservation of a peaceful middle ground and the absence of extremism. The government could not allow revolutionaries to undermine the image of democratic stability which Venezuela presented to the rest of the world, and so they used oil revenue, in Ana Teresa Torres's (1999, 55–66) terms, effectively to 'neutralise' writers. Both Francisco Sesto in *¿Por qué soy chavista?* [Why Am I Chavista?] (2006) and Mario Sanoja Obediente and Iraida Vargas Arenas in *La Revolución Bolivariana: Historia, cultura y socialismo* [The Bolivarian Revolution: History, Culture and Socialism] (2008) criticise the use of state funds in this period to win the compliance of formerly revolutionary intellectuals with grants, subsidies and cultural jobs, claiming that this money should have been put to better use serving 'the people' as a whole.

At the same time, it became increasingly difficult for writers to remain politically committed because their potential readership, the newly affluent middle-class emerging from the sudden rise in oil wealth, was not interested in their leftist ideals (Rama, 1982, 174). Consequently, Ana Teresa Torres (1999, 60) argues that authors from the later stages of Punto Fijo should not be judged on whether they were 'committed' or not because the political and economic stability of the time did not lead to the kind of polarisation seen in other periods. The failure of the revolutionary movements of the 1960s and early 1970s caused a deeply felt disillusionment among the intelligentsia. Writers' optimism at the fall of Pérez Jiménez was so strong that when they were unable to achieve the revolution that they so ardently hoped for many abandoned political commitment altogether (Barrera Linares, 2006a, 801; Britto García, 1999, 39). The failure of revolutionary movements in the context of the rise of the middle classes and the continued presence of traditional elites in positions of power led many disillusioned authors both to criticise national politics and to distance themselves from national narratives. Iraida Casique (2006, 620) highlights the bitterness, disillusionment and resentment evident in many works of this time, which distanced themselves for the image of triumph and heroism promoted by consecutive Punto Fijo governments. Casique discusses Renato Rodríguez as the prime example of this type of writing, but also points to Salvador Garmendia and Adriano González León, whose exploration of the rapid urbanisation, *País portatil* (1968), became one of the defining books of the generation.

Authors' desire to distance themselves from official nationalism, together with the spirit of aesthetic renovation of the time, led to experimentation with language and style influenced by international literary movements, including nihilism, Dada, surrealism and the Beatniks. However, Salvador Garmendia (2006, 597) noted that these complicated writing styles made literature inaccessible to all but educated elites. In this way, their writing was not only in opposition to official nationalism, but also incompatible with the socialist ideals these authors professed. The development of Venezuelan literature during Punto Fijo thus set the stage for the extreme polarisation of the literary field with the emergence of the Bolivarian Revolution. Having focused on introspection and literary experimentation in a way that alienated them from much of the population, the writers of the Punto Fijo period left a void – for national narratives, political concerns, and simple texts with mass appeal – which the Bolivarian government saw as its duty to fill.

By the end of the Punto Fijo period, the democratic and economic stability which had characterised the era was crumbling, as demonstrated by the Caracazo riots of February 1989 and the increasing claims of corruption against the government, and many people were calling for radical change (Smilde, 2011; Silva-Ferrer, 2014, 71–90). Hugo Chávez's victory in the 1998 presidential elections ushered in an era of transformation in Venezuela, beginning with the new Constitution in 1999 through which the name of the country was officially changed to the Bolivarian Republic of Venezuela. The ensuing decade can be thought of as a series of stages or turning points in terms of cultural policy, which often coincided with electoral victories (Brown, 2018). Little changed in terms of culture until 2001, when Chávez launched a 'war' on former cultural elites, including the televised mass firing of the directors of state cultural institutions on 21 January, accusing them of having kidnapped culture (Méndez, 2013; Silva-Ferrer, 2014, 117–118). Following this symbolic gesture, little changed again until 2004, when the figure of Minister for Culture was created, a position first held by Francisco Sesto, followed in 2005 by the creation of the Ministry for Culture. Sesto asserted the need for a radical break with the past, claiming that, to 'refundar la República' [relaunch the Republic], the cultural system would need to be redesigned (Wisotzki, 2006, 17). In many ways, the cultural policy introduced at this time was a backlash against the experience of Punto Fijo, during which period literature was the preserve of elites and detached from national concerns. This was made explicit in the Ley Orgánica de la Cultura, which also appeared in 2005, in which it is stated that the law was necessary to counteract:

> [El] deterioro constante sufrido en los últimos años del acervo cultural venezolano tradicional, por la acción erosiva de los antivalores del individualismo y el mercantilismo más exacerbados, inducidos por una cultura de masas globalizadora, guiada primordialmente por el espíritu de lucro y de dominación. (Comisión Permanente de Educación, 2005, 3)

> [The constant deterioration suffered by Venezuelan traditional cultural heritage in recent years, because of the erosive action of the anti-values of individualism and the most aggravated commercialism, induced by a mass culture of globalisation, guided above all by a spirit of profit and domination.]

All the themes which reappear in Bolivarian cultural policy and in statements by authors about the context in which they write are here: protecting cultural heritage, which does not include the cultural production of the preceding Punto Fijo years; the individual versus the collective; literature and the market; and globalisation. The document then presented a long list of ways in which national culture had suffered in the preceding 40 years and which would need to be rectified through the work of the new cultural ministry and related institutions. Many value judgements were implicit in this law: that political position and social commitment are more important for a manager of a cultural institution than knowledge of the market, training in management, or having many useful connections; that providing access to international art and literature is a threat to national identity rather than an opportunity for dialogue and innovation; that concentrating funding on cultural elites rather than on the widest range of people is both unfair and wasteful.

This discourse is emblematic of how the Bolivarian government discredited not only the opposition but the cultural production and activities of the previous 40 years (Kozak Rovero, 2008). Sesto condemned previous cultural policy as one by and for elites (Wisotzki, 2006, 8), vowing that the new Ministry of Popular Power for Culture would instead support culture by and for 'the people'. This reaction against the elitism of the literary system during Punto Fijo is also evident in the belligerent rhetoric of Iván Padilla Bravo, former vice-minister for Culture, who celebrated the radical break with previous conceptions of culture that has taken place as part of the Bolivarian Revolution, asserting in 2005 that 'la hegemonía de la clase dominante y explotadora es enfrentada y vencida por la hegemonía de los dominados, de los explotados, del proletariado' [the hegemony of the dominant and exploitative class is faced and defeated by the hegemony of the dominated, the exploited, the proletariat] (Kozak Rovero, 2007b, 108).[4] It is striking that Padilla Bravo could not conceive of culture without there being one group dominating another. In this way, the transition from Punto Fijo to the Bolivarian Revolution can be seen as a series of substitutions: 'the people' took the place of the favoured elites; individualism and cosmopolitanism were replaced with nationalism and socialism; and experimentation with form and language gave way to an imperative to make writing as simple and clear as possible.

The next turning point was in 2007, with the formation of the Plataforma del Libro y la Lectura [Platform for Books and Reading], which brought together publishers, printers, distributors and other state literary institutions. Their manifesto, resulting from a meeting of regional coordinators in Caracas from 27 to 29 June 2007, set out the vision for the platform:

> Participamos en la construcción de una poderosa Plataforma que propone al libro como medio de comunicación, recurso de formación ciudadana, de emancipación de la conciencia social y de preservación del patrimonio creativo de nuestro pueblo, y actuamos fundamentados en el convencimiento de que la lectura y la escritura constituyen prácticas socialistas. (Plataforma del Libro y la Lectura, 2007)

> [We are participating in the construction of a powerful Platform which puts forth the book as a means of communication, a resource for the instruction of citizens, for the emancipation of social conscience and the preservation of the creative heritage of our people, and we act based on the conviction that reading and writing are socialist practices.]

---

4 For a more detailed analysis of the popular counter-hegemony proposed by Bolivarian cultural policy, see Brown, 2018.

From this mission statement, the pillars of the Bolivarian vision for literature become clear: nationalism, socialism, the democratisation of literature, and a focus on literature as a way of documenting and transferring information more than as a creative endeavour. This statement also illustrates the conception of the Venezuelan people as one and united, with a shared history which must be preserved and reproduced. Although Paula Vásquez Lezama (2014, 14) maintains that Chavism cannot be reduced to populism, populist methods have been a key factor in Chávez's success, as studies such as Ryan Brading's *Populism in Venezuela* (2013) and Barry Cannon's *Hugo Chávez and the Bolivarian Revolution: Populism and Democracy in a Globalised Age* (2009) describe. Moreover, the writing workshops and mass publishing schemes introduced in this period by the Bolivarian government match those described as populist by Néstor García Canclini in *Hybrid Cultures* (1995). The primary example of these populist measures is the formation of a new state publishing house, El perro y la rana, in 2007, which, through schemes such as 'Cada día un libro' [One Book Every Day], published books by thousands of previously unpublished writers, stating that a will to participate was all that was necessary to be a writer. This scheme will be analysed in more detail in Chapter 1. Finally, in 2009, Chávez launched the Plan Revolucionario de la Lectura [Revolutionary Plan for Reading], designed to bring about 'a collective act to promote socialism' (Primera, 2009). Through the use of 'squadrons' of readers, sent out into communities to promote the reading of specific material on national identity, socialism and military history, the Plan aimed to inculcate support for the Bolivarian Revolution.

In one of the most complete studies of Bolivarian cultural policy to date, *El cuerpo dócil de la cultura: poder, cultura y comunicación en la Venezuela de Chávez* [The Soft Body of Culture: Power, Culture and Communication in Chávez's Venezuela], Manuel Silva-Ferrer (2014) argues that the Bolivarian definition of inclusion is contradictory, as it uses state institutions and resources to benefit those groups aligned with the Revolution while excluding others. The claim that Bolivarian cultural policy is exclusionary is one that appears repeatedly in the press and the academic studies to have broached the subject. This claim should be nuanced, however, by considering two factors. On the one hand, while there is no official censorship, certain writers feel excluded as the government wages war on elite culture. On the other hand, some writers exclude themselves, choosing not to publish in a state system that is bound by an ideology that they oppose, and that cannot offer them cultural or economic capital for their work. At the heart of this polarisation of the literary field are differences in the values attributed to literature. Those who make, implement or support Bolivarian cultural policy and those who oppose it hold competing ideas about what literature is or should be, does or should do.

Ideological divisions have split writers and readers, mirroring the conflict in Venezuelan society under the Bolivarian Revolution. From the way authors write – not only the themes they address, but the language they use and the form of their texts – judgements are made about their political positions. As Luis Barrera Linares (2006b, 881) affirms, 'Nunca la palabra tuvo mayor peso como portadora de etiquetas políticas y posiciones presuntamente ideológicas' [The word has never had more weight as a bearer of political labels and supposedly ideological positionings]. Writers who do not necessarily identify themselves with the Right are classified as Right for the way that they write (Torres, 2006, 915). However, there is a similar tendency among members of the opposition to assume that those who publish through the state support the regime. One author, who wishes to remain anonymous, reported to me that opposition critics had questioned them about their political beliefs after they published with state publisher El perro y la rana.

In many ways, looking back to the debates over culture in revolutionary Cuba, beginning in the 1960s, can help us to understand the tensions within Bolivarian Venezuela, as I explore further in Chapter 2. The language used by Hugo Chávez and Francisco Sesto to attack writers who do not support the Bolivarian Revolution or distance themselves from the nation echoes José Antonio Portuondo's speeches and essays from the early 1960s and the declaration by the 1971 Congreso de Educación y Cultura that 'El arte es un arma de la Revolución' [Art is a weapon of the Revolution]. Similarly, Venezuela's literary isolation in the 2000s recalls the difficulties experienced in Cuba in the 1980s including 'lack of access to contemporary world literatures and literary theories' and an inefficient distribution system (Kumaraswami, 2007, 76). As Jean Franco describes in *The Decline and Fall of the Lettered City* (2002), following the Cuban Revolution, a rift grew among Latin American authors between those who remained committed to the Revolution and those who believed in the autonomy of art, particularly after the Padilla affair in 1971. Franco (2002, 4) explains, 'A writer's disaffection from left-wing cultural politics was in many cases a tacit rejection of the rigidity of Soviet-inspired aesthetics'. The most noteworthy example of this is Mario Vargas Llosa's transformation from young socialist to critic of Castro, caused by his belief in personal liberty above any kind of totalitarianism, whether of the Left or Right. A similar disaffection is visible in contemporary Venezuela, where writers who identified with the Left, including Gisela Kozak Rovero, Israel Centeno and Ana Teresa Torres, have become outspoken opponents of the government's use of culture. Fully aware of this literary history, Torres (2006, 914) notes that with Chávez's declarations of war on literary elites, fear spread that the literary community would fracture like in previous totalitarian states.

In reaction to the Bolivarian Revolution and the many ways in which it has changed the Venezuelan cultural landscape, some writers have penned letters of protest. In *Cartas a la batalla* [Letters to the Battle], Harry Almela (2004) brings together a collection of letters – some individual, some collective – by Venezuelan writers about the political situation. In a letter entitled 'Grupo de escritores venezolanos denuncia el fascismo del régimen de Hugo Chávez' [A Group of Writers Denounce the Fascism of Hugo Chávez's Regime], written in 2002, 18 writers, including Alberto Barrera Tyszka, Israel Centeno, Juan Carlos Chirinos, Gisela Kozak Rovero, Juan Carlos Méndez Guédez and Slavko Zupcic (all analysed in this book), denounced the contempt shown by the government towards cultural processes and institutions (Almela, 2004, 36–39). The idea of writing as a tool for building a socialist nation was particularly painful for some Venezuelan writers for whom the ideal of literature as a means of individual expression had become deeply rooted since the Punto Fijo years. According to Luis Barrera Linares (2006b, 880), writing in Venezuela under Chávez was overshadowed by an emphasis on collective communication rather than individual expression. Yet it is precisely in the context of partisan antagonism that individual creation is necessary as a space for reflection. Manuel Silva-Ferrer (2014, 139) suggests that the focus on the individual he observes in contemporary Venezuelan fiction allows writers to avoid the tensions and threats of the outside world. As part of this demand for individual creative space, Ana Teresa Torres (2006, 922) objected to the insistence on nation-building narratives, asserting, 'Me gustaría defender el derecho a seguir construyendo los propios mundos narrativos. Vernos requeridos como testimoniantes sería, en verdad, una obligación nacionalista que no tendríamos por qué asumir' [I would like to defend the right to keep constructing our own narrative worlds. Being required as witnesses would, truly, be a nationalist obligation that we should not have to assume]. Given that the state envisioned writing as a tool in the socialist, nationalist revolution, writing an apolitical text became a political choice, a sign of defiance.

Whether the writers addressed in this book choose to write about politics or not, they distinguish themselves from the Bolivarian idea of culture, in which politics is the utmost priority, through their focus on literary quality. Even books which can be described as politically committed in theme or tone share a primordial concern with style, language, genre and storytelling. These are readerly writers or writerly readers, who read to be better writers and write the kind of books that they would want to read. This is evident in non-fiction statements from the authors – academic articles, interviews and blog posts – but above all in their fiction, in which the processes, purposes and values of literature are a key narrative theme.

Reading and writing outside of the state system

Julia Buxton (2011, xx) observes, 'the Bolivarian model, like the Punto Fijo system, is structured around networks of privileged access and loyalty', only those in favour swapped from an intellectual elite to 'the people'. Consequently, opposition to Bolivarian cultural policy could be seen as an example of what David Smilde (2011, 23) calls 'the dismay and frustration of formerly dominant social sectors at the new ascendency of formerly marginalised people and ways of being'. Such a negative reaction to democratising measures was previously witnessed among literary elites in revolutionary Cuba, who felt that attempts to create a mass movement of writers was a threat to 'the status of the author as individual – or at least minority – figure and skilled specialist creator' (Kumaraswami, 2012, 105). It would be reductive, however, to suggest that writers objected to the way in which the state literary system was run simply because they feared losing their privileged status. The authors and critics who expressed their dissatisfaction with Bolivarian cultural policy did not suggest that there was no merit to the state's efforts to democratise culture or that these should cease, but rather that these projects needed to be reconciled with space for professional, skilled writers. Seven years into the Bolivarian Revolution, Ana Teresa Torres (2006, 921) insisted that there still needed to be a discussion about how to balance the mass publication and distribution of literature with private initiatives to produce 'los libros que queremos leer y escribir' [the books that we want to read and write]. Private initiatives is the key term here. The perceived limits of state publishing forced its critics to be innovative, to move beyond the state, creating their own new publishing houses or looking for audiences beyond national borders. Manuel Silva-Ferrer (2014, 118) attributes this migration from public to private publishing to the loss of symbolic capital of state publishing resulting from the privileging of ideology over aesthetic quality, and the reduced capacity of the state-run publishing houses to offer legitimacy and prestige. He adds that this increased dramatically with the appointment of Francisco Sesto as Minister for Culture in 2004 (Silva-Ferrer, 2014, 119). In this way, one of the unintended outcomes of Bolivarian cultural policy was the development of a literary community in opposition to the state.

In spite of state control of resources including ink and paper (Fermín, 2013b) and having to compete against heavily subsidised state-produced books which made privately produced books seem unnecessarily expensive, private publishing increased exponentially since the start of the Bolivarian Revolution. While the commercial successes of Venezuelan writers, especially in international markets, remained slight compared with other Latin American authors, by 2012 critics were speaking of a 'Boom' or 'Golden Age' in Venezuelan literature (Vidal, 2012; Colmenares Gil, 2012). In his introduction to *Las voces secretas* [The Secret Voices], an anthology of contemporary Venezuelan short stories, Antonio López Ortega (2006, 16) highlighted the aesthetic quality of the generation born since the 1960s, their search for new themes and styles, and their commitment to writing as a vocation. More recently, Daniel Fermín (2013a), arts and culture reporter for *El Universal*, again suggested that a new generation of writers, this time born since the 1970s, were reinvigorating Venezuelan literature. Fermín (2013a) pointed to Roberto Martínez Bachrich, Carolina Lozada, Eduardo Sánchez Rugeles, Gabriel Payares, Willy McKey and Enza García Arreaza as must-read authors. Despite their insistence on writing as an act of individual self-expression, this new generation recognised the importance of promoting one another. Israel Centeno stated in an interview that authors need to name one another, to show that Venezuelan literature exists and encourage academics to research it

(Montañez Cortez, 2013). Part of the reason that Venezuelan writers do not enjoy as much success as they deserve, Centeno argued, is that, when asked in interviews about their influences or what they enjoy reading, Venezuelans name foreign authors rather than their compatriots, perhaps wanting to distance themselves from official nationalism, or to attach themselves to better recognised authors. As recognition of Venezuelan writers has increased in recent years, individual writers have achieved a certain measure of fame. A striking example of this is Eduardo Sánchez Rugeles, whose returns to Venezuela to promote his books were met with great excitement. According to online Venezuelan literary magazine *Qué Leer* (2013a), he became a literary 'rock star'. Similarly, Héctor Torres pointed out that, while the average Venezuelan novel or short story collection sold between 600 and 800 copies in Venezuela, certain works, including *La otra isla* [The Other Island] by Francisco Suniaga (2005), *La enfermedad* [The Sickness] by Alberto Barrera Tyszka (2006) and Torres's own *Caracas muerde* [Caracas Bites] (2012) sold upwards of 5,000 copies. 'Nuestro mercado es pequeño, pero con lectores fieles' [Our market is small, but our readers are loyal], Torres (2015) affirmed, noting how there was always a receptive audience at readings.

Looking at the lists of writers mentioned by Torres, López Ortega, Fermín and others, one common factor is that they are all published outside of the state system. Some, like Alberto Barrera Tyszka, were able to publish with the large multinationals such as Alfaguara and Anagrama. Manuel Silva-Ferrer (2014, 138–139) explains that these private publishing houses knew how to take advantage of the limits placed on importing books, searching for young, upcoming authors and taking on the more established names who had left state publishers. The much smaller international publishing house, Ediciones B (Bruguera), founded in Barcelona in 1986, was instrumental in the careers of Venezuelan writers including Eduardo Sánchez Rugeles and Fedosy Santaella. Santaella explains that he was approached by Silda Cordoliani at Ediciones B who was looking for new Venezuelan writers to publish, given that bringing foreign writers into the Venezuelan market was proving too expensive for them.[5] Under editor Beatriz Rozados, Edicions B Venezuela published a variety of genres, from literary fiction to self-help, including a notable collection of crime fiction. These examples demonstrate the interplay between national and international factors in contemporary Venezuelan publishing; if importing books to Venezuela had not been limited by the currency controls put in place by the Bolivarian government (Lionetti, 2012; Valery, 2009a), it is less likely that these Venezuelan authors would have been published. The limits on imports therefore proved effective at increasing the publishing of Venezuelan books in Venezuela, as Bolivarian cultural officials desired.

---

5 Santaella made these comments as part of a class on contemporary Venezuelan literature led by Raquel Rivas Rojas at Universidad Simón Bólivar, 29 September 2015.

As well as the internationals, Venezuelan publishing houses founded during Punto Fijo – including Alfa (founded in 1958), Oscar Todtmann (1973) and Equinoccio, belonging to the Universidad Simón Bolívar (1973) – made the most of the changes to publishing under the Bolivarian Revolution by publishing authors who would not be, or would not want to be, published by the state. Equinoccio, for example, released books by Mario Morenza, Miguel Gomes, and Gisela Kozak Rovero, while Alfa published some of the best-selling fiction by Venezuelans in the past decade, including Ana Teresa Torres's *La escribana del viento* [The Wind's Scribe] (2013) and a re-edition of *Falke* by Federico Vegas (2014, first published by Jorale in Mexico in 2004, and later by Mondadori in Caracas). Oscar Todtmann achieved notable success with Francisco Suniaga's *La otra isla* (2006), which has had 12 editions. *Qué Leer* (2015) praised the publisher for making their books available on Amazon and in Kindle form, thereby allowing authors easier access to international markets. It should be noted that these innovations began after the period studied in this book (2004–2012), but they can be seen as an extension of the increase in private publishing and reaching out to international markets which began during this period.

In addition to these established publishing houses, the Bolivarian period saw the birth of several small, independent publishers. Bid & co. launched in 2002, filling the market for translated classics as well as Venezuelans old and new, including José Balza and poets Eugenio Montejo and Rafael Cadenas. Lector Cómplice, founded by Lesbia Quintero, began life in 2006 with workshops, seminars and other literary discussions, branching into publishing in 2011. They describe themselves as committed to the promotion and dissemination of emerging literature. Puntocero, spawned from Alfa in 2009, also breaks down distinctions between Venezuelan writers (including Héctor Torres, Lucas García París and Camilo Pino) and writers from other parts of Latin America. Founder Ulises Milla explained that they wanted to change the scope of Venezuelan publishing with a focus on contemporary design, universal content and distribution across Colombia, Mexico, Chile, Uruguay and Argentina, as well as Venezuela (Ediciones Puntocero, 2010). Like Puntocero, Lugar Común, formed in 2011 by Luis Yslas and Rodrigo Blanco Calderón, had a clear editorial vision, which could not be further from the Bolivarian approach of publishing as much as possible in short runs. They did not accept manuscripts, insisting instead that they knew what they liked and would only publish that, including works by Rubi Guerra and Juan Carlos Méndez Guédez (Montilla, 2015). Lugar Común announced in September 2015 that they had to cease publishing, but Yslas has since returned with Editorial Madera Fina, which launched with the release of Méndez Guédez's novel *Y recuerda que te espero* [Remember that I'm Waiting for You] in October 2015. Meanwhile, the staff of the Lugar Común bookshop launched their own publishing house, El Estilete, named after *The Stylus* magazine which Edgar Allan Poe planned but never launched. Through an online magazine and the books that they publish, they aim to promote the tradition of cultural criticism in Venezuela. Their collection, focusing on poetry and essays, is united by a strong editorial design. Similarly, Libros del Fuego, founded in December 2013 by Alberto Sáez, Rodnei Casares, César Oropeza and Elías Farache, aims to encourage high-quality production despite the economic crisis. Graphic designer Juan Merceron reportedly reads each book three times before beginning work on the cover, and such attention to detail won him the 2016 Latin American Prize for Editorial Design, beating 800 other entries from across the continent (Lozada, 2016). With its name alluding to book burning, the publishing house also aims to make a stand against censorship (*Qué Leer*, 2013b). The survival of these private publishing houses is thanks to the initiative and determination of the individuals who run them and support from loyal readers, but it has not been easy. *El Universal* reported in 2013 that, unlike state publisher Monte Ávila, private publishers had been struck by a large rise in costs and paper shortages, which limited what they could print. Equinoccio, for example, could only print two of the six books it had planned for that year (Fermín, 2013b). Moreover, while these publishers grew in the period following Chávez's death, the growing economic crisis in Venezuela, which caused extreme shortages and hyperinflation in 2018, combined with increasing emigration levels, put into question the survival of the publishers in the future.

The products of these publishing houses drew readers to those independent bookshops which managed to survive difficult economic conditions.[6] These included Lugar Común, Alejandría, Kalathos and El Buscón in Caracas, and Ballena Blanca in Mérida. Kalathos described itself as a bookshop, café and meeting place, while staff at Lugar Común called the bookshop a mini cultural centre (Montilla, 2015). They offered regular talks and workshops, as well as Skype conversations with authors abroad, helping to keep the community together virtually. In this way, such bookshops became vital meeting points for a burgeoning literary community outside of the state system. An important factor in this development was increased access to and use of the internet, especially social media, to promote new releases and events such as readings. The internet also became a space for literary criticism and the promotion of new writing, the lack of which has been seen as a failing of the Venezuelan literary system. Dayana Fraile (2012a) claimed that, in the printed press and other mass media, books were seldom reviewed.

---

6 In 2011, Prodavinci reported that independent bookshops were in crisis due to rises in rent and the cost of importing books under the new currency and import controls. As a result, the once celebrated Caracas bookstore Lectura closed after 60 years (Falcón and Gómez, 2011). Rodnei Casares from Librería Alejandría told *El Universal* that sales had fallen by 30 per cent between 2005 and 2010, because bookshops were struggling to acquire the books that people wanted and those they did stock had become so expensive that people could no longer afford to buy many of them (Falcón and Gómez, 2011).

As a result, general readers got little information about works available and little temptation to read them. In this context, as well as the enhanced publicity efforts of private publishing houses and independent bookshops, literary websites became a way for Venezuelans to inform themselves about new writing. The success of literary sites, such as *Letralia*, *Qué Leer* [What To Read] and the rather unconventional *Nalgas y libros* [Bums and Books],[7] is due in part to the sense of community that these created, as readers could comment on articles and share them through social media.

One of the most influential websites in terms of literature in Venezuela is *Prodavinci*.[8] Although not a specifically literary website – it also hosts articles about current affairs, economics, science and technology, and lifestyle – *Prodavinci* publishes extracts from novels and short stories as well as introductions to new releases and essays. It has become a popular place for authors to share a taster of their latest work before publication. Notably, authors including Gisela Kozak Rovero, Willy McKey and Ana Teresa Torres also contribute opinion pieces about contemporary politics to the site. As with *Prodavinci*, many authors choose to premiere their new works on *Ficción Breve* [Short Fiction], which features extracts from both classics and new publications, as well as news, interviews and reviews.[9] The site is one of the activities of the Ficción Breve Venezolana civil association, run by Lennis Rojas, who set it up with Héctor Torres in 1999. The association describes itself as a not-for-profit NGO dedicated to the dissemination of Venezuelan literature. Since 2009, Ficción Breve has run the Premio de la Crítica de la Novela [Critics' Prize for the Novel], whose winners to date are Gustavo Valle (2009 and 2014), Victoria de Stefano (2010), José Napoleón Oropeza (2011), Eduardo Sánchez Rugeles (2012), Ana Teresa Torres (2013) and Krina Ber (2015). As the name suggests, the prize is a celebration not only of writing but of literary criticism, aiming to defend the position of the critic as a specialist (Ficción Breve, 2015). Winners gain not only a cash prize but the cultural capital that comes from recognition by those with specific training and expertise in judging literature. The prize is open to any book by a Venezuelan author published in Venezuela in that year; authors can self-nominate or be nominated by their publisher (Ficción Breve, 2015). Although the same names often reappear on the annual longlist of 12 to 15 nominees (Eduardo Sánchez Rugeles, Fedosy Santaella and Sonia Chocrón, for example), lesser-known authors have also found exposure through appearing on the list. Other highly regarded new prizes include the Premio de Cuento Policlínica

7 See https://letralia.com/; https://web.archive.org/web/20180224071719/https://queleer.com.ve/; https://nalgasylibros.com/.
8 See https://prodavinci.com/. Although viewing figures are not available, the Prodavinci page has nearly 100,000 'likes' on Facebook and its articles are regularly shared across social media.
9 See www.ficcionbreve.org.

Metropolitana para Jóvenes Autores [Short Story Prize for Young Authors], which has been run since 2006 by Héctor Torres, and the annual Premio Transgenérico [Cross-genre Prize] awarded by the Fundación para la Cultura Urbana [Foundation for Urban Culture] since 2001. The awarding of new literary prizes has been a valuable publicity tool for Venezuelan literature in recent years, especially given the lack of Venezuelan winners of international literary prizes.

Along with Ficción Breve, the Fundación para la Cultura Urbana has been a driving force behind interest in Venezuelan literature since it formed in 2001 with funding from the brokerage firm Econoinvest. The foundation publishes its own books, covering many different genres, as well as producing music and audio-visual content and housing a photography collection. One of their central literary activities from 2005 to 2010 was the annual Semana de la Nueva Narrativa Urbana [Week of New Urban Narrative], coordinated by Héctor Torres and Ana Teresa Torres, which led to the collections *De la urbe para el orbe* [From the City to the World] (2006), *Quince que cuentan* [Fifteen Storytellers] (2008) and *Tiempos de ciudad* [City Times] (2010). The story of Cultura Urbana is an enlightening example of how obstacles to private literary initiatives put in place by the government have cemented a literary community in opposition to the Bolivarian Revolution. After Econoinvest was seized on 20 July 2010 by order of the Comisión Nacional de Valores [National Values Commission], the Cultura Urbana offices were shut down, the staff were sent home and the locks were changed. All the foundation's work-in-progress and all their assets were locked away, meaning that staff could not continue with their work and could not be paid (see Vidal, 2010; Hernández G., 2010). Given that the foundation was legally autonomous from Econoinvest and functioned independently, this forced closure was illegal, as the foundation and its many supporters asserted repeatedly. Writers took to the internet in protest, praising the work of the foundation and criticising the state monopolisation of culture. Gabriel Payares, for example, posted that closing down Cultura Urbana 'apunta hacia una nauseabunda monopolización del rótulo "cultura" por parte del Estado' [points towards a nauseating monopolisation of the label 'culture' by the state] (Vidal, 2010). Similarly, Kira Kariakin affirmed that the reaction against the closure from the cultural community in Venezuela was not only due to their respect for the work of the foundation itself, but a sign of growing frustration at the government's increased power over the cultural field, through which institutions could be shut down and individuals arrested on a presidential whim (Vidal, 2010). By 25 July, 905 signatures had been added to a solidarity campaign, forming the basis of what became the Sociedad de Amigos de la Cultura Urbana [Society of Friends of Cultura Urbana].[10] At a press conference on 5 August, the

---

10 See http://solidaridadfcu.blogspot.co.uk/.

new Board of Directors, led by poet Joaquín Marta Sosa, announced that Cultura Urbana would continue to operate, funding their activities through events, workshops, private donations and selling their books, as soon as the Comisión Nacional de Valores returned their possessions (*Prodavinci*, 2010). The Cultura Urbana example highlights the importance of a sense of community, based on a shared appreciation of literature, in opposition to the Bolivarian government's control of culture. From discussions across social media and message boards to meetings in bookshops-cum-cafés, reading has become an increasingly social practice, as people define their community through what they read. There are obvious similarities between this social reading and the Bolivarian government's vision for reading as a social practice, as put forward in the Plan Revolucionario de Lectura [Revolutionary Plan for Reading] (2009). The difference is in the focus of the reading; the PRL explicitly stated that reading should inculcate Bolivarian values, whereas the community of readers formed outside the state system was more interested in specifically literary qualities.

What emerges from an overview of the current Venezuelan Boom is that a consequence of the governmental monopoly on publishing has been an adhesion to the rules of the market by many writers and emerging publishing houses (Silva-Ferrer, 2014, 24). This includes employing publicity techniques like new literary prizes, book launches as social events, the use of social media, and a focus on design to make books desirable objects. As Montague Kobbe and Adolfo Calero (2009) highlight, in this way, 'Chávez had served as a catalyst to trigger a capitalistic bonanza in the publishing business in Venezuela'. In response, Bolivarian cultural officials have adopted the discourse of the market to rebuke those writers who complain that only socialist texts are promoted by state-run institutions. In 2011, Christian Valles, President of the Centro Nacional del Libro [National Centre for Books], notably justified the overwhelming presence of texts with a socialist message at the state-run Filven book festival by asserting, 'Es un hecho editorial y de mercadeo que si en Venezuela hay una revolución de izquierda, los libros de izquierda tienen salida' [It's a fact of the market and of publishing that if there is a leftist Revolution in Venezuela then leftist books will sell] (Paullier, 2011). Such a statement reinforces Nicolas Kozloff's (2008, 97) claim that, despite promotion of socialism by the Bolivarian government, 'rejecting consumerist society is a hard sell in Venezuela'.[11]

As well as unintentionally encouraging private initiatives in Venezuela, the Bolivarian Revolution has caused a wave of emigration, with an estimated 1.5 million Venezuelans living abroad by 2014 (Olivares, 2014). This phenomenon is giving Venezuelan authors increased opportunity to publish in Europe and the United States. Silda Cordoliani (2013, 9) sees the proliferation of

---

11 Kozloff observes the abundance of shopping malls and designer labels in Venezuela, concluding that 'Venezuela seems to have a more insatiable desire for the trappings of US consumerism [than other Latin American countries]' (Kozloff, 2008, 97).

Venezuelans across the globe as an opportunity for Venezuelan literature to reach out to international audiences. This is evidenced by writers such as Israel Centeno, Juan Carlos Méndez Guédez and Juan Carlos Chirinos publishing with Spanish houses. Moreover, Sudaquia Editores, set up in New York by Venezuelan emigrant Asdrúbal Hernández in 2011, has begun to publish many Venezuelan texts in the United States, making them widely available internationally for the first time.[12] Gustavo Guerrero suggests that, for Venezuelans abroad, sharing their literature with their new neighbours is a way of remaining connected to their homeland. He explains, 'Dar a leer algunos libros de autores venezolanos, y participar en su reconocimiento, han sido dos de las maneras en que he podido asumir performativamente mi identidad venezolana en el extranjero' [Giving people books by Venezuelan authors to read and participating in its recognition have been two of the ways in which I can assume my Venezuelan identity abroad performatively] (Guerrero, 2013a, 20). Guerrero (2013a, 20) adds that promoting literature in this way is, for him, a form of resistance, celebrating unity in diversity rather than the one-dimensional model of national identity offered by the government. Guerrero's comments draw attention to similarities and differences in the ways that different groups value literature. Bolivarian cultural policy looks inwards, providing Venezuelan books to Venezuelan people, creating an 'imagined community' of readers (Anderson, 2006). By contrast, for critics such as Guerrero, building interest in Venezuelan literature abroad is a matter of national pride, letting others see what is good about their home country.

The search for other opportunities in the face of the limitations of state publishing recalls that experienced in the pre-Boom period by the Latin American writers who would go on to form the Boom. The many parallels between the pre-Boom period and Venezuela under the Bolivarian Revolution help us to understand the frustration certain contemporary authors feel, despite there being no official bars to them writing, at having lost the recognition for individual expression and aesthetic experimentation won by earlier generations. As José Donoso (1972) describes in his memoir *Historia personal del 'Boom'* [Personal History of the 'Boom'], the pre-Boom period in Chile and elsewhere was characterised by official demands for national narratives:

> Mientras el mundo de los jóvenes se expandía mediante lecturas y compromisos que tendían sobre todo a borrar las fronteras, los criollistas, regionalistas y costumbristas, atareados como hormigas, intentaban al contrario reforzar esas fronteras entre región y región, entre país y país, de hacerlas inexpugnables, herméticas, para que así nuestra *identidad*, que evidentemente ellos veían como algo frágil o borroso, no se quebrara o escurriera. (Donoso, 1972, 23)

---

12 See www.sudaquia.net. For an interview with Hernández, see Brown, 2014b.

[While the world of the young was expanding through reading and political commitments which aimed, above all, to remove borders, the *criollistas*, regionalists and *costumbristas*, working away like ants, tried by contrast to reinforce these borders between regions, between countries, to make them impregnable, hermetically sealed, so that our *identity*, which they obviously saw as something fragile and blurry, would not break or slip away.]

A similar insistence on protecting national identity is at the core of Bolivarian cultural policy. Like their Boom predecessors, the authors studied in this book counter demands for nation-building narratives with stylistic, linguistic and thematic experimentation. As well as emphasising local identity, political commitment was another key criterion in judging literary worth in countries such as Mexico, Chile and Peru, as novels were expected to be important, serious and in direct contact with real social issues (Donoso, 1972, 24). The result was limited possibilities for literary experimentation within the state publishing system. Donoso (1972, 25) notes, 'Las indagaciones formales estaban prohibidas. Tanto la arquitectura de la novela como el idioma debían ser simples, planos, descoloridos, sobrios, y pobres' [Formal experimentation was not allowed. Both the structure and the language of the novel had to be simple, flat, colourless, restrained and poor]. In such a context, Mario Vargas Llosa remembers, form became for him 'almost like a theme or character' (Shaw, 1998, 20). Even after the Boom, Donald L. Shaw (1998, 15) notes, there has been much criticism by left-leaning writers, including Antonio Skármeta, Henán Vidal and Juan Manual Marcos, of the Boom authors' linguistic and stylistic experimentation, for encouraging elitism and distracting readers from political concerns. This attitude reappeared in Bolivarian cultural policy, which demanded that writing be accessible – that is, understandable – to all, so that it could serve to educate the masses about the need for revolution. Donoso (1972, 51) adds that, before the Boom, any authors who wished to put their individual aesthetic concerns above the needs of the national community were made to feel excluded, and the term 'intellectual' became a stigma. Again, this is highly reminiscent of the many declarations against 'la cultura exquisita de las élites' [exquisite culture of the elites] (Sesto, 2006, cited in Kozak Rovero, 2007b, 105) by Bolivarian cultural officials that made those Venezuelan writers who aspired to be recognised for their literary talents feel ostracised. These multiple parallels suggest a need to rethink the Boom, and Venezuela's absence from it, as responses to specific sets of circumstances. Throughout this book, I propose reading the thematic and stylistic choices of the authors studied as responses to changes to the publishing landscape and to the official uses of writing in the Bolivarian Revolution.

Introduction to the authors and texts studied

This book focuses on novels published between 2004 and 2012. The year 2004 marks the start of major attention to culture in Bolivarian policy, while 2012 was the final full year of Hugo Chávez's life. Although the Bolivarian Revolution continues under Nicolás Maduro, who became president upon Hugo Chávez's death in 2013, there are notable differences between the two presidencies. First, although some of the programmes put in place under Chávez such as Misión Cultura continue, many have been abandoned, either through lack of resources or simply from lack of follow through. Secondly, the Maduro period has been characterised by crises: hyperinflation, shortages of food and medicine and continued protests, in which over 200 people were killed between 2014 and 2017. Authors such as Juan Carlos Méndez Guédez did continue to write metafiction in this period, but responding to different circumstances.

The corpus of novels studied here does not pretend to be in any way a representative sample of contemporary Venezuelan literature. Instead, I focus on a selection of novels, published outside the state system, in which the protagonists are writers, through which contemporary authors express their reactions to the conditions of literary production in Venezuela. The works analysed are: *El niño malo cuenta hasta cien y se retira* [The Naughty Boy Counts to 100 and Runs Away] (2010 [2004]) by Juan Carlos Chirinos, *Círculo croata* [Croatian Circle] (2012 [2006]) by Slavko Zupcic, *Bajo las hojas* [Beneath the Sheets] (2010) by Israel Centeno, *Chulapos Mambo* [Madrid Mambo] (2011) by Juan Carlos Méndez Guédez, *Transilvania unplugged* (2011) by Eduardo Sánchez Rugeles, *Rating* (2011) by Alberto Barrera Tyszka, *Todas las lunas* [All the Moons] (2013 [2011]) by Gisela Kozak Rovero and *La fama, o es venérea, o no es fama* [Fame is Sexually Transmitted or It's Not Fame] (2012) by Armando Luigi Castañeda. Some of these authors, notably Méndez Guédez, have written repeatedly about fictional authors and literary production. To allow for greater depth of analysis, I have chosen one example of each of their texts. This is not an exhaustive list of such metafictional production by Venezuelans since the start of the Bolivarian Revolution. Other notable examples from outside the state system include *La tarea del testigo* [The Task of the Witness] by Rubi Guerra (2012), written in the voice of poet José Antonio Ramos Sucre; *Un vampiro en Maracaibo* [A Vampire in Maracaibo] by Norberto José Olivar (2008), which follows a historian writing a book about local vampire legends; and *Lluvia* [Rain] by Victoria de Stefano (2002), in which an author resembling de Stefano – but named Clarice after Clarice Lispector – recounts the gestation of her new novel. Metafictional novels have also been published by the state. Notably, El perro y la rana published *Pie de página* [Footnote] by Humberto Mata in 2007. An introduction by Sael Ibáñez celebrates the novel for its complexity and intellectualising, comparing Mata to Borges and Kafka. This is a good example of how state publishing practice sometimes contradicted the messages set out in speeches and policy documents. However, in this book, I am more concerned with those messages than with practice. I have limited analysis to books published outside of the state system, as I wish to demonstrate the impact of national policy and official ideology on privately produced literature.

The eight authors addressed in this book are spread across a range of ages and experience, from Israel Centeno and Juan Carlos Méndez Guédez, who began publishing in the early 1990s, before the Bolivarian Revolution, to Eduardo Sánchez Rugeles, who only published his first book in 2010. They are all middle-class, educated professionals, the demographic often criticised by Chávez and Sesto. They have all moved away from Venezuela at different stages – Gisela Kozak Rovero was the last to leave, in 2017 – but they all publish both inside and outside the country. I will not consider these books within the framework of exile writing, however, partly because several of the books were written when their authors still lived in Venezuela, but primarily because they do not display the nostalgia for and longing for a return to the homeland which is a key feature of Hispanic exile writing. Very limited scholarship about these authors and their novels exists, so it is pertinent to introduce them briefly.

Juan Carlos Chirinos and *El niño malo cuenta hasta cien y se retira*

Juan Carlos Chirinos (b.Valera 1967) lives and works in Spain, having left Venezuela for doctoral study in Salamanca in 1997. He has enjoyed a varied writing career, having published three collections of short stories and four biographies, as well as three highly experimental and fantastical novels: *El niño malo cuenta hasta cien y se retira* (2004), *Nochebosque* [Nightwood] (2011) and *Gemelas* [Twins] (2013). His most recent work is a book-length essay called *Venezuela: biografía de un suicidio* [Venezuela: Biography of a Suicide] (2017). Chirinos won the prize for short stories in the José Antonio Ramos Sucre Literary Biennial in 2002 and was a finalist in the Juan Rulfo International Competition in 2009. His work displays a fascination with language, literature, fantasy, sensuality and evil. An introduction to his work is featured in Corral, de Castro and Birns's edited volume, *The Contemporary Spanish American Novel* (Stanco, 2013a).

Before *Biografía de un suicidio,* Juan Carlos Chirinos refused to write about Venezuelan politics explicitly because he felt unable to do so. In a 2012 blog post, he explained that his decision not to write about political realities was a question of respect: 'La desgracia de mi país tiene nombres, apellidos y topónimicos; yo – todavía – no puedo hacer literatura con eso' [My country's tragedy has names, surnames and place names; I – still – can't make literature with that] (Chirinos, 2012a). Moreover, for Chirinos (2012b), literature is a game, a 'territorio de libertad absoluta' [space of absolute freedom] in which to escape from the unrelenting politicisation of Venezuelan society. Nonetheless, certain stylistic and thematic choices in Chirinos's novels still seem to have been influenced by the context of Venezuelan politics and specifically the Bolivarian approach to culture, such as his representation of the political power of a charismatic storyteller.

El niño malo is the story of D.Jota, a young radio DJ from Caracas and the events of his brief stay in the mysterious town of El Pueblo with a young shepherdess called Fanny and her grandmother Derdriu. D.Jota leaves Caracas to find himself, and eventually finds his identity in what he calls 'la capsúla del mal' [the capsule of evil]. The novel switches focus between those three characters, as well as Fanny's grandfather Eugenio – inspired by one of Venezuela's most celebrated poets, Eugenio Montejo – and local storyteller Svevo, creating a complex multilayered narrative. *El niño malo* blurs generic borders, mixing prose, oral storytelling, poems, letters and diaries. This mixture of genres, bringing together indigenous and European, popular and elite culture, prompts an examination of hybridity as part of Latin American identity. The novel also blurs the frontier between dream and reality. While one scene is referred to as a dream explicitly, the whole story has an otherworldly quality which makes it all seem not quite real. The story is set in a 'no-place', a snowy north, populated by bears and people with Viking roots, but where the locals all speak Spanish. The dream, on the other hand, has more elements of the real, such as locations in Caracas and mundane interactions. First published in Caracas in 2004 by Editorial Norma, *El niño malo* was republished in Madrid in 2010 by Ediciones Escaleras.

Slavko Zupcic and *Círculo croata*

A psychiatrist and writer, Slavko Zupcic (b.Valencia, Venezuela 1970) was chosen by the Hay Festival in 2007 as one of the Bogotá 39, the 39 most promising Latin American writers under the age of 39. He has written four short story collections, essays, poetry and stories for children, and three novels: *Barbie*, *Círculo croata* and *Pésame mucho* [I'm So Sorry for Your Loss], published together as *Tres novelas* [Three Novels] (2006). The son of a Croatian immigrant, Zupcic explored his father's stories in *Dragi sol* (1989). Luis Britto García (1999, 45) notes that Zupcic writes about the ambivalence of growing up between two cultures and sometimes invents a mythical past for his ancestors in their country of origin, as can be seen in *Círculo croata*. He won the Bienal José Rafael Pocaterra in 1990 and the Ciudad de Valencia Municipal Prize in 1991. Zupcic currently resides in Valencia, Spain.

Círculo croata began life as the short story 'Amor que a otro puerto perteneces' [Love Belongs to Another Port], which appears in translation by Janet Hendrickson in the anthology *The Future Is Not Ours* (Trelles Paz, 2012). Hendrickson also wrote a chapter for the volume *New Trends in Contemporary Latin American Narrative* (2014), in which she uses Zupcic's story as a case study for the problematic relationship that contemporary Latin American authors have with readers' expectations and with their literary past. We are told on the first page that *Círculo croata* is a novel 15 years in the making, the product of young writer Zlatica Didič's obsession with writing the story of the father he will never meet, a Croatian immigrant to Venezuela. With the help of a Croatian writer, Salvador Prasel, Zlatica reconstructs the story from a photo album and a pile of letters in Serbo-Croatian that he will never be able to read. The narrative alternates extracts from the various versions of the novel that Zlatica writes with first-person narration of the writing process. Zlatica's novel is a humorous account of two Croatian soldiers (Zlatica Sr. and Salvador Prasel) in the Second World War who are charged with taking the bones of San Desiderio from Italy back to Croatia on the whim of a mad Austro-Hungarian prince. When Zlatica finally meets his father, the latter claims to have no knowledge of San Desiderio, suggesting that the story is just a product of Zlatica's imagination. The key themes of the novel are reading, writing and questions of identity. Originally published by El otro y el mismo in Mérida, Venezuela, in 2006, *Círculo croata* was republished with *Barbie* by Sudaquia in New York in 2012.

Israel Centeno and *Bajo las hojas*

With the release of *Calletania* in 1992, Israel Centeno (b.Caracas 1958) won immediate critical success, including the Consejo Nacional de la Cultura Prize. However, following the publication of his novel *El complot* (2002), which describes an attempt to assassinate the president – recognisably Chávez, although not named as such – Centeno received physical abuse and threats against his family, which eventually led him to leave the country in 2010 (Sainz Borgo, 2014). In response, City of Asylum in Pittsburgh offered him a place as a writer-in-residence until the end of 2014. He is still resident in the United States. A prolific writer, Centeno has published 11 novels, most recently *La Marianne* (2015), four short story collections and four translations from English, with many more manuscripts still unpublished. *El complot* was published in English as *The Conspiracy* in 2014, translated by Guillermo Parra.

In *El complot*, Centeno explores what happened to far-left revolutionaries – those remnants from the guerrillas and radical movements which flourished in Venezuela following the end of the Pérez Jiménez dictatorship in 1958 – once the 'Revolution' came to power. Having grown up surrounded by radical activism, Centeno was disillusioned by 'the Process', as the novel expresses. It is deeply critical of power-hungry former radicals turned ministers, who abandon their Marxist beliefs to form part of the establishment. At the same time, the novel shines a light on the sinister undercurrent of this process, the ruthless violence necessary to cover up any traces of former 'undemocratic' behaviour by those now in power. In the background bubbles a criticism of 'el Presidente' himself, his populism, his reliance on the military and his use of the media to secure his power. In *Bajo las hojas* (2010), Centeno turns this critique of the Bolivarian government to the literary field, exploring how the government's control of the literary system allows them to maintain and extend their power.

As Jason Maldonado (2010) highlights, *Bajo las hojas* is a novel that demands commitment and concentration from readers. The first forty pages of Centeno's 400-page novel are a relatively straightforward, if self-reflexive, account of a middle-aged novelist, struggling to make ends meet in Venezuela, who seizes the opportunity to run off to London with his young and beautiful mistress. The novel then becomes increasingly complicated, after Julio agrees to take a job with the government, which involves him writing one scene every 45 minutes. Julio turns out to be a pawn in a grander scheme involving his mistress, his son, his old revolutionary colleagues turned police officers, an Italian dancer, and a death-worshipping cult of psychologists. The narration switches constantly between these disparate but linked characters and a mysterious omniscient power. As the name of the cult – Los argonautas jungianos de los últimos días [The Latter-day Jungian Argonauts] – illustrates, the novel is replete with erudite references to Greek myths and legends, psychology and religion, as well as British history, Latin American poetry and more. At the same time, Centeno experiments with many popular genres – mystery, fantasy, Gothic, suspense, crime and eroticism – using them to hook readers while also subverting generic expectations. Published in Caracas by Alfaguara, *Bajo las hojas* was shortlisted for the 2010 Iberoamericano Planeta – Casa de América Prize, out of over 500 entries.

Juan Carlos Méndez Guédez and *Chulapos Mambo*

Juan Carlos Méndez Guédez (b.Barquisimeto 1967) has lived in Spain since 1996 and holds a PhD in Latin American literature from Universidad de Salamanca. A prolific writer, he has published ten novels from *Retrato de Abel con isla volcánica al fondo* [Portrait of Abel with Volcanic Island] (1997) to *La ola detenida* [The Blocked Wave] (2017), six short story collections, two children's books, and the travel narrative *Y recuerda que te espero* [Remember I'm Waiting for You] (2015). He won the Ciudad de Barbastro international prize for short fiction in 2009 for *Tal vaz la lluvia* [In Case of Rain] and the Premio de los Libreros [booksellers' prize] in 2013 for *Arena negra* [Black Sand]. Through dark humour, his work explores themes of rootlessness, travel, relationships and politics. His stories and novels, which he calls 'autogeographical' (Brown, 2013), often feature Venezuelans in Spain. A brief summary of Méndez Guédez's work appears in *The Contemporary Spanish American Novel* (Stanco, 2013b).

In Méndez Guédez's writing, Antonietta Alario (2006) argues, politics is ever-present, but as a background rather than the main subject. She suggests that the characters are all affected by the convulsive political context, but do not engage in political debate themselves (Alario, 2006, 32). Significant moments in Venezuelan recent political history, such as the *Caracazo* riots of 1989 or the 2002 failed coup attempt, appear in the novels, but the characters only think about how these affect their own lives rather than wider political consequences. In his contribution to the collection of essays by Venezuelan writers abroad, *Pasajes de ida* [One Way Tickets], Méndez Guédez (2013b, 35) admits, 'Solo en la ficción consigo hablar de Venezuela sin que me falte el aire, sin que suceda el dolor o la emotividad extrema o la perplejidad absoluta' [It is only in fiction that I can talk about Venezuela without getting short of breath, without pain or extreme emotion or absolute bewilderment]. Although writing is a way for him to tease out ideas about Venezuela and its politics, Méndez Guédez does not want to be overbearing in his novels. In an interview, he explained his belief that people are subjected to so many different pressures and to so many people or organisations who want to use them for their own gain, that they need literature as a solitary space (Sánchez Aparicio, 2012). For him, literature is 'un lugar donde el ruido del mundo no entra con brusquedad, sino que es parte de una música de fondo donde la subjetividad explora nuevas reglas, nuevas sensaciones y sentimientos' [a place where the noise of the world does not enter abruptly, but as part of the background music where subjectivity explores new rules, new sensations and feelings] (Sánchez Aparicio, 2012). Literature can draw attention to certain events or issues but should ultimately leave readers with space to think.

Chulapos Mambo is an absurd, ironic and darkly humorous novel following the misadventures of three rather unsavoury characters in Madrid: Alejandro, the womanising businessman, Simao, the scrounger, and Henry, who believes himself to be God's gift to writing – if only he could write anything. While Henry puzzles over how the literary world has yet to recognise his genius and writes his 'MASTERPIECE', Alejandro and Simao's scheming gets them all caught up in violence, prostitution, stalking and kidnapping. Much of the humour of the story derives from the caricatured protagonists and the farcical situations in which they find themselves, but those aware of Bolivarian cultural policy will also appreciate the deeply sarcastic and ironic portrayal of the relationship between literature and the Venezuelan government which is the novel's primary concern. In a review for the journal *Letras*, Juan Manuel Romero (2013, 146) calls *Chulapos Mambo* a very important book in contemporary Venezuelan literature, in which 'se reinventan ópticas, se desconocen ciertas comodidades y se complejiza los ángulos más sencillos' [perspectives reinvent themselves, certain interests are disregarded and simple angles become more elaborate]. First published by Casa de Cartón in Madrid in 2011, a Venezuelan version was released by independent publisher Lugar Común in 2012. A French translation, *Mambo Canille* (trans. Nicole Rochaix-Salmona) was published by Zinnia in 2014.

Eduardo Sánchez Rugeles and *Transilvania unplugged*

Eduardo Sánchez Rugeles (b.Caracas 1977) rose to fame after winning the Arturo Uslar Pietri Prize for his first novel *Blue Label/Etiqueta Azul* (2010). *El Universal*'s literature correspondent Daniel Fermín (2013a), for example, listed Sánchez Rugeles in his top six young Venezuelan authors to read.

Since 2007, Sánchez Rugeles has lived, studied and written in Madrid, but still publishes his work in Venezuela. His first three novels – *Blue Label*, *Transilvania unplugged* and *Liubliana* (2012) form an unofficial trilogy documenting the complex relationship between Venezuelan youth and their homeland. He has also written a book of creative non-fiction, *Los desterrados* [The Rootless] (2011c), *Jezabel*, written for Ediciones B's crime fiction collection (2013), and *Julián* (2014), a retelling of the Orpheus story by a young boy with cancer. *Liubliana* won the Venezuelan Premio de la Crítica de la Novela [critics' prize] and the international Sor Juana Inés de la Cruz Prize.

Of all the writers addressed in this book, Eduardo Sánchez Rugeles is the most openly critical of the Bolivarian government in his novels. His novels written before Chávez's death were all narrated from a post-Chávez near future, from which the protagonists recall their life during the *chavista* period. While in *Blue Label/Etiqueta Azul* (2010) and *Transilvania unplugged* (2011a), Chávez is only inferred,[13] *Liubliana* (2012) is full of references to Chávez by name, and particularly to the way that outsiders view him as a hero or an inspiration. By *Jezabel* (2013), the criticism of Chávez voiced by the characters had become even more vitriolic. We are told, for example, that 'Para Amanda, todos los infortunios del mundo tenían un único responsable: Chávez' [For Amanda, there was only one person responsible for all the woes of the world: Chávez] (Sánchez Rugeles, 2013, Kindle loc. 619). Outside of his fiction, Sánchez Rugeles used his acceptance speech for the 2010 Uslar Pietri Prize to argue for novels of artificial democracies in the tradition of the novels of dictatorship by Arturo Uslar Pietri and Miguel Ángel Asturias. In the same speech, Sánchez Rugeles (2011c, 142–143) asserted, 'Tengo la convicción de que la literatura es inmune a la censura y al agravio, al grito feraz del ignorante' [I am convinced that literature is immune to censorship and insult, to the full cry of the ignorant]. For him, writing is in itself a political act, a resistance against the government's power over the literary system.

The opening of *Transilvania unplugged*, asking how a Latin American ended up in a Moldavian refugee camp, introduces the main themes of the novel, namely the unexpected links between Latin America and Eastern Europe, and the idea of being out of place, while at the same time establishing a mystery that the reader will have to solve through the novel. The Latin American in question is José Antonio Galleti, or Iosep Antoniescu Lacatusu Calinescu, a twentysomething 'de nacionalidad plural' [of plural nationality] (13), the son of Romanians, raised by an Italian step-father in Venezuela. José Antonio travels to Romania to meet his uncle Lucien Calinescu, accompanied by his friend Emilio Porras, who will teach cookery in Sibiu, European Capital of Culture 2007. Lucien is convinced

---

13 For analysis of how Chávez's government is referred to in *Blue Label/Etiqueta Azul*, see Brown, 2014a.

that someone named Luzny Hervasy was responsible for both his personal disgrace and the fall of Ceaușescu. This sets José Antonio off on a surreal journey through Romania in which he confronts not only Romania's history but the concept of Venezuelan national identity, and issues of contemporary Venezuelan politics and society. *Transilvania unplugged* is the novel which has received most critical attention of those studied in this book. Laura Chirinos Castellanos (2014) provides a hermeneutic reading of migration in the novel, while Patricia Valladares-Ruiz (2013) considers the movement of characters in the novel as a form of political dissent. Belkis Barrios (2011) offers a wide-ranging analysis of recurrent themes and stylistic elements in the novel, including the similarities drawn between Venezuela and Romania and the fusion of romanticism, naturalism and the absurd. *Transilvania unplugged* was first published by Alfaguara in Venezuela in 2011, then republished by Ediciones B Venezuela in 2015 with a new prologue by Sánches Rugeles explaining the book's inception.

Alberto Barrera Tyszka and *Rating*

Beginning his career as a poet and later a successful *telenovela* (television soap opera) writer, Alberto Barrera Tyszka (b.Caracas 1960) has written novels, short stories and co-authored a biography of the Venezuelan President, *Hugo Chávez sin uniforme: una historia personal* (2006) [*Hugo Chávez: The Definitive Biography of Venezuela's Controversial President* (2008)], as well as teaching literature at the Universidad Central de Venezuela and writing for Venezuelan newspaper *El Nacional*. He currently lives in Mexico. While his first novel, *También el corazón es un descuido* [The Heart is also a Mistake] (2001), did not achieve much critical recognition or commercial success, his second, *La enfermedad* (2006), won the Premio Herralde, and has since been translated into English, German, French and Italian. The English translation by Margaret Jull Costa, *The Sickness* (2010), was shortlisted for the Independent Foreign Fiction Prize. His short story collection *Crimenes* (2009) was published in English as *Crimes* in 2015. His latest novel, *Patria o Muerte* [Fatherland or Death], which explores the socio-political situation in Venezuela under Chávez, won the 2015 Tusquets international prize, and is forthcoming in English with Maclehose Press. According to Miguel Gomes (2010, 826), Barrera Tyszka's writing style stands out for its use of popular novel and *telenovela* techniques, such as suspense and switching points of view, and for its appropriation of the lexical specificities of the Venezuelan press, creating a blend of high and low registers.

With his third novel, *Rating*, which was runner-up for the 2011 Premio de la Crítica de la Novela, Barrera Tyszka brings his experience of writing for television to the page. It is the story of literature student Pablo Manzanares who becomes the assistant of Rafael Quevedo, Vice President of Special Projects for a major television channel. Obsessed with ratings, Quevedo dreams up a cross between a *telenovela* and a reality show with those left homeless by flooding as contestants. Veteran screenwriter Manuel Izquierdo is hired to script the programme and his ruminations on life, death, literature and *telenovelas* complement Pablo's youthful concerns about sex and social status. The novel switches continually between first person narration from Pablo or Manuel and an impersonal, third-person narration, juxtaposing the three. As well as traditional prose, the novel incorporates fragments of television scripts and technical reports, questioning the border between reality and fiction and the absorption of television into everyday lives. The main theme of the novel is *telenovelas* as a key Venezuelan cultural expression. *Rating* examines the rules of *telenovelas*, their purpose, and how these reflect the Venezuelan people. It presents television as aspirational, serving to distract people from their problems, allowing Barrera Tyszka to consider the poor conditions in which a large number of Venezuelans live despite being an oil-rich country. Other prominent themes of the text are the division between high culture (poetry/literature) and low culture (mass media), which draws on the classic civilisation and barbarism divide, and the commodification of culture. *Rating* is the subject of an article by Edgar Mejía Galeana (2015), which analyses the novel through the lens of biopolitics and discusses the similarities between Cuba and Venezuela evident in the text. *Rating* was published by Anagrama in Barcelona in 2011.

Gisela Kozak Rovero and *Todas las lunas*

Gisela Kozak Rovero (b.Caracas 1963) is one of Venezuela's most prominent literary scholars. She is a professor of Latin American literature at the Universidad Central de Venezuela, and has written extensively on Venezuelan literature and cultural politics, including the book *Venezuela, el país que siempre nace* [Venezuela, A Country Always Reborn] (2008). She also frequently writes articles for many publications including *Tal Cual* and *Prodavinci*. As a creative writer, she has published the short story collections *Pecados de la capital y otras historias* [Capital Sins and Other Stories] (2005) and *En rojo* [In Red] (2011), the novels *Latidos de Caracas* [Caracas Heartbeats] (2007) and *Todas las lunas* (2012), and the collection of *crónicas*, *Ni tan chéveres ni tan iguales* [Not So Cool nor So Equal] (2014). As a supporter of radical leftist movements before Chávez came to power, but opposed to Chávez and his methods, Kozak Rovero evidently resents the way that the opposition are treated in Venezuela, which is reflected in both her academic work and her fiction. Inma Chacón (2009) describes Kozak Rovero's writing as founded in her political commitments, her feminism and her belief in unity in diversity.

Todas las lunas weaves together disparate writings – *crónicas*, letters, and diary entries – by a 'family' of orphans in response to the disappearance of Loren, a poet and the youngest member of the group. The protagonists, all from diverse ethnic and linguistic backgrounds, live together in Estefania, a Utopia where immigrants from around the world live in harmony. Their love goes beyond familial bonds to romantic and sexual relationships, upon which Loren's disappearance forces them to reflect. The tone of the novel is intimate and confessional, as the characters reassess their lives and the meaning of home. Each of the protagonists is in some way creative (a musician, an architect, a writer, an engineer, a poet and a doctor with a unique approach to healing), so the nature of creation, and the motivations behind it, are key themes in the novel. Roberto Martínez Bachrich (2013) recounts how *Todas las lunas* began life in a literary workshop led by Carlos Noguera in Caracas. Bachrich (2013) calls it the happiest of her novels, which 'se alejaba, felizmente, de la realidad circundante y la monótona sinfonía de sangre del país, para explorar tiempos y lugares remotos (en el pasado, en el futuro, en la imaginación), sensibilidades voraces, personajes insólitos' [was, thankfully, removed from the surrounding reality and the monotonous symphony of blood in the country, to explore remote times and places (in the past, the future, the imagination), raging feelings and unusual characters]. *Todas las lunas* was finished in 2004 but was not published for the first time until 2011, by Equinoccio in Caracas, and republished by Sudaquia in New York in 2013. Kozak Rovero noted in an interview with Inma Chacón (2009), before *Todas las lunas* was published, that, as time passed, the novel increasingly spoke to the situation in Venezuela: 'Al ser un relato que se propone una idea radicalmente antiautoritaria del mundo, creo que su relación con la abusiva situación de poder del estado venezolano actual sale a la luz' [As it is a novel which proposes a radically anti-authoritarian idea of the world, I think its link to the abusive use of power of the current Venezuelan state is coming to light].

Armando Luigi Castañeda and *La fama, o es venérea, o no es fama*

Armando Luigi Castañeda (b.Valencia, 1970) is a writer, lawyer and photographer. He has completed five masters' degrees and a doctorate (in literature, law and international development, between Venezuela, Spain and France), and now lives in Paris. As he describes in his autofictional novel, *La fama, o es venérea, o no es fama*, his first book was published after winning the national biennial Miguel Ramón Utrera Prize in 1997 (Castañeda, 2012, 264). His books include *Mujer desnuda mirando a un enano negro arrodillado* [Naked Woman Looking at a Kneeling Black Dwarf] (1994), *La crisis de la modernidad* [The Crisis of Modernity] (1997), *Historia de la burra y la motocicleta* [The Story of the Donkey and the Motorcycle] (1998), and *Guía de Barcelona para sociópatas* [Guide to Barcelona for Sociopaths] (2007). In May 2015, Castañeda published a three-part interview with himself on his blog, in which he explained his ideas about himself as a writer. He stated that having spent the first 28 years of his life in Venezuela leant certain characteristics to his writing, particularly his sense of humour, but that in an age of globalisation it is difficult to feel part of a local or national tradition.

Like most of Castañeda's work, *La fama, o es venérea, o no es fama* began life as a series of posts on his blog between 2006 and 2009.[14] In *La fama*, an author, unnamed yet bearing many biographical similarities to Castañeda, flits between struggling to write a conventional crime thriller, which bores him, and recounting his travels, his sexual exploits and his dead-end job, interspersed with literary experiments, ideas for adverts and random notes. The 'antinovel' also includes imaginary conversations with readers and a reader's report from a Spanish publisher. Much of the novel is therefore the author–narrator's reflections on literary value and the process of writing. *La fama* was published by Sudaquia in New York in 2012.

Metafiction, autofiction and intertextuality

What unites the novels addressed in this book is their use of writers – amateur or professional, real or fictional – as protagonists. Although he never refers to himself, or to his parade of ex-lovers, by name, Armando Luigi Castañeda states throughout *La fama, o es venérea, o no es fama* (2012) that it is a work of 'autofiction', and the events described follow his own biography, as posted on his blog in 2006. Indeed, that biography ends 'El resto de la historia está en una novela' [The rest of the story is in a novel], and the final four paragraphs of the biography appear verbatim in *La fama* (Castañeda, 2012, 264–265). Throughout, readers are encouraged to interpret *La fama* as Castañeda's musings on the writing process and ideas of literary quality. The protagonist of *Bajo las hojas* (2010), Julio, can similarly be read as a fictional version of its author, Israel Centeno. He is a professional writer who struggles to make ends meet in Venezuela by teaching creative writing classes. Feeling oppressed by the government, he goes to live abroad. Julio ends up in London, a city he had briefly enjoyed as a young man, 26 years earlier. Julio's memories of London are based on Centeno's time squatting in Brixton Hill in the 1980s. Like Centeno, Julio resents the Bolivarian government for betraying the Revolution and for forming an alliance with the military (Centeno, 2010, 15–16). The multiple parallels between Julio's life and Centeno's own prompt readers to interpret Julio as Centeno's mouthpiece, expressing his own attitudes towards the Venezuelan literary system. By contrast, the protagonist of *Chulapos Mambo* (2011), Henry, is on the other side of the political divide to author Juan Carlos Méndez Guédez. *Chulapos Mambo* offers a deeply ironic portrait of a terrible writer who is supported and promoted by the government thanks to his blind loyalty to 'the Process', the very opposite of Méndez Guédez himself. It is Henry's arch-nemesis in the story, Saúl Junco, who recalls Méndez Guédez, a talented and critically acclaimed novelist living in Spain and spurned by the Bolivarian government and its supporters. In *Rating* (2011), Alberto Barrera Tyszka depicts two very different kinds of professional writer: Pablo Manzanares, an aspiring poet and literature student,

---

14 See http://armandoluigi.blogspot.com/.

and Manuel Quevedo, a veteran scriptwriter. Through the juxtaposition of the two characters and the dialogue between them, Barrera Tyszka raises questions of the value of different kinds of writing and the various motivations behind them. Barrera Tyszka has stated that his ambition was to write a novel with a mixture of elements of himself, of people he knows and of invention (Linares, 2012). Like Pablo Manzanares, José Antonio Galleti in *Transilvania unplugged* (Sánchez Rugeles, 2011a) and Zlatica Didič in *Círculo croata* (Zupcic, 2012) are aspiring writers who have studied literature, enter literary competitions and try to get published, in the hope that writing will bring them fame and a sense of self-worth. *Transilvania unplugged*'s other protagonist, Emilio, although not a writer by trade, at times becomes an 'author–narrator' (Cazzato, 1995, 31), as he writes the story of what happened to him and José Antonio in Transylvania for a journalist and comments upon this writing process at the same time. In Emilio's frequent criticisms of José Antonio's writing, one can read Sánchez Rugeles's own thoughts about literary quality. Zlatica Didič, meanwhile, shares many biographical details with his writer, Slavko Zupcic. Like his protagonist, Zupcic is half-Croatian, and has spent most of his life rewriting the same story. At 19, Zupcic published *Dragi Sol* (1989), a much more autobiographical exploration of his absent father, in which he uses his real name (Saavedra, 2012, 138–139). In *Círculo croata*, the protagonist becomes Zlatica Didič, but events from *Círculo croata*, such as Salvador Prasel dying just as the young writer is about to meet him, are real events from Zupcic's life, as described in his collection of essays, *Máquinas que cantan* [Singing Machines] (2005). Nonetheless, *Círculo croata* is above all about writing, specifically the influence that other writers have on the narrator and how writing becomes a way for him to define his own identity. As Gisela Kozak Rovero's *Todas las lunas* (2013) is a patchwork of memoirs, diary entries and letters, all the protagonists are, in some sense, writers and narrators. Only one, however, Robin, is a professional – and very famous – writer of *crónicas*. This mixture of professional and amateur writers allows Kozak Rovero to explore the processes and values of writing from a range of different angles, juxtaposing private and public forms of writing. Finally, the protagonist of Juan Carlos Chirinos's *El niño malo cuenta hasta cien y se retira* (2010), D.Jota, fits least neatly into the definition of writer. A radio DJ by profession, the only reference to him writing before the events at the heart of the story is a recollection of evenings spent writing surrealist poems with his friend (Chirinos, 2010, 202–203). However, the second half of the novel is written as D.Jota's first-person account of what happened to him, written in a stolen notebook as he takes the train back to Caracas. In addition, other lead characters of *El niño malo* include real-life poet Eugenio Montejo and local storyteller Svevo, through whom Chirinos explores the power of words and storytelling.

As well as these writer–protagonists, other literary references – explicit or oblique – abound, and as readers we are constantly made aware that what we are reading is a fabrication. Such self-reflexivity, as Carmen Bustillo describes in *La aventura metaficcional* [The Metafictional Adventure] (1997), has been a key feature of Latin American literature, with Manuel Puig, Mario Vargas Llosa, Felisberto Hernández, Álvaro Mutis and Alfredo Bryce Echenique as, in her eyes, its greatest proponents. Elzbieta Sklodowska (2003, 103) equally observes that 'one of the most salient characteristics of the Boom was the ubiquity of metafictional texts exploring mechanisms of their own making'. For Latin American writers since the Boom, a significant challenge has been how to distinguish themselves from their predecessors without denying their influence, especially in the context of commercial demands for texts similar to those produced in the Boom (Hendrickson, 2014). This tension was notably expressed by the Crack and McOndo groups in the mid-1990s. In the Crack manifesto Miguel Ángel Palou asserts, 'Nada más fácil para un escritor que escribir sobre sí mismo; nada más aburrido que la vida de un escritor' [Nothing is easier for a writer than writing about oneself; nothing is more boring than the life of a writer] (Volpi et al., 1996, 3), while Ignacio Padilla notes a 'cansancio de las letras que vuelan en círculos como moscas sobre sus propios cadáveres' [weariness of works that fly in circles like flies above their own cadavers] (Volpi et al., 1996, 5). In his introduction to *The Contemporary Spanish American Novel*, William H. Corral (2013, 12) considers the legacy of the Boom authors' experimentation with metafiction and intertextuality on their successors, noting an 'awareness that those devices were daring and amusing but now they have to work better'. Both Corral's analysis and his use of the term 'devices' are reductive, minimising the value of these attempts by the Boom authors to give literary form not only to the new realities that they were experiencing, but also, as Carlos Fuentes (1969, 30) affirmed, the centuries of experience which had been silenced. Fuentes (1969, 32) argued, 'Nuestra literatura es verdaderamente revolucionaria en cuanto le niega al orden establecido el léxico' [Our literature is truly revolutionary in that it denies the established lexical order]. Fiction about fiction and literary experimentation fought against the model of nation-building narratives and the linguistic legacies of Spanish colonialism. As discussed previously, I maintain that the similar conditions for writers in countries such as Chile and Peru in the pre-Boom period and those in Venezuela under the Bolivarian Revolution led to similar literary cultures. Just as metafiction and intertextuality were more than mere novelties for the Boom authors, contemporary Venezuelan works of literature – including but not limited to those which make up the corpus of this study – 'foreground their own production, their authorship, their intertextual influences, their reception or their enunciation' (Stam, 1985, xiii) in response to their socio-political context. In these novels, metafiction and intertextuality allow authors to comment on the uses and values of literature for the Bolivarian government and offer their own opposing ideas about reading and writing.

First used by William Gass in the late 1960s to describe 'recent fictions that were somehow about fiction itself', the term metafiction began to be used regularly during the 1970s to describe 'fiction with self-consciousness, self-awareness, self-knowledge, ironic self-distancing' (Currie, 1995, 1). However, while the term is relatively new, the literary practice it describes is well-established. Mark Currie (1995, 6) has linked the advent of metafiction to modernism, in its problematising of traditional, realist narratives and their presumption of truth and authority. Although modernism implies a specific historical period, the late nineteenth and early twentieth centuries, the 'conventions of realism', which Currie (1995, 6) lists as 'traditional narrative forms, principles of unity and transparent representational language', still dominate the Bolivarian idea of literature, while the preferences of the modernists for self-referentiality and alienating readers as described by Currie are shared by many contemporary Venezuelan novelists. Other scholars see metafiction as a specifically postmodern phenomenon. Luigi Cazzato (1995, 27), for example, defines metaculture as the 'ultimate product of the Western historical cultural process', manifesting 'the predominance and the importance of self-consciousness in postmodern culture'. Again, the novels in this study share features often described as 'postmodern', such as disillusionment with grand narratives and moral relativism. However, my aim here is not to classify the novels according to these categories (modernist/postmodernist), but to highlight how, in a large range of literature from different genres, traditions and time periods, self-reflexivity has been used to challenge dominant narratives. Within Venezuelan literary history, as Rivas Rojas (2010, 16) describes, reactions to the lack of literary freedom under the Pérez Jiménez dictatorship (1948–1958) led to a wave of literature characterised by metafiction, self-reflection, parody, distancing and rewriting. Renato Rodríguez's *Al sur del Equanil* [South of the Equanil] (1963) has been considered one of the first Venezuelan novels to engage seriously with metafiction (Barrera Linares, 2012). The aesthetic legacy of literature from the Punto Fijo period is evident throughout the metafictional texts discussed in this book, which assert a continuity of literary tradition.

The preference for metafiction among the authors in this corpus can in part be attributed to their high levels of literary and critical knowledge. One common definition of metafiction is as the place within narrative where fiction meets criticism. Currie (1995, 2) views metafiction 'as a borderline discourse', which, positioned between fiction and criticism, explores the relationship between the two, while Patricia Waugh (1995, 39) considers metafiction as the exploration of 'a theory of fiction through the practice of writing fiction'. Currie (1995, 3) attributes this critical awareness within fiction to the fact that 'academic literary critics have been increasingly successful as novelists', as evidenced by the authors in this study. Gisela Kozak Rovero and Alberto Barrera Tyskza, for example, have taught literature at university level. Those who are not currently engaged in literary criticism still have this grounding from their education: Juan Carlos Méndez Guédez, Juan Carlos Chirinos and Eduardo Sánchez Rugeles have all carried out doctoral study of literature at the Universidad de Salamanca. In this way, the writer–critic becomes 'a dialectical figure, embodying both the production and the reception of fiction in the roles of author and reader' (Currie, 1995, 3).

Through its self-criticism, metafiction demonstrates to readers the ways in which they can engage critically with the text itself (Hutcheon, 1984, 6). In the novels analysed here, the narrators and characters, and by extension the novelists who wrote them, both reflect on their own creative choices during the writing process and comment on other books that they read, establishing their own ideas about literary quality with which readers can engage. Through such reflections, authors such as Juan Carlos Méndez Guédez, Eduardo Sánchez Rugeles and especially Armando Luigi Castañeda try to pre-empt and counter criticism of their own writing within their novels, even though it is ultimately impossible to control all criticism. As Bolivarian cultural policy has focused on delegitimising literature (speaking always of books and suggesting cultural elites are out of touch with the needs of the nation) and the privileged status of authors, while increasing the value and legitimacy of other types of culture, particularly music (Gaspar Károsy, 2005), authors use the main tool at their disposal, their novels, to, in Bourdieu's terms, take a position within the literary field, which they hope will increase their standing within the hierarchy (Bourdieu, 1993, 30–31). In a context where discussion of literary quality is dismissed as elitist, by discussing literary quality within their novels these authors make a claim to be 'legitimately entitled to designate legitimate writers' (Bourdieu, 1993, 41).

A subset of metafiction found in the novels studied in this book is autofiction. Armando Luigi Castañeda describes his work as autofiction, and refers to various examples of autofiction from world literature through his text. Autofiction is a form of autobiographical writing that incorporates the techniques and characteristics more commonly associated with fiction (Dix, 2017, 160). The term was coined by Serge Doubrovsky in 1977 to described his book *Fils* (Dix, 2017, 157; Reisz, 2016, 74), although Diana Diaconu (2017, 41) emphasises that Doubrovsky did not invent the genre, he just gave it a name. Rather than thinking of Doubrovsky as an individual genius, Diaconu (2017, 45) advocates questioning the specific socio-historical context in which autofiction appeared which led to the need for such a form of expression. According to Jacques Lecarme (1994, 227), autofiction is characterised by the author, narrator and protagonist sharing a nominal identity (a name) and basic facts, such as being the author of a certain book, or born in a certain city. Susana Reisz (2016, 77–78) critiques critics' insistence on the author in this equation as the 'implied author', or the concept of authorship, in the place of the real, living author. She argues that it makes little sense for a reader to compare a character with the concept of authorship, whereas it is easy to note similarities between a real author's biography and that of a protagonist. Other common features of autofiction are stream of consciousness, an unreliable narrator and elusiveness (Dix, 2017, 161), all elements which characterise *La fama*.

Although Hywel Dix (2017, 158) states that autofiction is a predominantly French genre, there has been significant interest in Hispanic autofiction in the twenty-first century, with notable studies including *La autoficción: reflexiones teóricas* [Autofiction: Theoretical Reflections] (2012) and *El yo fabulado: nuevas aproximaciones críticas a la autoficción* [The Invented I: New Critical Approximations to Autofiction] (2014), both edited by Ana Casas, as well as *El pacto ambiguo: de la novela autobiográfica a la autoficción* [The Ambiguous Pact: From the Autobiographical Novel to Autofiction] (2007) by Manuel Alberca. The 'ambiguous pact' of Alberca's title places autofiction between the autobiographical pact described by Lejuene (through which readers expect the truth) and the fictional pact (through which readers suspend disbelief). In this way, according to Susana Reisz (2016, 74), autofictions are discourses which transgress literary boundaries and aim to frustrate the reader's desire to distinguish between the real (lived experience) and the imaginary. Marjorie Worthington (2017, 474) asserts that 'autofictions consciously play with readerly expectations about memoir and fiction, thwarting both, thereby simultaneously calling into question – and ultimately, making a case for – the importance of distinguishing between fact and fiction'. Worthington (2017, 476) stresses that the difference between memoir and autofiction is that autofiction questions the unproblematic equation of the narrator–protagonist with the real-life author. She adds that autofiction offers not 'the truth' but a particular version of the truth. The use of autofiction techniques in the novels studied is particularly pertinent to the Venezuelan context where, as I explore in Chapter 6, questions of truth and objectivity are political.

Diaconu (2017, 42) rejects the idea that autofiction is the experimental expression of autobiography, arguing instead that it is born from a dissatisfaction with the form of the novel, specifically the novel's ability to convey inner truths. With reference to the work of Roberto Bolaño and Fernando Vallejo, she argues that autofiction is a way for the novel to maintain a critical edge, to assert an individual identity, and to escape from the conventions of novels for mass consumption. Reisz (2016, 87–89), meanwhile, suggests that the implied reader of autofiction is part of the intimate circle of the author, and therefore likely to be a literary insider; autofiction, she argues, is written for these insiders who can distinguish the fact from the fiction (recognise the real characters and events), although the book can be read in a different way by outsiders. Not only in *La fama*, but in other, less overtly autofictional novels studied in this book, are there references to the Venezuelan literary system which would only be recognised by those familiar with it.

As well as metafiction and autofiction, I look at references to other authors and their works within these novels, through quotation, allusion, and using real-life authors as characters, to ascertain how the value of literature is judged, whether literature is shown to have any effect on people's lives and to what extent writers engage with wider literary tradition. I ask how intertextuality adds new layers of meaning to the novels, following Graham Allen's (2000, 38) assertion that 'the meaning of texts is always at one and the same time "inside" and yet "outside" the text'. Definitions of intertextuality range from textual borrowings to the idea that society itself is a text whose meanings are interwoven into every utterance, building on twentieth-century linguistics, particularly the work of Saussure, Bahktin, Kristeva and Barthes, as Allen (2000) describes. My analysis here employs what Gérard Genette (1997, 5) defines as 'hypertextuality', that is, 'any relationship uniting a text B [the hypertext] to an earlier text A [the hypotext], upon which it has been grafted in a manner that is not that of commentary'. Genette (1997, 5) specifies that the hypertext may speak about the hypotext directly or owe its existence in some way to the hypotext, and that it is still considered literature, usually fiction. Both the origin of the quotation or allusion and the ways in which it is incorporated into the hypertext affect the meanings that readers take from it. Michael Riffaterre (1990, 57) maintains that 'the urge to understand compels readers to look to the intertext to fill out the text's gaps [and] spell out its implications'.

To understand the novels in this corpus better, I have looked to the works cited or alluded to, as well as to the lives of their authors (Mario Vargas Llosa, Alfredo Bryce Echenqiue, Eugenio Montejo, Salvador Prasel and William Faulkner). The ways in which authors use intertextuality is indicative of the audience they imagine for their novels, an audience which has read widely enough to recognise the intertexts and to understand the meanings they confer on the new text. These authors refuse to make their texts simpler to reach a mass audience. Instead, according to Catalina Gaspar Károsy (2005), 'más que apelar a un compañero de ruta, a un lector cómplice, [la literatura contemporánea venezolana] exige no sólo su participación sino también su responsabilidad en la generación de la significación, en la activación del complejísimo proceso intertextual' [more than appealing to a fellow traveller, a complicit reader, contemporary Venezuelan fiction demands of readers not only participation but also responsibility in making meaning, through activating a very complicated intertextual process]. The novels studied in this book incite readers to seek out works by other authors, both Venezuelan and international, who have been condemned as elitist in Bolivarian rhetoric. By using the term coined by Trotsky, 'fellow travellers', Gaspar Károsy implies that it is a particularly socialist trait to expect readers to share a common ideology. However, the authors of these novels seek their own kind of complicit readers, ones who share, or seek to share, their literary knowledge and tastes.[15] In this respect, 'both axes of intertextuality, texts entering via authors (who are, first, readers) and texts entering via readers (co-producers) are [...] emotionally and politically charged', as Worton and Still (1990, 2) note. By drawing attention to the interconnectedness of cultural productions, these intertextual novels undermine the self-sufficiency espoused in Bolivarian policy, according to which culture should be rooted in the national geography and history (Wisotzki, 2006; Plataforma del

---

15 One of the new private publishing houses to have emerged in Venezuela in recent years is even called Lector Cómplice: http://www.lectorcomplice.com.ve/.

Libro y la Lectura, 2007). In addition, the intertextuality in these novels allows the authors to place themselves within the literary field. According to Bourdieu (1993, 183), referencing other authors is both 'grateful homage' and 'self-valorising annexation', both an acknowledgement of their debt to other authors and a way to associate themselves with the authors they admire in the minds of readers. Following Harold Bloom's (1997, 5) claim that 'weaker talents idealize, figures of capable imagination appropriate for themselves', the authors in this corpus demonstrate their literary talent by making other authors' work part of their own.

As well as the narrative content and themes of these novels, their form is in itself metafictional and intertextual, drawing attention to the writing process and the influence of other texts or authors. Formal experimentation signals defiance of the condemnation of 'elite' culture by the Bolivarian regime and support for literature as an artistic endeavour grounded in a long literary tradition stretching far beyond Venezuela's borders. Of particular interest here is how writers who are seen by the Bolivarian regime and its supporters as elitist both appropriate and subvert the tropes of certain 'popular' genres, such as detective fiction, fantasy or comedy. Avoiding an overly simplistic elite/popular dichotomy, the writers examined here play with generic conventions to create works that are innovative and challenging, yet still entertaining. They offer plenty of material for socio-political analysis but can just as easily be read for the joy of an absorbing story. Such engagement with popular genres is not a recent development, but rather, as Philip Swanson (1995) explores, a common characteristic of the so-called 'new novel' in Latin America.[16] Nonetheless, the distinctions drawn between the popular and the elite in Bolivarian rhetoric add a new dimension to this merging of popular and high culture.

Each chapter of this book explores a way in which these novels reflect on writing, from the protagonists as writers in different contexts (Chapters 1–3), through appearances from real-life writers (Chapter 4), to experiments with style and popular culture (Chapter 5) and questioning the boundaries between fiction and reality (Chapter 6).

Chapter 1 examines how *Chulapos Mambo* (Méndez Guédez, 2011) and *Bajo las hojas* (Centeno, 2010) condemn the connections between a successful or unsuccessful writing career and Bolivarian politics. The protagonist of *Chulapos Mambo*, Henry, is a talentless writer promoted by the government. The novel explicitly criticises the populist measures put in place by the Bolivarian government to make Venezuela a nation of writers, as well as suggesting that Bolivarian cultural policy rewards those who are loyal to the

---

16 As Swanson (1995, 2) explains, 'new' is not necessarily defined chronologically, as the term has been applied to books from the 1920s to the 1980s, but instead refers to works which 'reject the premises and formal structures of conventional realism'.

Revolution. Moreover, the rivalry between Henry and critically acclaimed but starving opposition writer Saúl Junco demonstrates the polarisation of the literary field, which reflects the polarisation of all aspects of society under the Bolivarian Revolution. *Bajo las hojas*, meanwhile, reflects criticism among certain writers and critics that Bolivarian cultural policy views writing more as a hobby than a profession, and does not offer writers the cultural capital required to make a successful career of writing, particularly in a globalised literary market. Protagonist Julio takes a job writing for the government, but ends the novel thoroughly disillusioned, as he dreams of writing 'great works' that have a profound effect on readers. Julio's complaints echo claims among writers that Bolivarian cultural policy has instrumentalised reading and delegitimised literary experimentation.

Chapter 2 considers both the protagonists and the authors of the novels in this study as 'writer–critics' who share their ideas about literary quality through discussion of both their own writing and other people's. As institutions set up during the Punto Fijo period (1958–1998) to endow writers with literary capital and raise the reputation of Venezuela in international literary circles, such as the Rómulo Gallegos literary prize and Monte Ávila publishing house, have been subsumed into the Bolivarian 'Platform for the Book', some writers are concerned that a focus on ideology will undermine literary quality. In *Transilvania unplugged* (Sánchez Rugeles, 2011a), *Todas las lunas* (Kozak Rovero, 2013) and *Rating* (Barrera Tyszka, 2011), characters both attest to the significance of well-written literature for them and display their literary knowledge and tastes as a sign of distinction. As professional writers move away from the state, they are faced with new challenges, in the form of the demands of international literary markets. Throughout *La fama, o es venérea, o no es fama* (Castañeda, 2012), the author–narrator is caught between an aspiration to write challenging and experimental fiction and a desire for commercial success.

With the resurgence of nationalism in Venezuela instigated by Hugo Chávez, cultural policy posits reading and writing as tools for building a national community. Chapter 3 examines how (auto)fictional writers counter this national narrative by asserting the place of the individual or the family (*El niño malo cuenta hasta cien y se retira*, *Todas las lunas* and *Rating*), or exploring the complexities of national identity (*Círculo croata* and *Transilvania unplugged*). This trend mirrors the 'subjective turn', which, according to Raquel Rivas Rojas (2010), characterised the texts written in opposition to the dictatorship of Marcos Pérez Jiménez (1948–1958). The chapter concludes that writing is used to explore the tension in terms of the national. The writers in these novels do not identify with the nationalism of the Bolivarian Revolution, but they cannot avoid questions about national politics and society, and use their writing to work through them.

Chapter 4 suggests that, by linking their own writing to that of an author they admire through quotation, allusion or reference, Méndez Guédez, Chirinos and Zupcic both counter Venezuela's literary isolation and explore issues of particular importance to them. Through playful references to other writers which his readers are expected to recognise, *Chulapos Mambo* draws attention to the disparity between the readers' own literary advantages and the limits to access and exposure faced by readers and writers in his native Venezuela. In addition, real Latin American writers appear throughout the story, most notably Mario Vargas Llosa and Alfredo Bryce Echinique, two writers who, like himself, have been judged negatively for their political beliefs. In *El niño malo*, as well as integrating fragments of Montejo's poems into the narrative and employing Montejian motifs, Chirinos turns one of Venezuela's greatest poets into one of the main characters of his story. As well as paying homage to Montejo, Chirinos contemplates his own experience of being Venezuelan abroad, and the importance of language and writing in this context. In *Círculo croata*, Zupcic honours Salvador Prasel, a Croatian emigrant who became a writer in Venezuela, while also linking Prasel to William Faulkner, allowing Zupcic to allude to Faulkner's appreciation for Venezuelan literature.

Chapter 5 proposes that, while the incorporation of aspects of popular culture in literary texts is not new, it takes on new significance in the context of the distinction between the popular as 'ours' and the elite as 'unpatriotic' in Bolivarian rhetoric. In addition, the 'popular' as celebrated by the Bolivarian Revolution is defined by the national and often the indigenous. Popular culture in terms of globalised media is condemned as neo-imperialist. *Bajo las hojas*, *Chulapos Mambo*, *Transilvania unplugged* and *El niño malo cuenta hasta cien y se retira* are all novels that blur the boundaries between elite and popular culture. Popular is understood here as genres such as the gothic, comedy and detective fiction with mass appeal and as global media and the internet. *El niño malo* also incorporates aspects of indigenous storytelling, asserting that indigenous culture is not the preserve of the Bolivarian Revolution.

Chapter 6 demonstrates how fiction that highlights its own constructed nature is not only a reaction against the delegitimisation of the author as an individual talent in Bolivarian cultural policy, but also a challenge to the grand narratives of nationalism and socialism propagated by the government. These metafictional texts encourage readers to recognise the blurring of the boundary between truth and fiction at the heart of the increasingly violent and destructive polarisation of Venezuelan society. The metafictional aspects of these novels are a message to readers to detect fiction outside of the novel: in official histories, 'reality' television, news reports and in political rhetoric.

CHAPTER 1

Writing for the State

Of the many ways in which authors comment on Bolivarian cultural policy in their fiction, the most explicit is through characters who work for the state as writers. This chapter examines how *Chulapos Mambo* (Méndez Guédez, 2011) and *Bajo las hojas* (Centeno, 2010) condemn the connections between a successful or unsuccessful writing career and Bolivarian politics. Juan Carlos Méndez Guédez's novel *Chulapos Mambo* (2011) parodies the Bolivarian approach to culture through the character of Henry, a talentless writer who is nonetheless promoted by the state thanks to his loyalty to the Revolution. Henry's self-delusion, fuelled by his determination to will himself into being a successful writer, is exacerbated by a cultural policy which celebrates everyone as a writer regardless of literary talent, or lack thereof. Henry is shown living the high life thanks to a government credit card in exchange for his loyalty to the party, embodying claims that writers are judged on their political orientation and activity, and criticism of the so-called '*boliburguesía*' [Boli-bourgeoisie], those who have become rich through their support of the government (Valery, 2009b). In addition, the rivalry between Henry and the critically acclaimed but starving opposition writer Saúl Junco reflects the polarisation of the literary field under the Bolivarian Revolution. Israel Centeno's novel *Bajo las hojas* (2010) also explores what it means to write for the state, but through the lens of Julio, a struggling writer who takes a job writing for the government out of desperation. Julio's complaints reflect claims among writers that Bolivarian cultural policy has instrumentalised reading and delegitimised literary experimentation.

In *Chulapos Mambo* (2011), Juan Carlos Méndez Guédez parodies the literary system in Venezuela under Chávez. Henry Estrada, who thinks of himself as the saviour of Western literature, is presented as wholly unappealing: a fat, ugly drunk whose writing sends women to sleep. Henry, however, refers to himself repeatedly as a genius (17, 95, 188, 271) and even emails various publishers announcing:

YA ESTÁ AQUÍ.
LLEGÓ LA BOMBA. ESPERE LA EXPLOSIÓN QUE CAMBIARÁ

PARA SIEMPRE EL CURSO DE LA LITERATURA UNIVERSAL. (62)

[IT'S HERE.
THE BOMB HAS DROPPED. AWAIT THE EXPLOSION THAT WILL CHANGE THE COURSE OF WORLD LITERATURE FOR EVER.]

Henry's brash emails show how little he knows about the conventions of international literary markets. The absurd exaggeration of Henry's negative qualities juxtaposed with his inflated ego provides much of the humour of the novel. Beyond a clever comedic device, this contrast allows Méndez Guédez to introduce a critique of various aspects of cultural policy and practice in contemporary Venezuela.

Over the course of the novel, Henry's outrageous self-belief is revealed to be a defence mechanism. Henry creates for himself an identity as a great writer to counteract his self-doubt (36). His lack of confidence stems from his parents' indifference towards him when he was a child. His mother did not want to listen to him, telling him, 'Callado estás precioso, criatura ...' [You're beautiful when you're quiet, child] (57). Writing, in his mind, becomes a route to fame, which will finally allow him to assert himself. Above all, fame will make his parents take him seriously and they will have to listen to him (57). It is not just his parents' admiration he craves, though, but that of the whole town – in the form of a library named after him (35) – and even the whole country. He dreams of the fictional Venezuelan Nobel Prize-winning author Ceramiga (perhaps a nod to José Saramago) praising his literary talent and 'GRAN OBRA' [great work] (77). Henry echoes the Boom novelists in their ambition to become recognised for a 'gran obra' (Blaustein, 2011, 162), a body of work that will make a real impact and be remembered. His aspiration to fame is also fuelled by a warped view of the lifestyle of writers, that is, a belief that writing will lead him quickly to material gains with minimum effort (61). His goal is to achieve the same standard of living as he perceives the Boom writers to have enjoyed, including relocation to Europe. He plans:

> Redondear una obra maestra y conseguir un dinero que le permitiese vivir con suma comodidad, con apartamentos en París, en Barcelona, en Londres; con asistente personal, con piscinas; repleto de medallas y de doctorados honoris causa; igual que los maestros del Boom. (188)

> [Crafting a masterpiece and getting some money, which would allow him to live in upmost comfort, with apartments in Paris, Barcelona, London; with a personal assistant, with swimming pools; covered in medals and honorary doctorates; just like the maestros of the Boom.]

This idealised picture of wealth and luxury evidences Henry's naivety and lack of real knowledge about the Latin American literary industry. At the time of the Boom, public interest in the Cuban Revolution 'played a major role in creating an environment favourable to the reception of the Boom novels' (de Castro and Birns, 2010, 2). In addition, the interest of the U.S. government in improving relations with Latin America led them to fund translation and promotion of Latin American literature. By the early 2000s, when the novel was set, Latin American authors operated within a very different context. Moreover, while writers like Gabriel García Márquez, Mario Vargas Llosa and Carlos Fuentes did become very wealthy, at the time that they were writing, they had to depend on other activities to live modestly (Donoso, 1972, 71). Their ultimate financial success owed as much to them being shrewd businessmen, undertaking lecture tours or writing for newspapers, as to the sales of their books.

Writing is something that Henry feels that he must do, even though it is not something he enjoys. This is evident in his comparison of his own writing process with that of his arch-nemesis, Saúl Junco, who 'tenía una actitud tan irresponsable con la escritura que parecía disfrutar con ella' [had such an irresponsible attitude to writing that he even seemed to enjoy it] (177). For Henry, by contrast, writing is a constant struggle, a battle against his lack of ideas (177). In this respect, Henry once again seems the opposite to Méndez Guédez, who professes greatly to enjoy writing and claims that writing has made him a very happy person (Volpini, 2011). Writing, for Henry, is such a chore because, deep down, he realises that his own work is terrible, even though he will never admit this out loud, as evident from the first chapter when he reads what he has written and then deletes the whole file in disgust (13).

Regardless, Henry retains a construction of himself as an important writer and believes that if he can just imitate the behaviour of successful writers he will become one himself. Even though he does not like alcohol, Henry drinks excessively because he has read in biographies that alcoholism is a trait of many famous authors (93) and even considers cutting off one of his hands to be like Cervantes and Valle Inclán (97). This idea that being a writer is more a matter of will than of talent is shared by the second protagonist of the novel, Simao, a layabout who in a former life back in Venezuela was a literature student, although the third main character, philandering Spanish businessman Alejandro, cannot comprehend this:

> [Alejando:] Un escritor que no puede escribir ... No lo comprendo, es como un cirujano que no puede operar. Entonces no es cirujano.
> [Simao:] Esto es distinto. Un escritor es una persona que dice que es escritor y ya. Lo es siempre. (175–176)
>
> [Alejandro: A writer who doesn't write ... I don't get it, it's like a surgeon who can't operate. Then he's not a surgeon.
> Simao: It's different. A writer is someone who says he's a writer and that's that. He will always be one.]

Throughout *Chulapos Mambo*, Bolivarian cultural policy is portrayed as responsible for instilling in people like Henry the belief that they are all writers, no matter what (or whether) they write. Henry's self-delusion, fuelled by his determination to will himself into being a successful writer, is reinforced and exacerbated by a cultural policy which celebrates everyone as a writer. One especially striking example of this in *Chulapos Mambo* is when Henry receives a Christmas card from the Ministry of Culture:

> La tarjeta iba dirigida al escritor Henry Estrada. Al fin alguien lo respetaba verdaderamente, pensó, sin saber que otras trescientas mil tarjetas similares habían sido enviadas y que a toda persona sin oficio conocido le habían colocado ese título porque a decir del Coronel encargado del Gabinete de prensa todo el mundo escribe y por lo tanto todo el mundo es escritor. (188)

> [The letter was addressed to the writer Henry Estrada. At last someone truly respected him, he thought, not knowing that another 300,000 similar letters had been sent and that the title had been given to every person with no known occupation because the Colonel in charge of the Press Office said that everyone writes and therefore everyone is a writer.]

Such descriptions satirise the official view of writing as a hobby that requires no skill, a fact of life or even a celebration of basic literacy. Observations like these are made throughout the book in such a deadpan way that the reader is left to wonder whether such events are real or a comic invention by Méndez Guédez. We can begin to answer this question by turning to the official discourse of the Bolivarian government in relation to literature.

One of the hallmarks of Bolivarian cultural policy, like all areas of the Bolivarian Revolution, is mass participation. This process of democratisation, according to Néstor García Canclini (1995), is typical of populist regimes. He maintains that 'Populists try to ensure that the people do not remain as the passive receiver of communicational actions. [Instead,] people appear participating and performing' (García Canclini, 1995, 192). Making the people active participants in culture is a way of legitimising rule because it gives 'the popular sectors the confidence that they are participating in a system that includes and recognises them' (García Canclini, 1995, 191). This begins with declarations, such as those of Francisco Sesto in *El pueblo es la cultura* [The People are Culture] (Wisotzki, 2006), about the government's belief in the creative power of the people. Sesto asserts, 'Todos, absolutamente todos, poseemos una capacidad creadora' [All of us, absolutely all of us, have creative potential] and 'Todo ciudadano es potencialmente un escritor' [Every citizen is potentially a writer] (Wisotzki, 2006, 24; 35). The cultural activities he instigated as Minister for Culture stem from these beliefs. As hyperbole is considered the prime example of 'ironic signalling' (Hutcheon, 1995, 156), such exaggeration in *Chulapos Mambo* alerts the reader that Méndez Guédez intends to 'transmi[t] both information and evaluative attitude other than what is explicitly presented' (Hutcheon, 1995, 11). By creating a picture of Bolivarian cultural policy that, while grounded in fact, seems too absurd to be true, Méndez Guédez obliges his readers to judge this cultural policy as itself absurd.

In the same way, *Chulapos Mambo* parodies the use of state publishing initiatives to inculcate socialist values and cast the government in a positive light. Henry describes a new collection he has heard about from his friends in the ministry, which will be launched in a few months:

> Se trataba de editar todo. TODO. TODO. Un proyecto igualitario en el que la totalidad de esos libros de autores nacionales que las editoriales habían rechazado en los últimos cinco años debería aparecer en un formato modesto. La idea es que se viera que el Proceso no censuraba, que el Proceso descreía del criterio comercial de los libros. Por muy malo que fuese un título siempre sería muestra del ingenio humano, de los poderes creadores de un pueblo. (78)
>
> [It was a case of publishing everything. EVERYTHING. EVERYTHING. An egalitarian project in which every single book by national writers that had been rejected by publishers in the last five years would appear in a modest format. The idea was for it to be seen that the Process did not censor, that the Process did not believe in the commercial criterion for books. No matter how bad a book was, it would still show human ingenuity, the creative powers of the people.]

Although the name of this scheme is not mentioned in the novel, readers aware of the Bolivarian literary system in Venezuela would recognise this as 'Cada día un libro' [One Book Every Day], the polemical initiative introduced by the Ministry of Popular Power for Culture to release thousands of previously unpublished writers in cheaply produced short runs.

The Cada día un libro collection was a key part of the Bolivarian strategy to democratise culture. The collection was first published by CONAC [the National Council for Culture] in 2005 and then by El perro y la rana in 2007 after CONAC was shut down. The introductory text, which is printed on the first page of every book in the collection and appears in a shorter version on the back covers, evokes the overall Bolivarian vision for culture. The 2005 text explains that the collection was created by the Ministry of Popular Power for Culture and CONAC to open up a new and better space for cultural participation. As the presentation explains, the texts published in the collection are winners of the Certamen Mayor de las Artes y las Letras, a vast, nationwide competition, which awards literature, theatre, dance and visual arts. Over the course of one month in 2004, people could deliver their book to an office in each region of the country. Some 360 books would be chosen to be published, promoted and distributed, making 15 books for each state, in line with the government's aim to decentralise literature, that is, to move away from Caracas as the centre of literary activity. Entrants had to submit their work under pseudonyms to ensure fairness in the decision making (Prensa-CONAC, 2005). The democratisation, or desacralising, of literature is evident in the use of 'libros' [books] rather than 'literatura' throughout the introductory text, and in the emphasis on ideas and dreams rather than any technical or stylistic qualities. The presentation also calls the programme 'un significativo acto de justicia' [a significant act of justice], reinforcing the radical break with the past that is at the heart of all Bolivarian rhetoric. The text aims to convince aspiring writers that the government cares for them when previous governments did not, affirming, 'Pero ahora los tiempos han cambiado y las puertas están abiertas también para ellos' [But now times have changed and the doors are open for them too]. The similarities between this text and the words used by Henry in *Chulapos Mambo* are obvious.

When the second Cada día un libro collection was published by El perro y la rana in 2007, the introduction incorporated military imagery and became more hyperbolic:

> Existe un encuentro que se hace golpe sobre papel, en todo lugar están las voces de nuestra gente que retumban desde tiempos ancestrales y se precisan susurro estridente, grito inevitable, respuesta urgente ante la convulsión de todos los mundos que forman al ser humano.

> [There is an encounter which is striking the page, in every place we find the voices of our people which have resounded since ancestral times and which need a piercing whisper, an unavoidable cry, an urgent response to the convulsion of all the worlds which make the human being.]

Compared with this presentation text, Méndez Guédez's imagined speech seems tame. This new introduction stresses more forcefully that a great number of Venezuelans who wanted to publish were excluded under previous regimes, equates this exclusion with their subjugation to capitalist elites and posits writing as a form of liberation. It once again places political drive and creative will over technical skill, comparing the written word to a weapon. Such hyperbolic language is designed to spark revolutionary fervour in readers and to encourage continued support for the Bolivarian 'Process'. As well as the introductions, the cover designs for the collection show the evolution of Cada día un libro as a tool for instilling the values of the Bolivarian Revolution. The 2005 design featured a block of colour (orange for fiction, red for *crónicas*, pink for theatre), with the name of the author and the title of the book prominently displayed as well as the logos of the Ministry for Culture and CONAC. The 2007 design, by contrast, visualised the idea that each writer was part of a collective: the cover was filled with names of authors and titles in the collection with the author and the title of that specific book in bold.

It is through an exaggerated, fictionalised version of this scheme that Henry's highly plagiarised short story collection, *Los cien años de Artemio* [One Hundred Years of Artemio],[1] is published, although Henry clearly views its

---

1 The title combines Gabriel García Márquez's *Cien años de soledad* [One Hundred Years of Solitude] and Carlos Fuentes's *La muerte de Artemio Cruz* [The Death of Artemio Cruz].

egalitarian approach to publishing as an affront to his 'talent'. When handed the 100 copies of his book along with 800 other writers, he feels despondent (78). His shame is evident in the fact when we first meet Henry, he is boasting about the thousands of copies of his book that have been published (29), and it is only later that he admits this is a complete lie (117). Moreover, Méndez Guédez questions the quality of the books produced by this system:

> Uno escribió en Esperanto las memorias de su abuela Ángela, la mujer que en los años cincuenta promovió una técnica de autoerotismo que consistía en frotarse el cuerpo con espinas de bagre; otro era autor de un recetario en el que se facilitaban cien maneras de comer arroz; y el último había escrito un análisis de *Popol Vuh* donde se demostraba que los hispanoamericanos eran una raza superior porque provenían del maíz. (79)

> [One wrote in Esperanto the memoirs of her grandmother Ángela, the woman who in the 1950s promoted an autoerotic technique that consisted of rubbing the body with catfish spines; another was the author of a cookbook offering 100 ways to eat rice; and the final one had written an analysis of the *Popol Vuh*, where he demonstrated that Hispanic Americans were a superior race because they came from corn.]

Behind the humorous absurdity of these examples lies a serious criticism of the perceived loss of literary value that results from a policy of inclusion. Méndez Guédez derides the mystification of the self, the 'heroic' past and national customs which the collection promotes. Although Méndez Guédez is highly critical of the scheme here, we must not disregard the benefits it offered in terms of opening up publishing opportunities. The main issue with *Cada día un libro* was that the sheer weight of books produced, combined with the lack of attention paid to promotion, made it difficult for any one book to be publicised and found by readers.

In a similar way, *Chulapos Mambo* suggests that any book, no matter what its subject, can be used as an ideological tool. The official guide to puberty that Henry is tasked to write warns girls that once their period begins, 'Tu principal prudencia debe ser evitar que desaprensivos oligarcas intenten conquistarte' [Your first concern should be to avoid letting the unscrupulous oligarchs try to conquer you] (113). The idea that every topic can be linked to the Bolivarian Revolution reflects real-life publishing practice. One particularly memorable example is *La segunda oportunidad* [The Second Chance], by Martiza Avilez, published in 2007 in the Cada día un libro collection. A mile-a-minute story of a hard-working Venezuelan mother who turns out to be a telepathic, genetically engineered Nazi hunter, the novel is described on the back cover as a metaphor for the resilience of the Venezuelan people, and the need to fight for change. In *Chulapos Mambo*, Henry is charged with writing a first aid manual and a guide to sexual orientation for mass distribution across schools and public squares. Thousands and thousands of copies of these books will be distributed as part of a 'bolsa patriótica' [patriotic bag] along with half a kilo of biscuits, some meat and a T-shirt emblazoned with the president's face (94). In this way, *Chulapos Mambo* parodies the mass distribution of books by the Bolivarian government, questioning whether people read these books at all, or just take them to get the other goods.

The 'massifying tendencies' (García Canclini, 1995, 90) of Bolivarian cultural policy are further satirised in *Chulapos Mambo* through Henry's role as a leader of one of the writing workshops in poor neighbourhoods which have been conceived to turn Venezuela into a nation of writers (Plataforma del Libro y la Lectura del Ministerio del Poder Popular para la Cultura, 2007). The description of these workshops in *Chulapos Mambo* implies an official approach of quantity over quality when it comes to writers:

> En una semana de cada taller sacamos diez nuevos escritores. Para el año que viene seremos el país con más escritores en el mundo. Todo el que quiera participar en los talleres se volverá escritor. Es un programa muy bonito. Explico todo en cinco sesiones de dos horas. (60)

> [In one week we get ten new writers from each workshop. By next year, we'll be the country with the most writers in the world. Anyone who wants to take part in the workshop will become a writer. It's a beautiful programme. I explain everything in five two-hour sessions.]

This is a deeply sarcastic account of the writing workshops which gained prominence in Venezuela under the auspices of the Plataforma del Libro y la Lectura. Both the Casa Nacional de las Letras Andrés Bello (Casa Bello) [National House of Literature] and the Centro de Estudios Latinoamericanos Rómulo Gallegos (CELARG) [Centre for Latin American Studies] put in place a variety of programmes, designed significantly to broaden participation in cultural activities. Casa Bello's activities served as a supplement to traditional education, and included running programmes or one-off events in schools, prisons and local communities, as well as ongoing writing workshops (Casa Bello, 2013a). One notable programme of theirs was 'La Comunidad y su escritura' [The Community and its Writing], whose main objective was to encourage people to write about their past experiences and daily life in the community (Casa Bello, 2013b). In this way, the government promoted the view of literature as a document of lived experience. Like Casa Bello, CELARG offered a range of free creative workshops. Whereas Casa Bello's classes covered literary subjects including poetry, narrative or journalism (Casa Bello, 2013c), CELARG's offering was much more obviously ideological, combining those traditional subjects with courses such as 'Límites del capitalismo rentístico y del paradigma del desarrollo' [The limits of rentier capitalism and the paradigm of development] (CELARG, 2013). In this way, participants were encouraged to equate literary production with political concerns.

These activities recall the 'workshops of popular creativity popularising not only the product but the means of production' which became prominent in Cuba in the period following the revolution (Canclini, 1995, 91). These workshops wanted Cubans not just to read more but to tell their own stories. The symbolic value of these workshops, as a sign of the recognition of all Cubans, is clear. However, while the Cuban popular workshops sat alongside the promotion and support of professional writers through organisations such as the Casa de las Américas, Bolivarian rhetoric promotes mass participation at the expense of developing the careers of professional writers. Gisela Kozak Rovero (2007b, 114), for example, claims that:

> La 'estética socialista' en lo que a literatura se refiere podría definirse entonces como la creación de un imaginario en el que ésta no es una actividad que requiere cultivo y esfuerzo sino la simple voluntad de considerarse escritor(a), una actividad aficionada que no sirve para ganarse la vida.
>
> [The 'socialist aesthetic' as applied to literature can be defined as the creation of an imaginary in which literature is not an activity which requires nurturing and effort but rather the simple will to consider oneself a writer, a hobby that does not allow one to earn a living.]

Those authors who see their work as having both an economic and an artistic value feel that producing books with little attention to how, or whether, they might be read undermines the value of their own work. Méndez Guédez's tone throughout *Chulapos Mambo* betrays his anger at having his position as an author undermined by a system that affirms over and again that writing is not a skilled profession. He further suggests that the Bolivarian workshops are mainly symbolic by describing how they were later cancelled and replaced with literacy classes. Henry explains, 'Como a la gente le pagan por asistir, los que originalmente eran mis cuasi novelistas ahora afirman que no saben leer ni escribir, y de nuevo reciben dinero por cada clase a la que acuden para aprender los vocales' [As people were paid to attend, those who had originally been my almost-novelists are now saying that they don't know how to read and write, and once again they get paid for each class they attend to learn their vowels] (61). According to Henry, either people were only attending the literacy workshops for money, taking advantage of the government's willingness to spend state funds, or the first workshops were trying to teach people who could not even read how to be writers, in which case they were even more redundant than they initially seemed. This episode recalls a study by Francisco Rodríguez and Daniel Ortega, which found that, where the government claimed to have taught 1.5 million people how to read, only 1.1 million were illiterate to begin with (*The Economist*, 2008).

Chulapos Mambo presents writers as promotional tools for the government, as Henry is tasked with writing patriotic texts and sent to represent the Revolution at national and international events, despite having only written one slender, plagiarised novel (78). In turn, *Chulapos Mambo* implies, these writers can exploit this system to their own advantage. In his introduction to *Venezuela's Bolivarian Democracy*, sociologist David Smilde (2011, 24) observes that, in all aspects of the Bolivarian system, 'those who support Chávez are favoured and those who are favoured support Chávez'. Given that Henry became a writer to win the acceptance and praise he had always felt the lack of as a child, he thrives on the positive attitude of the government towards his writing and consequently feels very grateful to them (151). In addition to the recognition he receives from the Ministry for Culture itself, in Henry's mind he will finally receive public adoration thanks to their promotional efforts. He proclaims proudly, 'Ahora en el país se lee mucho y se nos valora a los autores nacionales, a los que interpretamos de verdad el poder popular y el sentir profundo de las verdaderas raíces ...' [Today in this country people read a lot and value us national authors, we who interpret the truth of popular power and the deep feeling of our true roots] (29–30). Such comments draw attention to the positive symbolism of mass publication programmes, designed to make people feel worthy and valued. However, in the novel, no one knows of Henry and his books sit in a box in his room. This suggests that mass publication is not sufficient and that concerted efforts at promotion are necessary. Nonetheless, for the Bolivarian Revolution, the symbolism of publication is more important than whether the books reach readers. Silva-Ferrer (2014, 27) maintains that the democratising measures introduced by Bolivarian cultural policy created a new form of subjugation. Although the stated motivations behind such initiatives – to make access to reading and writing fairer, and to give those with fewer resources and less education the opportunity to express themselves – were honourable ones, they could lead to reliance on and thus loyalty to the government.

More pragmatically, *Chulapos Mambo* suggests that writers who supported the government also benefited from material advantages, promotion and travel abroad. Henry's companions in Madrid, representing the Revolution, are Morella, Parménides and Silvio. Henry describes how the ministry paid for a face-lift for Morella so that he could still attend events for young writers, and published an unfinished novel by Parménides, even though it was only ten pages long, with the excuse that Kafka also left his novels unfinished (19). This is just one example of a system riddled with corruption. In exchange for his loyalty to the Process, Henry has been given a gold card and is living in luxury. During an early encounter with Henry, Simao notes his expensive clothes and concludes, 'Henry seguro estaba vinculado al gobierno de mi país y era uno de esos enchufados que manejan buenos viáticos, cuentas secretas y excelentes contactos' [Henry was surely linked to my country's government and was one of those well-connected people who managed generous expenses, secret bank accounts and excellent contacts] (49). Simao's assertion that a rich person must be with the government exposes the paradox at the heart of the Bolivarian system; that, in a nationalised economy, supporters of the socialist regime are the ones with material advantages. The phenomenon became so widespread that its beneficiaries became known as the *boliburguesía* (Valery, 2009b). In such a context, Méndez Guédez suggests, it was more lucrative to support the state than to attempt to sell books on the market. This is highlighted through Henry's arch-nemesis, Saúl Junco, who has won literary prizes and critical acclaim (180), yet he lives in a slum (181), stacking supermarket shelves (179), and busking in the metro (12) to survive. The source of his misfortune is having the wrong politics. *Chulapos Mambo* proposes that, beyond the content of their writing, writers are judged on their political orientation and activity. This reflects claims that officials responsible for culture assumed that authors would sign up to the socialist party, the PSUV (Kozak Rovero, 2007b, 106). Minister for Culture Francisco Sesto, moreover, made it clear that he judged writers on their political positioning. With implied reference to the poet Rafael Cadenas, who refused to be published by the state, Sesto asserted that one could not be a good poet if one was against the revolution. He notably asked, '¿Cómo es posible ser un buen poeta y, al mismo tiempo, un ciudadano de comportamiento tan dudoso?' [How is it possible to be a good poet and at the same time a citizen with such suspect behaviour?] (Kozak Rovero, 2007b, 116). Sesto's comment is striking not only for its fusion of culture and politics, but even more for the naturalised assumption that opposing the 'Process' is not a political choice but a moral aberration. One cannot help hearing in those declarations by Francisco Sesto equating political commitment with literary value echoes of Fidel Castro's avowal at the First Congress of Education in 1971 that 'Nuestra valoración es política. No puede haber valor estético sin contenido humano' [Our judgment is political. There can be no aesthetic value without human content]. However, looking back further to Castro's famous 'Palabras a los intelectuales' [Words to the Intellectuals] speech from 1961, it is notable that he spoke to intellectuals with respect and logic, rather than with the antagonism displayed by Sesto. Castro (1961) affirmed that he understood demands for artistic freedom, but reasoned with intellectuals that the government had to put the needs of the revolution above all.

Beyond antagonistic rhetoric, authors and critics perceived division and discrimination at all stages, from what gets published, via who has access to ink and paper, to which books certain bookshops will sell (Roche Rodríguez, 2013). Ana Teresa Torres (2006, 913–914) claimed that there was an ideological basis for selection of participants for literary events, stating 'solo son requeridos los escritores oficialistas, casi siempre los que forman parte de la nómina burocrática' [only the official writers are required, usually those on the bureaucratic payroll]. Her use of the word 'requeridos' here suggests that the government could argue that no one was excluded because no one was told that they could not come, but only those who supported the regime were invited. At the same time, 'requeridos' recalls how state institutions call writers necessary for the success of the revolutionary 'Process'. In *Chulapos Mambo*, the description of Saúl Junco's situation echoes Torres's comments:

Hacía años que en el Ministerio de Cultura no le daban un billete de avión a Saúl para que asistiese a ningún evento; hacía años que a nadie se le ocurría otorgarle una ayuda económica para que escribiese un libro; hacía años que ninguna biblioteca del país compraba ninguna de sus publicaciones; hacía varios años que a ningún organismo del estado se le ocurría ofrecerle un trabajo. (55)

[It was years since the Ministry for Culture had given Saúl plane tickets to go to any events; it was years since it had occurred to anyone to give him any financial help to write a book; it had been years since any library in the country had bought one of his publications; it had been many years since it had occurred to any state organisation to offer him a job.]

The repeated use of 'se le ocurría' to assert that Junco's treatment is not an example of censorship, but merely forgetfulness, implies just the opposite.

The feud between Henry and Saúl caricatures the polarisation of the literary field. According to Guillermo Parra, it is often writers themselves who encourage this polarisation, insisting on calling each other *chavista* or opposition, 'real' or 'fake' (Payares, 2012). In an article considering how the situation of Venezuelan literature would change in the wake of Chávez's death, Gustavo Guerrero (2013b) noted how deeply ingrained these divisions had become, adding that any attempts at reconciliation had failed. In *Chulapos Mambo*, despite Henry's evident material advantages over Saúl, he still insists on referring to his rival as a 'perro oligarca, depravado burgués' [oligarch dog, depraved bourgeois] (134), because he is in the opposition. On the other side, Saúl signals Henry out by screaming, '¡Este es una de esas mierdas, este es uno de esos parásitos!' [He's one of those shits, he's one of those parasites] (152). Throughout the novel, it is made abundantly clear that irrational anger and hatred on both sides impedes any – potentially mutually beneficial – moves to promote Venezuelan literature internationally.

This feud takes a more sinister turn when Henry considers adding Saúl's name to an online list of traitors of the Process: 'Vio que Saúl ya aparecía en esas listas. En una de ellas un grupo anónimo le pedía a Junco y a otras diez mil personas que abandonaran el país o no responderían por su seguridad' [He saw that Saúl already appeared on those lists. In one of them an anonymous group told Junco and another ten thousand people to leave the country or they would not be responsible for their safety] (56). The scale of this list is probably exaggerated for effect, like Gabriel García Márquez's famous description of the *bananera* massacre in *Cien años de soledad*.[2] Nonetheless,

---

2 Eduardo Posada-Carbó (1998, 396) recounts how García Márquez's fictional account of 3,000 workers having been slaughtered came to be seen as historical fact, whereas Márquez himself stated that he 'decided on 3,000 dead because that filled the dimension of the book [he] was writing'. Posada-Carbó advises literary critics not to read such fictional accounts as historically accurate. The exaggeration can be seen as symbolic of the author's attitude towards the events described.

the exaggeration demonstrates the scale of feeling about real life cases, such as the death threats sent to Israel Centeno. Moreover, the idea that people who did not support the Process did not belong in Venezuela conforms to Gisela Kozak's (2013) assertion that the opposition were seen as 'el no-pueblo' [non-citizens] in Bolivarian rhetoric.

Incorporating elements of autofiction, Israel Centeno brings his experience of the changes in what it means to be a professional writer in Venezuela to the page in *Bajo las hojas* (2010). The novel presents the point of view of a professional writer who is suffering from a lack of opportunities. Centeno has maintained that in Venezuela he faced ideological barriers to publishing, asserting that independent thought is not allowed (Montañez Cortez, 2013). The writer–protagonist Julio begins the novel bemoaning the lack of work in Venezuela for writers and worrying about how he can continue to support his family in such a situation, especially if his children will need to go abroad to find a good quality education (12). He takes on whatever vaguely literary odd jobs he can find – teaching workshops, copy-editing, and reporting celebrity gossip – but these opportunities are drying up:

> No era una referencia interesante para ser incorporada en el currículum de nadie; haber asistido a un curso suyo podría convertirse en algo parecido a haber perdido el tiempo, poco a poco se fue transformando en el hombre invisible, en el escritor inexistente. (19)

> [He wasn't an interesting reference to include in anybody's curriculum; having been in one of his classes would be something like a waste of time, little by little he was becoming the invisible man, the non-existent writer.]

Julio's wife urges him to be pragmatic, give up his scruples, and ask for work in television for the sake of the family (20). Julio, however, is not ready to abandon his literary dreams. Julio clearly conceives of literature as a form of distinction (an idea which will be analysed in the next chapter). Despite the obstacles, 'él debe seguir soñando con escribir la gran novela' [he kept dreaming of writing the great novel] (20). While Julio shares the ambition to write 'la gran novela' with *Chulapos Mambo*'s protagonist Henry, his definition of 'great' is not a best-seller or prize-winner, but a novel of true aesthetic quality. Having been considered once 'un escritor de renombre' [a renowned author] is a matter of great pride for Julio, even though he has now fallen into obscurity (21). He distinguishes himself as a 'real' writer, that is, in his terms, someone who 'concibe las grandes historias y logra contarlas con una voz particular y una propuesta estética bien definida' [conceives great stories and manages to tell them in an individual voice with a well-defined aesthetic strategy] (21–22).

The character of Julio is an example of someone who became a writer during the Punto Fijo period, who is now struggling to adapt to the change in regime. Writing was professionalised in Venezuela during the Punto Fijo period, with the formation of the Instituto Nacional de Cultura y Bellas Artes [National Institute of Culture and Fine Art] (INCIBA, 1966) and the foundation of the Monte Ávila and Biblioteca Ayacucho publishing houses (1968 and 1974 respectively). In 1975, the Consejo Nacional de la Cultura [National Council for Culture] (CONAC) was formed by presidential decree as an autonomous institution affiliated with the president's office, taking over the rights and responsibilities of the INCIBA (Congreso de la República de Venezuela, 1975). The decree dedicated CONAC to the production, specialised training, promotion, research, conservation and enjoyment of all aspects of culture (Congreso de la República de Venezuela, 1975). The creation of CONAC represented the institutionalisation of the whole literary process, not just publishing but training writers, promoting books and fostering collaboration between intellectuals (Torres, 2006, 919) During the Punto Fijo period, the state not only provided the necessary resources to be a professional writer, but also recognition and symbolic capital. In *Bajo las hojas*, the situation Julio finds himself in under the Bolivarian Revolution, by contrast, seems deeply unfair to him. Julio grumbles, 'Otro lugar, un mundo justo, eso me basta' [Another place, a fair world, that would do me] (21–22). He acknowledges that there is no market for his work as the reading public in Venezuela is very small to begin with, and the state publishers have no interest in his kind of writing. When the state does not consider writing a profession, and private publishing houses struggle to compete with them financially, it is very difficult for writers to support themselves through their work. Of course, this is not a new problem, nor one unique to Venezuela. Nonetheless, authors in Venezuela wishing to earn money from their writing also had to contend with a government that symbolically equated capitalism with U.S. neocolonialism and did not invest in the promotion or international distribution of literature. This particularly affected opportunities for authors to gain international recognition. In addition, as Slavko Zupcic (2015) told me in response to a question about the invisibility of Venezuelan literature internationally, the international reputation of literature is a question of markets, and the currency controls imposed by the government took Venezuela out of those markets.[3] As explored in the introduction, Venezuela hardly exported any books, as the Bolivarian government was more concerned with making citizens feel included in the national publishing system than reaching international audiences. The omniscient narrator scoffs at Julio's literary ambitions, claiming, 'Nadie se va a creer esa vaina de que un escritor en Venezuela despertara oleadas de pasiones, un hombre que tenía rotas las suelas de los zapatos' [Nobody is going to believe that a writer in Venezuela could awaken waves of passion, not a man with holes in his shoes] (39–40). Venezuela is not seen to have the kind of prestige in world literary space as enjoyed by countries such as Mexico and Argentina. Instead, the narrator suggests, it is considered a poor backwater. I will return to the need to improve recognition for Venezuelan literature in Chapter 4.

---

3 See *El Universal* (2015) for an introduction to currency controls and how they have affected the Venezuelan economy.

Even outside of Venezuela, Julio admits, it is difficult for an author to succeed unless he is a big name. When Julio considers pretending that the money he has been given for his secret government job is an advance on a book, he convinces himself otherwise, telling himself that no publisher would ever pay so much to an unknown writer (92). In the global literary market of the twenty-first century, only a handful of international literary superstars can command large advances. These combined obstacles make Julio want to give up. He must admit to himself, 'que has escrito demasiado, que tus expectativas han sido defraudadas y que lo que iba a suceder no sucedió' [you have written too much, your hopes have been let down and what you thought would happen did not happen] (27). In one of the many self-reflexive moments of the novel, the omniscient narrator refers to Julio as the kind of pathetic character he would usually mock in his own writing (37).

If he has not yet given up, it is because the principal motivation behind his writing is not money or fame – as much as he would enjoy these – but a desire to affect his readers' lives in some way, to move them with his work. He maintains that, 'Logradas con maestría, [las novelas] cambian la vida de quien la vive, porque ha dejado de leerla para vivirla' [When masterfully done, a novel can change the life of the person who lives it, because they have stopped reading it to live it] (365). He sees the novel as a transcendental experience, something which captures readers' attention entirely and touches them on an emotional level. Julio's insistence on readers contrasts the focus on the production of writing in Bolivarian cultural policy with the limited attention to whether this writing would be read. Julio shares this attitude towards writing with his friend Pepe Libedinski, who 'insistía en que nunca se escribe por deporte o de manera ingenua, ni siquiera para solazarse en el lenguaje, se escribe porque quieres mover la emoción de alguien, cambiarle el día, el estado de ánimo, la vida' [insisted that one must never write as a sport or in a naive way, not even to take pleasure in language, one writes because one wants to move somebody emotionally, change their day, their state of mind, their life] (379). The Bolivarian idea of literature as a hobby, a political tool, or a way of documenting lived reality cannot fit with these characters' aim to create literature which affects readers personally, intimately. Faced with this dichotomy, the third member of their group, Rubén Tenorio, distinguishes clearly between public or political and private writing. While working for the police, altering reality through what he writes in his reports, and, more importantly, what he omits from them, Rubén spends his spare time endlessly writing and deleting his novel, crafting a perfect piece of literature which no one will ever read (379).

Julio is scornful towards those writers who, in his eyes, compromise their artistic integrity in exchange for the security of working for the government. When he is offered a government job he asks, '¿Y por qué yo? ¿Por qué no echan mano a ese ejército de escritores que está pudriendo con su culo un sillón en los despachos del Ministerio de Cultura?' [Why me? Why don't you reach out to that army of writers whose backsides are rotting the chairs in the offices of the Ministry for Culture?] (24). However, out of economic necessity, he takes the job, which takes the idea of altering reality through writing to a new level – in this fantastical novel, in both a political commentary and a reference to the book of the Fates, scripts written by government employees become reality. We often see Julio writing these scripts, but he is also described as writing books, war propaganda and pamphlets for global lobbies (259). In the fantasy of the novel, the forces he works for use superhuman powers to put pressure on Julio, combined with threats to his loved ones. Although their mind control is an exaggeration, *Bajo las hojas* conveys the pressure felt by many civil servants to conform to the needs of the Bolivarian Revolution rather than face unemployment and hardship. By the end of the novel, as Julio finishes the scenes that he has been commissioned to write, he is disillusioned and resigned to the loss of his literary ideals. He also feels guilty that his writing has been used for unjust and violent ends. Tired and fed up, 'puso al lado la culpa y se atrevió a llegar sin pausa hasta el punto final. Ya no escribiría más por un tiempo' [he put his guilt to one side and dared himself to get to the end without stopping. He would not write again for some time] (394). Knowing that it is impossible for him to write the way that he wants to in the current political context, and afraid of becoming further implicated in a regime he is fundamentally opposed to, Julio decides it is better not to write at all, presenting failure as a legitimate reaction to an unjust situation.

Through two very different characters, the self-serving Henry and the disillusioned Julio, *Chulapos Mambo* and *Bajo las hojas* create a picture of a state literary system that promotes mass participation to encourage loyalty to the Bolivarian Revolution but delegitimises the writer as a skilled professional. By employing irony, exaggeration and absurdity throughout *Chulapos Mambo*, Méndez Guédez delivers a cutting criticism of the literary system in contemporary Venezuela, especially the practices of state publishing and writing workshops designed to project an image of cultural openness at odds with the practice of rewarding political loyalty over literary merit. In this way, the novel demonstrates Ross Chambers's (1990, 18) claim that irony is a 'possible model for oppositionality whenever one is implicated in a system that one finds oppressive'. *Bajo las hojas*, in contrast, is more overtly critical, as protagonist Julio realises he cannot fulfil his literary ideals in such a system and submits to writing only the practical texts required of him, before giving up altogether. The only alternative for professional writers is to take their chances on the international market, as explored in the next chapter.

CHAPTER 2

Writing and Distinction

At the heart of the polarisation of the literary field under the Bolivarian Revolution, in the period analysed, was a set of competing value judgements: authors who prioritised aesthetic concerns clashed both with the Bolivarian government, whose priority was inculcating a national, socialist community, and with the demands of the international publishing industry, which judges books on how well they sell or meet the perceived needs of the market. In this context, the writer–protagonists of the novels discussed in this chapter become writer–critics, 'dialectical figure[s]', in Mark Currie's (1995, 3) terms, who engage simultaneously in the production and reception of literature. Through their writing, they make judgements about both their own work and other texts. This chapter begins with analysis of how characters in *Transilvania unplugged* (Sánchez Rugeles, 2011a), *Todas las lunas* (Kozak Rovero, 2013) and *Rating* (Barrera Tyszka, 2011) all make judgements about literary quality as a form of distinction. It then considers Armando Luigi Castañeda's fragmentary, disjointed anti-novel *La fama, o es venérea, o no es fama* (2012) as an example of the tensions between literary ideals and the demands of the international literary market in a context where state publishing no longer offers distinction or support for writing as a profession.

As Pierre Bourdieu (1993, 42) argues, 'The fundamental stake in literary struggles is the monopoly of the power to consecrate producers or products'. Under the Bolivarian Revolution, institutions put in place during the Punto Fijo period to facilitate, promote and reward literary quality were subsumed into the Bolivarian literary system. The two key examples are the publishing house Monte Ávila and the Rómulo Gallegos literary prize. Monte Ávila was formed in 1968, under the leadership of Simón Alberto Consalvi. Despite belonging to the state, it was run as an autonomous company. Alexis Márquez Rodríguez (1999, 90) claims that the creation of Monte Ávila marked the major turning point in the history of Venezuelan literature. Likened to Mexico's Fondo de Cultura Económica (Nuño, 2014), Monte Ávila's wide editorial offer ranged from works by consecrated authors which had gone out of print, to unpublished and often highly experimental new writers. However, as stated on the website of the publishing house, 'Comprometida con la actual transformación histórica venezolana, iniciada en 1998, [Monte Ávila] redimensiona su línea editorial a partir de 2003, para atender nuevos retos, vincularse con amplios públicos y construir un puente para llegar a las grandes mayorías' [Committed to the current historic transformation of Venezuela, which began in 1998, Monte Ávila has been reshaping its editorial line since 2003, to meet new challenges, relate to wider audiences, and build a bridge to the great majority]. Israel Centeno, among others, has criticised this strategy, suggesting that, while the state-run publishers do include some independent voices, in general, 'ideologizaron sus estrategias, sesgaron su producción y terminaron haciéndose instituciones de propaganda gubernamental' [they have ideologised their strategies, distorted their production and ended up becoming institutions of governmental propaganda] (Centeno, 2013). 'Sesgaron' here suggests that Monte Ávila were on the right path before and went wrong by changing their output to fit the aims of the Revolution. Monte Ávila's realignment to fit in with the mission of the Bolivarian Revolution was a particularly troubling occurrence for authors and critics who once saw it as a shining example of publishing standards across the continent. In an article for the Colombian *Revista Arcadia* about the effect the Bolivarian Revolution has had on some of Venezuela's leading pre-Chávez cultural institutions, María Gabriel Méndez (2013) claims that the 'gusto intelectual impecable y un espíritu progresista' [impeccable intellectual taste and spirt of progress] which once characterised Monte Ávila have been negated in recent years. She goes on to quote Antonio López Ortega, who complains that the number of collections of political thought have increased, that they have stopped publishing authors who take a public position against the government and that they reject manuscripts of new editions of books which are critical of the government or in praise of the Punto Fijo period. Méndez's assessment is laden with implicit value judgements, based on the idea that taste is innate and can either be right or wrong. Similarly, López's Ortega's complaint that Monte Ávila collections now have a lower profile reveals the importance of cultural capital for writers wanting to publish with Monte Ávila and their regret that publishing with Monte Ávila is no longer a sign of distinction. The Rómulo Gallegos literary prize, meanwhile, was founded by presidential decree in 1964 to honour the memory of the novelist and president, and to support creative writing in Spanish. Anadeli Bencomo (2006, 763) describes the creation of the prize as a key example of the modernising discourse in Venezuela at the time, and the state's desire to be seen as a leading actor in this modernisation. The Rómulo Gallegos Prize became a symbol of the state's commitment to culture and desire to institutionalise democracy. Gallegos himself symbolises the conjunction of literature and democracy in Venezuela, as in 1948 the author became president of the Republic, ruling for nine months until he was overthrown by a military coup. The Rómulo Gallegos Prize became one of the most prestigious and sought-after literary prizes in Latin America, with winners including Mario Vargas Llosa for *La casa verde* [The Green House] in 1967, Gabriel García Márquez for *Cien años de soledad* [One Hundred Years of

Solitude] in 1972, Carlos Fuentes for *Terra Nostra* in 1977, and, more recently, Elena Poniatowska for *El tren pasa primero* [The Train Passes First] in 2007 and Ricardo Piglia for *Blanco nocturno* [Nocturnal Target] in 2011. To date, there has only been one Venezuelan winner, Arturo Uslar Pietri, who was recognised for *La visita en el tiempo* [The Visit in Time] in 1991. Consequently, the prize became a way for Venezuela to impose itself on the Hispanic literary field, providing international publicity to the newly democratic state and their support for culture (Bencomo, 2006, 763). The prize was a reaction against the years of dictatorship and resultant exclusion from what Pascale Casanova (2004) calls the 'world republic of letters'. Despite its prestige in the Punto Fijo period, however, the prize came under discussion during the Bolivarian period, with claims from previous winner Roberto Bolaño (2001) and Venezuelan writers such as Gustavo Guerrero (2005) that decisions were being made on an ideological basis.[1]

To understand the tensions around writing in Venezuela under the Bolivarian Revolution, it is instructive to look back to Cuba in the 1960s, a 'period of intense discussion surrounding the importance of aesthetic and ideological elements and their relationship to each other' (Kumaraswami, 2007, 72). At that time, critic José Antonio Portuondo promoted Soviet realism, suggesting that each period of history has a type of art which is appropriate for its social and political structure, and realism was the appropriate form for Revolutionary Cuba: 'un arte esencialmente comunicativo, concreto [...] que manifieste la realidad en su trascendencia histórica y social' [an essentially communicative, concrete art which shows reality in its historical and social significance] (1963, 59). This attitude was not shared by all in the Cuban Revolution, as even Che Guevara rejected socialist realism in his 1965 essay 'El socialismo y el hombre en Cuba.' Nonetheless, the Declaration of the 1971 Congreso Nacional de Educación y Cultura placed 'the people' over professional writers, stating, 'Rechazamos las pretensiones de la mafia de intelectuales' [We reject the pretensions of the intellectual mafia] (Kumaraswami, 2007, 74), language strikingly similar to that used in Venezuela by Francisco Sesto over 30 years later. Néstor García Canclini (1995, 91) describes the approach to writing in this period of the Cuban Revolution as 'involuntary aesthetic terrorism by those who believe that the best creative method is participative good-will, that quality is measured by ideological clarity and that clarity by the uncritical adherence to an ideology'. Focusing on ideological factors, Canclini argues, leaves no space or support for more literary aspects of writing, such as style or language. Looking back at Cuban history, we can see growing dissatisfaction with the ideological being valued over the aesthetic. By the 1990s, Cuba saw the 'rejection of the stale and officialist testimonial imperative of the 1970s and 1980s in favour of more

---

[1] See Brown, 2018 for a more detailed analysis of the controversy surrounding the Rómulo Gallegos Prize.

personal and universal styles and themes which engaged with post-structuralist and postmodernist deconstructions of language, subjectivity and reality' (Kumaraswami, 2007, 77).

Cuban history illustrates the fears of some contemporary Venezuelan writers about the loss of space or recognition for literary concerns. These fears are evident in the discussions of literary quality that take place within the narratives analysed in this chapter, which can be read as the authors claiming a space for aesthetic considerations and their own 'power to consecrate producers or products' (Bourdieu, 1993, 42). We can perceive a cycle of reactions here: Bolivarian cultural policy reacted to the elitism of the state cultural system in the Punto Fijo period and some authors, publishers and critics in turn react to the lack of support and recognition for literary writing. As Gabriel Payares (2013, 172) noted, 'Frente a la épica bolivariana promulgada desde el aparato estatal, ciertas iniciativas culturales independientes [...] sintieron la necesidad de promover sus propias etiquetas culturales con las que distinguirse' [Faced with the Bolivarian epic spread through the state apparatus, certain independent cultural initiatives felt the need to promote their own cultural labels with which to distinguish themselves].

In *Transilvania unplugged* (Sánchez Rugeles, 2011a), the portrayal of Emilio as the reader of José Antonio's writing, from his earliest stories to his increasingly deranged accounts of his investigations through Romania, allows Eduardo Sánchez Rugeles to discuss ideas of literary quality. Emilio is very critical of José Antonio's writing style and literary aspirations. He describes with disdain how, ever since he was a child, José Antonio 'aspiraba a crear textos épicos e interminables' [aspired to creating epic and unending texts] (48), suggesting that good writing by contrast should be focused and tightly plotted. He also values originality or individuality of narrative voice, regretting that, in José Antonio's case, 'La búsqueda de una lengua, de una geografía propia, perdió su espacio ante la retórica cancerígena de la prensa democrática y los discursos humanitarios de los ecologistas' [the search for his own language, his own geography, lost out to the carcinogenic rhetoric of the democratic press and the humanitarian speeches of ecologists] (49). José Antonio is later shown to criticise Venezuelan journalism too, calling it 'mediocre' (75). However, this remark, made in the context of his having received low marks in his journalism course, seems more like a defence mechanism than a judgement based on any objective criteria for quality journalism. Emilio reveals more about his attitudes towards literature by judging José Antonio for his reading preferences and influences:

> [José] siempre sintió una profunda atracción por los cuentos de José Rafael Pocaterra. Descubrió el castellano con ellos, contrastó los timbres impersonales de su casa con las historias urbanas del venezolano de la decadencia, una de tantas decadencias. Pocaterra es horrible. (49)

> [José always felt a deep attraction to the stories by José Rafael Pocaterra. He discovered Castilian with them, he contrasted the impersonal tones of

his home with the urban stories of the Venezuelan in decline, one of many declines. Pocaterra is awful.]

Pocaterra (1889–1955) was a writer and journalist who participated in two attempts to overthrow the dictator Juan Vincente Gómez, in 1919 and 1929. Elvira Macht de Vera (1979, 3) explains that all the structural elements of his novel *Vidas oscuras* (1912) work towards exposing the moral and material decadence in Venezuela during the Gómez dictatorship. By calling Pocaterra 'horrible', Emilio rejects such moralistic writing. Pocaterra has also been described as insular and cut off from the world (Gomes Porras, 2017). Given Emilio's frustration with Venezuela and sense of rootlessness at this early stage of the story, it is unsurprising that he would criticise this insularity. By stating 'Pocaterra es horrible' without qualification, Emilio implies that it is not a matter of personal taste, but a fact. Emilio appears to consider himself 'legitimately entitled to designate legitimate writers' (Bourdieu, 1993, 41). His matter-of-fact contrast of his own taste with José's, where he is right and José is wrong, is a method of distinction, of asserting his superiority over José. Acting as a critic of José's writing, Emilio puts himself into a position of power.

Emilio continues his assessment of José complaining that as he grew older his desire for fame adversely affected the quality of his writing. He complains, 'El Nuevo José, el moralizante, aspiraba, más que todo, al mercado. José quería ser un Paulo Coelho o, mejor aún, un Dan Brown' [The New José, the moraliser, aspired, above all, to the market. José wanted to be Paulo Coelho, or, better yet, Dan Brown] (49). With this deprecating tone, Emilio implies that these authors do not write well, yet they appeal to a wide international market, raising questions about the incompatibility of commercial and aesthetic concerns. These are not new questions, but common to struggling writers across the globe. However, they take on added significance in a context where state support for literary production had been replaced by programmes for mass participation in writing. As the novel progresses, José joins Emilio as a critic of his own writing. He does not realise at first that source material alone cannot make a good story, as 'entre la realidad aburrida y el imaginario romántico, José Antonio escribió un cuento malo que en su primera lectura le pareció brillante' [between the boring reality and a romantic imagination, José Antonio wrote a bad story which, when he first read it, seemed brilliant to him] (60). However, as the book progresses, he admits to himself, 'Soy un escritor malo' [I'm a bad writer] (166). His self-criticism is focused on the technical aspects of crafting a story: 'Carecía de intención, de estructura, de sensibilidad' [He lacked intention, structure, feeling] (166). José proves with his own failure that writing well requires qualities including feeling and intention that cannot be forced or easily learnt.

Not only literary knowledge, but books themselves, are shown as status symbols in *Transilvania unplugged*. María Gabriela's mother is portrayed as part of the intellectual elite vehemently opposed to and opposed by Chávez and his Bolivarian government. She is a political consultant to anti-Chávez candidates – referred to as 'perdedores entusiastas' [enthusiastic losers] (32) – and for many years was the editor of the *Papel Literario* literary supplement for the newspaper *El Nacional* (32). For her, books are objects which are there to confer prestige rather than to be read:

> Practicaba distintos fetiches literarios. En principio, no compraba ediciones de bolsillo. La estantería gigante, desde el suelo hasta el techo, copaba dos habitaciones y estaba repleto de títulos de editoriales caras – muy caras – que en su mayoría aún se hallaban cubiertos de plástico. (33)
>
> [She practised various literary fetishes. Above all, she would not buy paperbacks. The enormous floor-to-ceiling bookcase took up two rooms and was filled with titles from expensive – very expensive – publishers, most of which were still covered in plastic.]

She collects books in English, French and even Hungarian to create a 'biblioteca exhibicionista' [exhibitionist library] (33), in which monetary value is more important than the effect a book might have on its readers. In this way, María Gabriela's mother exemplifies the wealth inequality and extreme elitism that the Bolivarian Revolution reacted against.

In an interview with Inma Chacón (2009, 37), Gisela Kozak Rovero stressed her respect for literary tradition, stating, 'Soy escritora porque soy lectora' [I am a writer because I am a reader], and listing a wide range of writers from across Europe and the Americas to whom she is indebted. Roberto Martínez Bachrich (2009) equally calls her novel *Todas las lunas* (2013) a novel for readers of literature. In the novel, literary tastes are linked to distinction, as Hans asserts that not everyone shares his ability to appreciate quality literature. As an angry young man, who feels misunderstood and undervalued, Hans sees his literary refinement as something he can be proud of. Hans takes on the role of critic in his discussions about writing by Guillermillo, a despised fellow voyager on the ship *La Luna*, talking with certainty about good and bad writing, as if these were fixed, objective qualities. Attitudes such as this reinforce the polarisation of the literary field and perceptions of elitism, implying that the ability to recognise and understand the value of literature is an innate and rare gift. As Peter Widdowson (1999, 9) maintains, 'a deeply exclusive and hence elitist, literary-critical stance lies at the heart of assumptive evaluative judgements'. Hans includes an extract of Guillermillo's writing in his second memoir, introduced with sarcasm and disdain:

> Veamos algunas de sus rutilantes reflexiones [...] sacadas de los libelos mal escritos y peor impresos que hace circular uno que otro ignaro de las nuevas generaciones:
> *La razón de la razón que es sinrazón, que por razón de ser vuestro, tengo para alabar vuestra sabiduría y reinado.* (112–113)

[Let's see some of the sparkling reflections taken from the poorly written and worse printed libels that every other ignorant youth passes around: *The reason of reason is unreason, which for being yours, I have to praise your wisdom and your reign.*]

Calling Guillermillo's fans ignorant, Hans distinguishes himself; he considers himself knowledgeable and possessing good taste by contrast. In his opinion, Guillermillo's writing is immature and dull or unimpressive, as implied by his sarcastic use of 'rutilantes' [sparkling]. By referring to these writings as libels, Hans is suggesting that the texts are so bad that they are insulting to readers. He also criticises the printing quality of these texts, suggesting that the physical form of the book reflects its literary quality, in a veiled comment on the cheaply produced books published by the state. By including this extract shortly after Lope de Vega's 'Sonnet 126', Hans encourages his readers to compare the two. He asks Jozef, '¿No te das cuenta de la diferencia entre esa lengua desertificada y funcionaria del Guillermillo y los versos de un gran poeta?' [Can't you tell the difference between this barren and functionary language of Guillermillo and the verses of a great poet?] (113–114). Although Guillermillo's writing is about emotion and desire, Hans suggests that it lacks feeling and passion. Comparing Guillermillo's language to that of civil servants reinforces Hans's belief that there is a distinct literary language which writers should use. Jozef, acting as a father figure to Hans, encourages him to be open to new voices. Jozef then cites the poem 'Prometeo' [Prometheus], by Julián de Casal (1863–1893), which he says reminds him of Hans, perhaps because the Prometheus myth refers to the quest for knowledge and the risks of taking this too far. The choice of poem illustrates how the modernists' emphasis on creating musicality and striking imagery above expressing emotions or relating to context was a significant change from poetic conventions in the late 1800s, but this does not mean their work is not of value.

Over the course of *Rating* (Barrera Tyszka, 2011), references to multiple avant-garde writers appear, from the early Venezuelan poet and playwright Salustio González Rincones (1886–1933) to the much better known Cuban baroque author José Lezama Lima (1910–1976) whose work Pablo is studying as part of his literature degree. While Pablo becomes more interested in the fame and fortune he can get from television production than baroque poetry, Manuel Izquierdo, the veteran scriptwriter, conversely reveals his pride in being well-read, as well as his fixed ideas about literary value. Manuel's early experience of working in the national library while at university was a formative time for him, reflecting the faith in the power of literature among students in the newly democratic Venezuela of the 1960s and 1970s. Losing his job there after an indiscretion in the stacks, Edgar Mejía Galeana (2015, 419) argues, symbolises the failure of these student movements, and Manuel's resulting move to television represents the disillusionment with writing this caused. Alberto Barrera Tyszka himself had after all been a poet as a student before working in *telenovelas*. Manuel is a firm believer in the classics, stating that 'la gran literatura ya está escrita' [the great literature has already been written] and that 'la humanidad ya escribió todo lo que podía escribir' [humanity has already written all it could write] (61). Manuel here displays the internalised, assumptive norms which Widdowson (1999) describes. He never explains what makes 'la gran literatura' so great. His assertion that nothing today is of value because everything has already been said in every possible way suggests that, for him, originality is an important part of literary value. Manuel proclaims, 'Hoy en día, no hay nada más fácil que escribir un mal libro' [Today, there is nothing easier than writing a bad book] (61). As well as the technical advances which make it easier to write and publish books today, this claim is particularly resonant in the Venezuelan context, where state-funded programmes such as Cada día un libro published thousands of titles. He does not specify what makes a bad book. Instead, he continues to advise against writing altogether, suggesting that aspiring writers would be better off going to a library or a bookshop. He adds, 'Ahí descubriría que lo que quiere decir, ya se dijo, ya se escribió. De mejor forma, además. Sólo puede pretender escribir aquel que no ha leído suficiente' [There he would discover that what he wants to say has already been said. In a better way too. Only those who haven't read enough can try to write] (61–62). Manuel maintains that rather than being encouraged to write, people should be encouraged to read. Such insistence on respecting literary tradition, which can be seen as conservative or elitist, counters Bolivarian cultural policy, which supports mass production of writing with little concern for whether these books are read.

In terms of writing, Manuel had never harboured any literary aspirations. He affirms that writing is nothing more than his way of earning a living (27). Having fallen into scriptwriting through an acquaintance when in need of a job, Manuel is disdainful of those who do not write to live, but 'desean *ser* escritores' [want to *be* writers] (62). In a monologue which recalls Bourdieu's (1993, 45) distinction between the two hierarchies of writers – the heteronomous or economic and the autonomous or aesthetic – Manuel observes:

> Ellos suelen ganarse la vida de otra forma. No saben lo que es estar atornillado en una silla, frente a una computadora, escribiendo todos los días diez horas seguidas. Ellos relacionan con las musas, nosotros lidiamos con un jefe. Ellos esperan a la inspiración, nosotros debemos cumplir un horario. [...] No buscamos trascendencia sino dinero. (62)

> [They tend to earn a living another way. They don't know what it's like to be bolted to a chair, in front of a computer, writing for ten straight hours every day. They relate to muses, we deal with bosses. They are waiting for inspiration, we have to meet a deadline. We aren't seeking transcendence, but money.]

While working in television, Manuel nevertheless continues to read with great intensity. One writer who Manuel particularly admires is F. Scott Fitzgerald, especially the short stories Fitzgerald wrote in 1940, the final year of his life, featuring a character called Pat Hobby. Manuel recalls, 'Hace años, cuando me dio una crisis y sentí unas, tan estúpidas como repentinas, ganas de escribir libros, tuve la suerte de tropezarme con esa breve recopilación de cuentos. [...] Ahí estaba todo lo que yo quería contar' [Years ago, when I had a crisis and felt the equally sudden and stupid desire to write books, I was lucky enough to come across this short collection of stories. There was everything I wanted to say] (72). Manuel clearly identifies with the pathetic but comedic Hobby, a once moderately successful, now washed up, screenwriter, who believes that scriptwriting is not art but industry. His belief that Fitzgerald has spoken for him reflects Harold Bloom's (2000, 22) assertion that people read to strengthen their sense of self. Hobby's observations about where the power really lies in Hollywood help Manuel to contextualise his own lowly status in the television studios, exploitative contracts, and how he must behave around mindless producers like Rafael Quevedo (73). In addition, by identifying himself with Fitzgerald despite being separated geographically, chronologically and in their relative levels of fame, Manuel is writing himself into the Western world.

As well as Fitzgerald, Manuel also recommends that his young apprentice Pablo read Budd Schulberg (43). Schulberg wrote novels – including *What Makes Sammy Run?* (1941), *The Harder They Fall* (1947), *The Disenchanted* (1950) and *On the Waterfront* (1955) – but is remembered primarily for his award-winning screenplays. Schulberg was well aware of the distinctions between scriptwriting and literary fiction, especially the limits imposed on a scriptwriter by the nature of film, as he discusses in his introduction to *On the Waterfront* (2013 [1955], 11–15). By mentioning Schulberg, Manuel therefore seems to be making Pablo aware of the limits of his new profession. Equally, readers familiar with Schulberg would recognise in *Rating* echoes of *The Disenchanted*, in which a faded writer (Fitzgerald in all but name) agrees begrudgingly to work with a young beginner on a script doomed to failure at the insistence of a know-it-all producer. In both *The Disenchanted* and *Rating*, the idea of apprenticeship plays a large role, drawing attention to what is involved in becoming a writer, and suggesting that writing is a craft to be passed on. In this way, *Rating* calls to mind Bloom's (1997, 13) concept of the 'anxiety of influence', which he defines as 'the melancholy of the creative mind's desperate insistence upon priority'. While Manuel knows that his writing will not have an influence, he hopes to at least influence Pablo through his mentoring.

Writing for the market

Bolivarian officials frequently reasserted the democratic and inclusive nature of the literary system brought about by the Bolivarian Revolution. In a 2011 speech to the National Assembly, for example, Francisco Sesto proclaimed,

'El Gobierno Revolucionario ha convertido la gestión cultural en una acción popular, masiva, democrática, desconcentrada, al servicio del pueblo. Pasó de una concepción de exclusividad, de élite a una de inclusión absoluta' [The Revolutionary Government has turned cultural management into a popular, mass, democratic, decentralised act, at the service of the people. It went from an idea of elite exclusivity to one of absolute inclusion] (Falcón, 2011). Critics, however, question this image of absolute inclusion. Introducing the current context of publishing in Venezuela to English-speaking readers in a special issue of *Words Without Borders*, Ana Nuño (2014) claimed that those who have 'chosen not to conform [and] are vocal in their criticism of the government's coercive methods [...] are treated as *personae non gratae*, and those who published there before 1999 ([Rafael] Cadenas, [Victoria] De Stefano, [Ana Teresa] Torres, [Israel] Centeno) have seen their titles expunged from the catalogue'.[2] Antonio López Ortega similarly cites the case of historian Germán Carrera Damas, author of *El culto a Bolívar* [The Cult of Bolívar] (2003), who presented to the media a letter from the director of Monte Ávila telling him that they would no longer be publishing his books (Méndez, 2013).

While Nuño and López Ortega talk of exclusion, however, it is often more a matter of self-exclusion by writers who do not want to be associated with the ideology to which Monte Ávila became inextricably linked. Gisela Kozak Rovero claimed that publishing with Monte Ávila is equivalent to showing support for and approbation of the Bolivarian regime (Méndez, 2013). Choosing where to publish can therefore be a political act. At the same time, writers had other, more pragmatic, reasons not to want to publish with Monte Ávila. López Ortega claimed, 'Publicar hoy en día en Monte Ávila es como habitar en un cementerio' [Publishing with Monte Ávila today is like living in a graveyard], citing how the publisher lost its international, especially Latin American, influence and was not featured in many of the large continental book fairs (Méndez, 2013). In addition, Manuel Silva-Ferrer noted that many of the most important intellectuals in Monte Ávila's catalogue – though he did not specify who – were driven away by frustration that their works were not being reprinted (Silva-Ferrer, 2014, 119). This self-exclusion, according to writer Montague Kobbe (2009), 'has none of the negative connotations of censorship, but shares many of its causes and consequences'. The differences in values here are evident: among those who criticised the changes to Monte Ávila were writers who considered themselves professionals and wanted not only the cultural capital of a publisher renowned for quality, but also the ability to sell books internationally, and thereby achieve wider recognition. The Bolivarian government, by contrast, was more interested in influencing people within Venezuela, publishing books by and for the Venezuelan people.

Having to look beyond the state for publishing opportunities meant writers had to contend with the demands of the market, which pose different threats

---

2 The authors mentioned all feature in the *Words Without Borders* Venezuelan issue.

to literary quality. This is the central theme of Armando Luigi Castañeda's autofiction *La fama, o es venérea, o no es fama* (2012). Many years ago, the author–narrator had found some success as an author in Venezuela: 'Gracias a un premio literario nacional casi importante, me publicaron mi primer libro y me convertí en joven promesa del exiguo y poco competido panorama cultural del país' [Thanks to an almost important national literary prize, my first book was published and I became a promising young voice within the meagre cultural panorama of the country, without much competition] (264). In the present, he is torn between writing a conventional novel for the international market, which he believes is likely to be a commercial success, and indulging his literary ambitions in the desire for transcendence. His attitude recalls Bourdieu's (1993, 98) distinction between long-term writers who aspire to recognition from their peers above all and short-term writers, 'professional writers who stick to the rules of a tried and tested aesthetic'. The author–narrator explains:

> Tenía dos opciones, escribir una novela con estructura, personajes, y etc., al gusto del mercado local, o continuar con la payasada que comencé hace diez años de escribir libros autobiográficos y experimentales.
> Me fui por la segunda opción, claro. (15–16)
>
> [I had two options, to write a novel with a structure, characters etc, to the taste of the local market, or continue playing about with autobiographical and experimental books as I had done for the last ten years.
> I went for the second option, obviously.]

In his mind, there is no common ground; he holds no illusion that experimental works would be to the local taste. He considers writing experimental autofiction ridiculous or foolish, suggesting that writing for the market is a far more rational decision. Nonetheless, he goes against his better judgement, in line with Diana Diaconu's (2017, 42) assertion that writers turn to autofiction when frustrated with commercial expectations. The word 'claro' is significant here. On the one hand, 'claro' refers to the evident fact that he chose the second option, as the very book we are reading is autobiographical and experimental. On the other hand, 'claro' also suggests that higher literary aspirations are the only legitimate option.

Castañeda engages critically with the question of how to balance introspective writing with writing as a profession. The author–narrator appears ambivalent about this self-reflexive writing. He acknowledges and seems to agree with suggestions that such writing is self-indulgent:

> Una amiga me dirá que no le gustan mis escritos porque siempre hablan de mí, y no sabe qué interés puede tener mi vida; que eso de hablar de sí mismo está bien para la gente importante, pero un tipo como yo, ¿para qué?, ¿a quién le puede interesar? (25)
>
> [A friend would tell me she didn't like my writing because I always talked

about myself, and she doesn't know why my life would be of interest. Talking about yourself is fine for important people, but a guy like me, why? Who would care?]

This reflection echoes Serge Doubrovsky's (1977) claim – with which he launched the term 'autofiction' – that autobiography is only for important people (Dix, 2017, 163). Castañeda here encourages readers to ask whose life stories are worth reading, why so many people think their stories are worth reading, and whether they are right or wrong to do so. While these are universal questions, they have added resonance in the context of the Bolivarian state publishing system, which focused on publishing as many people's stories as possible.

The narrator admits that he never reads similar writing by other people as he does not care at all about other people's lives and often finds them ridiculous (43). Following this reflection, he decides that 'obras estirilizadas' [sterilised works] are the correct thing to do: impersonal, universal and scientific narratives (43). He then begins to weave reports of scientific experiments, explicitly marked by the subtitle 'Experimento', in among the other strands of the narrative for the next 25 pages (43–68). These experiments are an illustration of the absurdity of the demand for objective or impersonal fiction. He begins with the typical experiments taught in a psychology class, such as a test of behavioural conditioning in chimpanzees (43–44), ending his account, 'Con este experimento se demuestra que las instituciones humanas se prolongan en el tiempo aunque ya no sirvan para nada. Se demuestra, también, que los chimpancés prefieren los frutos secos para alimentarse' [This experiment has shown that human institutions endure through time even if they are useless. It has also shown that chimpanzees prefer to feed on dried fruits] (44). Each experiment ends with 'Con este experimento se demuestra que ...', parodying how scientific writing justifies itself by explicitly stating its utility. This is always followed by 'Se demuestra, también, que...', mocking the claims to objectivity of such writing by demonstrating how different spins can be put on the same facts.

By the third 'experiment', a description of a piece of experimental theatre (46–48), the narrator's attempts at impersonal, objective writing are already giving way to the personal and subjective again. In his conclusion, he mimics the discourse of theatre practitioners and cultural commentators, imposing his own opinions, stating 'Con este experimento se demuestra que la creación es el lenguaje, y no al revés. Se demuestra, también, que un churro intelectualoide puede dar de comer si has nacido en el lugar adecuado' [This experiment has shown that creation is language and not the other way around. It has also shown that a pseudo-intellectual mess can make you money if you were born in the right place] (48). While directing his typical cynicism towards this kind of production, he nevertheless highlights the geographical disparities in the cultural market. It is far easier to make a living out of art – even bad art – in other countries than it is in Venezuela. He treats experimental film (52–54) and visual art (54–55) in the same way, contrasting mimicry of artspeak with his own cynicism towards the art market. In the subsequent set of experiments, the narrator attempts to describe a painting (57), a sound (60–61) and a sexual encounter (62). Each conclusion follows the format, 'Con este experimento se demuestra que sí, muchas veces, una imagen dice más que setenta y ocho palabras. No se demuestra nada más' [This experiment has shown that yes, often, an image says more than seventy-eight words. It has not shown anything else] (57). Maintaining the guise of scientific objectivity, the narrator has returned to the introspective, autofictional concerns which pervade the entire book, specifically the nature of cultural production and the difficulties of the writing process.

Having doubted the value of autofiction by other 'normal' people, the narrator nonetheless continues to write about himself. At first, he makes excuses for this choice of subject matter, confessing that he has always taken the easy option (22). As the book progresses, however, it becomes increasingly clear that, behind his cynicism, the narrator yearns for approval from readers. In one notable scene (122–124), in which the narrator fights with his wife about the reasons for writing, from money and fame to having something transcendent to say, she mocks him for wanting to be read after his death. He responds that he is always impressed when he discovers that something he has enjoyed reading was written by someone long dead and he wants to be part of that chain of people.

Throughout *La fama*, the author–narrator displays disdain for the conventional novel form, referring repeatedly to his own attempt at a popular crime/action novel as 'la novelita' (16, 117, 131, 132, 187, 260), the diminutive emphasising how trivial he finds it. Despite being poor and unemployed himself, he harbours elitist ambitions for his readership. In his opinion, those who would choose to read a conventional crime novel are not worthy of his effort. He admits that one of the reasons he failed to complete such a novel was that he kept slipping into condescension towards his prospective readers:

> Insultaba al lector por leer el librito en el transporte público que lo llevaba a su trabajo. Le preguntaba si no le importaba ver pasar sus días trabajando para unos tipos que lo despreciaban o, si tenía suerte, lo ignoraban. (16)

> [I insulted the reader for reading the silly little book on public transport on their way to work. I asked whether he minded seeing his days go by as he worked for some guys who looked down on him or, if he was lucky, ignored him.]

Not having a stable job himself, the author–narrator makes himself feel better by distinguishing himself from these readers, positioning himself as superior because he has committed himself to art. Such comments also exemplify the impossible desire to control the audience, as the type of audience an author attracts reflects well or poorly on him. Being chosen by an elite audience who are very knowledgeable about literature confirms that his work holds up against other works and is therefore of literary value. As Bourdieu (1993, 50) argues, for the non-commercially successful writer, recognition among peers becomes the 'sole legitimate profit'.

Despite his earlier condescension towards readers of popular novels, the author–narrator criticises such novels for treating their audience as stupid, deriding the oversimplified action:

> Hecho, ya presenté al personaje, acaba de terminar la primera parte de la receta feliz para fabricar noveles simpáticas. Se supone que con lo dicho hasta ahora el lector puede entender por qué el tipo va a hacer lo que hace en lo que queda del libro. Entonces, siguiendo siempre la receta feliz, me dispongo a introducir la situación que da origen al conflicto. (68)

> [Done, I've introduced the character, I've finished the first part of the happy recipe for writing nice novels. We can suppose that with what I've said so far the reader can understand why the guy is going to do what he does in the rest of the book. Now, still following the happy recipe, I'm getting ready to introduce the situation which gives rise to the conflict.]

As Linda Hutcheon (1995, 11) explains, 'irony is the intentional transmission of both information and evaluative attitude other than what is explicitly presented'. The author–narrator's ironic comments not only describe the recipe for a bestselling novel, but imply that such novels lack literary quality, that 'good' literature is more complicated. Similarly, the author–narrator is very cynical about what one should hope to achieve with a book. He muses, 'Se supone que ahora toca introducir la trama para que el lector se enganche, siga con el librito, lo acabe, quede más o menos contento, y se acuerde de decir a sus amigos que lo compren' [Supposedly I now have to introduce the plot so that the reader gets hooked, carries on with the book, finishes it, is more or less happy, and remembers to tell his friends to buy it] (117). The implication of this sarcastic comment is that a book should do more than just make people happy. Later, his stance is more nuanced as he suggests that a book can make readers happy and still be of high literary quality. He refutes 'la creencia general de que las cosas bien hechas son serias, y lo chistoso es mal hecho' [the general belief that things done well are serious and funny things are done poorly] (180). The reader is left to ponder what it is that makes a funny book well or poorly written. In a similar vein, the author–narrator wonders why people choose to read books which make them unhappy (195). He first considers Aristotle's answer to the paradox of tragedy, a necessary catharsis, then quickly adds that many other explanations have followed, and none can be verified (195–196). He realises, however, that a cynical, market-driven approach to writing is likely to fail, as by the time the first people to buy the book have read it it will no longer be in the shops, as stock changes every few months (118). It is notable that the author–narrator never considers libraries or alternative ways of finding books; he can only think of books being bought from shops. He concludes from this that the quality of the writing does not matter, as it will not help him to sell books, and all that is important is what could catch the attention of the few readers who might come across the book upon its release (118). Contrary to the aphorism, the narrator maintains that consumers will judge a book entirely by its cover. He should not be worrying about writing the book, he decides, he just needs to think of an eye-catching title. He might be right, as 15.1 per cent of Venezuelans interviewed for CENAL's reader behaviour study said that they choose what to read because they are attracted by the title (CENAL, 2013, 45). Nonetheless, the narrator soon contradicts his neat conclusion, as he does throughout the book, remembering that for there to be a book to have a cover to judge he first needs to write something good enough to convince agents to, in turn, convince publishers it will sell (118). The fate of his book, he determines, is in the hands of a very restricted number of people. Writing for the market means catering to the tastes of the agents and editors who hold the monopoly on the market. It is implied that these people do not share his high literary tastes, given the type of books that they have made bestsellers. In the hopes of winning their favour, he tries to follow successful models, reading the *Da Vinci Code* and Steig Larsson novels for inspiration (131, 260), but soon gets bored of generic action scenes:

> Corrió hasta el balcón y joder, ya me aburrí. Este rollo cinematográfico del estilo *best sellers*, para escribir, fastidia. Que el personaje salte, corra, se esconda, haga lo que le dé la gana, me da igual. Tendría que dejar la idea de la novelita del robo con allanamiento aquí. (132)
>
> [He ran to the balcony and fuck, I'm bored already. This best-seller style cinematographic shit is so dull to write. Whether the character jumps, runs, hides, does whatever he wants, I just don't care. I'll have to leave the idea for the armed robbery story here.]

The narrator is torn between the commercial pressure to conform and his desire to stretch his creativity and challenge his readers. This is further emphasised as his action novel becomes increasingly convoluted. He expresses concern that his novel is getting too complicated, 'y eso no es bueno, puede que el lector se atosigue y suelte el librito y, ¡susto!, adiós las recomendaciones' [and that's not good, the reader could fret and give up the book and – horror! – goodbye recommendations] (187). He suggests the commercial taste for easy-to-follow books leaves little space for intellectually challenging narratives. This is not an analysis of the Venezuelan literary system, but of international markets, as shown by the kind of authors to which he refers (Dan Brown, Steig Larsson).

As well as lengthy discussion about the process of writing the 'novelita', the author–narrator also reflects frequently on the book we are reading, particularly its structure, and what to include or cut out. One of the interwoven strands of the book is a fragmentary recollection of his visit to China, but he cuts it off midway when he thinks it is getting too long. He writes, 'Dejo

Xian, Luoyang, Zhenzhuo, Chulin, Kaifen, Beijing, Shangai y Hanzhou para otro libro; uno que no escribiré' [I'll leave Xian [...] and Hanzhou for another book; one that I won't write] (107). In this way, the narrator suggests that the story does not matter. He is not working towards a climax if he can just cut the narration part-way through. He seems not to have selected the anecdotes from his trip that would work best as a story, but just started at the beginning. In that case, why did he choose to include part of the trip at all? The fact that he will never write the book about the second part of his trip implies that it is the narration itself, the ways in which places and events are described, that is more valuable than the information being imparted. The author–narrator further questions narrative conventions by skipping ahead to describe a kiss, defying conventions of linearity:

> Pero me adelanto, porque lo de su beso con bocanada fue en nuestra tercera salida y tendría que narrar, antes, las otras dos, por respeto al lector, a los valores literarios, a la moral y a las buenas costumbres, a la coherencia estricta de este librito, a la vida como experiencia lineal, y a todo eso. (268)

> [But I'm getting ahead of myself, because the kiss with a puff of smoke was on our third date and I should recount the other two first, out of respect for the reader, for literary values, for morals and good manners, for the strict coherence of this book, for life as a linear experience, and all that.]

Once again, his ironic tone implies that literature should not be confined to a simple, linear structure, as life is not. His reference to morals and good manners makes linearity seem overly conservative, safe and boring, and while he, by contrast, views himself as daring and innovative.

Increasingly obsessed with the reception of the autofictional anti-novel he is writing, the author–narrator imagines a conversation with readers, saying 'Quisiera saber si estáis a gusto con nuestro librito' [I'd like to know if our little novel is to your liking] (249). The diminutive appears once again, perhaps this time to appear humble to his imagined interlocutors so that they judge his work kindly, even though he swears that he wants their honest opinion. His use of 'estáis' rather than 'están' suggests that he is imagining Spanish rather than Latin American readers. This demonstrates the power which Spain still exerts over the publishing industry in the Hispanic world. As William Corral (2013, 5) notes, even where publishing houses like Alfaguara and Anagrama have regional offices in each country, they abide by rules set by their Spanish headquarters. The imagined Spanish readers ask him why he writes in such a confusing, difficult to read way:

> Los lectores: [...] Se hace usted a veces un poco, cómo decirlo ... ¿agotador?
> El autor: [...] ¡Yo sólo he intentado escribir un librito divertido!
> Los lectores: Pues, no se moleste con nosotros, pero puede que no lo haya conseguido. (294–295)

[Readers: You can sometimes be a bit, how to put it ... draining?
Author: I was only trying to write a fun little book!
Reader: Well, don't get annoyed with us, but you might not have succeeded.]

This is the first of many examples in *La fama* of writing in what Luigi Cazzato (1995, 37) calls the 'criticgraphic mode', in which 'the author–narrator includes comments about his/her works or about literature and criticism in general in order to channel or prevent or caricature criticism'. The concerns about structure and ease of reading which the author–narrator had raised earlier reappear. The exchange is his way of affirming that writing a confusing text is not the result of any lack of skill on his part but a conscious artistic decision, fitting what he has already made clear is his taste for a challenging narrative structure requiring an engaged reader. In another lengthy exchange with his imagined readers, they state that they do not like the way he treats his characters, explaining, 'A veces parece que odiara usted a la Humanidad' [Sometimes it seems like you hate humanity] (298). By including this comment, the author–narrator further proves that he is aware of how his book will be received. He first tries to justify his unflattering portrayals of his lovers, his readers and humanity in general by declaring his taste for black humour and cheekiness (298). Even so, as the imagined readers keep insisting that he will never succeed as a writer unless he can create an emotional link with his audience, he becomes increasingly agitated and retorts, 'Puede ser que no quiera llegar a ningún lado' [Perhaps I don't want to get anywhere] (299). In their third and final intervention, the readers reveal their conservatism by asking the author why he does not write about 'normal' people who work steady jobs and raise a family, to inculcate the correct moral values (316–317). The narrator counters that he does not think that his characters are abnormal, suggesting that the readers' views are outdated (317). Unconvinced, the readers continue to advise him to write about simple things (318). They completely miss the sarcasm in his response, 'Seguramente saldrá un bestseller' [It will surely be a bestseller] and affirm that that is exactly what they want for him (318).

La fama draws to a close with a readers' report, later revealed to be from a Spanish publisher. The power of the readers from the Spanish publisher over the fate of a text is emphasised by the ironic title, 'HUMILDE INFORME' [humble report] (385). The report begins with a synopsis of the book (385–387), which describes the digressions about the writing process as 'una peculiar lucha entre la humildad y el ego del escritor' [a strange fight between the humility and the ego of the author] (385). This comment suggests that readers are expected to recognise this self-reflexivity as the most important aspect of the book. In the following six pages of 'INFORME DE LECTURA' [readers' report] (387–392), the readers list, page by page, the things that they like and dislike about the book. The same points reappear: the book is too heavy, too confusing and there seems to be no overall point or goal. They note that the book starts well but then dries up (390) and advise the author that he needs to work on unity to keep readers interested (391). The readers further complain, 'Se hacen repetitivas las escenas de sexo. [...] Al ser muy parecidos entre sí, es poco lo que aportan al relato' [All the sex scenes are repetitive. As they are all quite similar, they bring little to the story] (388). What is it that the multiple sex scenes are supposed to add to the book? It could perhaps be the shock value; although graphic sex scenes are not uncommon in contemporary Venezuelan literature, those in *La fama* are strikingly explicit. Perhaps readers are expected to enjoy such scenes, to then keep reading and to recommend the book to friends, in line with the author–narrator's design for commercial success. A further explanation is that the narrator's life is punctuated by sex, and so an autofictional novel should reflect this. Notably, the readers do not complain about the explicit nature of the sex scenes, but rather the fact that they are too repetitive, suggesting that commercial success requires spectacle, exaggeration and narrative progression. The readers' final advice is that if the author–narrator wants his novel to be published it will require many cuts to make it more commercial (391). They warn him, 'Nos parece complicado lograr un editor que apueste por tu relato tal como está en estos momentos' [We think it will be difficult to find a publisher who will take a risk on your story as it is now] (392). In this way, commercial publishers are portrayed as unwilling to take risks, preferring to stick with more traditional narratives which are more likely to produce financial gains.

The author–narrator counters the criticisms outlined in the readers' report by following it with a letter in response from an ex-girlfriend who offers a much more sympathetic reading (393–396). She is suggested to have higher literary tastes and knowledge than the authors of the report, as she notes the fragmentary novel is an accepted, even celebrated, trend in world literature (395). By asserting her superior knowledge over the writers of the report, she delegitimises the criticisms of the book presented in the report, pre-empting further criticism from readers of the final version of *La fama*. The ex-girlfriend's letter continues to suggest that the report writers did not fully understand what the author was trying to achieve, highlighting, 'De entrada, el texto no busca ser una novela tradicional sino la traducción de una visión del mundo' [For a start, the text isn't trying to be a traditional novel but the translation of a world view] (397–398). This is an argument often found in the theory of autofiction (Diaconu, 2017; Reisz, 2016). The comparison between the two implies that the traditional novel is outdated and limited, while *La fama* is far more ambitious. She compares the author–narrator's self-reflexive writing to that of successful, respected writers, both recent – J.M.G. Le Clezio, Patrick Modiano, Paul Auster, J.M. Coetzee, and Amos Oz – and less recent – Giani Stuparich, Sherwood Anderson and Jack Kerouac (395). Inspired by these comparisons, the author–narrator believes that this kind of writing could allow him to achieve his literary aspirations and to write himself into the world literature canon.

La fama ends with the author–narrator's own response to the readers' report. Marjorie Worthington (2017, 480) notes that whereas 'contemporary literary criticism does not usually afford an author the opportunity to explicate his own work, [autofiction] allows for the insertion of authorial interpretation, but under the cover of the author-*character* rather than the author himself'. The author is permitted to defend his novel in a way that might not otherwise be accepted or acknowledged. The author–narrator of *La fama* ends his response with criticism of the Spanish publishers behind the readers' report. He suggests that handing his novel over to them 'es como producir vino y tener que poner la producción en manos de comercial experto en coca-cola que no tiene puta idea de vinos' [is like producing wine and having to put the production in charge of an expert in Coca-Cola who doesn't have a damned clue about wine] (398). The analogy of wine and cola further emphasises the author–narrator's perception of literature as a mark of distinction; he ignores that wine, like literature, can also be a mass product depending on how it is made and marketed. The author–narrator had wanted to publish in Spain because the Latin American market is not prestigious enough. As Pascale Casanova (2004) argues, the European capitals – London, Paris and Barcelona – remain at the centre of world literary space, and so to become consecrated at home an author must first be recognised by one of these centres. The author–narrator affirms, 'Me interesa entrar a España y salir del circuito académico de Sudacalandia, pero tampoco quiero desmadrar lo que he hecho' [I want to break into Europe and get out of the academic circle of South America, but I also don't want to lose control of what I've created] (398).[3] His insistence that he would rather not be published than compromise his artistic vision exemplifies what Bourdieu (1993, 50) calls 'bad faith'. Bourdieu (1993, 50) maintains that authors often 'experience the incomprehension of the audience as an effect of the prophetic refusal to compromise with the demands of an audience attached to the old norms of production'. The author–narrator asserts that the Spanish publishers do not really know what readers want, as he can tell from the number of visits to and comments on his blog that many Spaniards are interested in his writing (398–399). *La fama* thus encourages readers to question the monopoly of a few commercial publishers and their adherence to formulae for commercial success. Contesting such a profit-driven approach to publishing is at the heart of Bolivarian cultural policy. Indeed, the statement announcing the launch of the Revolutionary Plan for Reading in 2009 explicitly states the need to 'abolir la hegemonía del mercado y la subordinación del libro al mismo' [abolish the hegemony of the market and the subordination of the book to it] (Ministerio del Poder

---

3 Note that Sudacalandia is an offensive, dismissive way of referring to South America.

Popular para la Cultura, 2009, 6). At no point, however, does the author–narrator of *La fama* consider Venezuelan state publishing as an alternative to trying to publish in Spain, presumably because it cannot offer him the recognition that he craves.

Two opposing notions of the value of literature dominate the literary field in the Venezuela of the Bolivarian Revolution. On the one hand, holding the monopoly on publishing in the country, the Bolivarian government delegitimises the figure of the professional author through the mass production of books with little attention to marketing and distribution. On the other hand, academics, literary critics, and other writers use their cultural capital to consecrate works that they consider to be of high literary value. This consecration is often symbolic, taking the form of positive reviews or recommendations rather than commercial success. In each of the texts discussed in this chapter, the protagonist considers him or herself 'legitimately entitled to designate legitimate writers' (Bourdieu, 1993, 41). Taking on the role of literary critics, these characters 'declare not only their judgement of the work but also their claim to the right to talk about it and judge it' (Bourdieu, 1993, 36). These characters, and their authors, pass judgement on writing to display the strength of their literary knowledge and supposedly superior tastes as a sign of distinction. In their explorations of literary quality, the writer-critics show concern not only about subject matter, but the way a story is crafted, its structure, feeling, and how it will affect readers. Such concerns take on a new significance when a writer must attempt to enter the private literary market due to the changing priorities of the state.

CHAPTER 3

Challenging the National Narrative

Metafiction, according to Luigi Cazzato (1995, 33), is a 'natural product of a general condition of anxiety'. Behind the desire to put oneself on the page lies a fear of the loss of individual identity in contemporary society. For David Lodge (1995), this anxiety is the product of the Barthesian 'death of the author'. Since the dawn of the novel, Lodge (1995, 149) argues, a key component of that literary form has been the idea of the author as 'a uniquely constituted individual subject, the originator and in some sense owner of his work'. Following Barthes and other structuralists' work, however, the author lost their place at the centre of literary criticism, as meaning began to be understood as the product of readers' interpretations based on their own experiences and wider societal discourse and relations. Consequently, Lodge (1995, 154) argues, 'the foregrounding of the act of authorship within the boundaries of the text [...] is a defensive response, either conscious or intuitive, to the questioning of the idea of the author'. The authors analysed in this chapter, well-versed in critical theory, are aware of structuralist criticism and the 'death of the author'. Nonetheless, the socio-political context of the Bolivarian Revolution, where individual expression is subsumed into the collective, adds an extra dimension to anxiety about the loss of an individual authorial identity theorised by Barthes. With the resurgence of nationalism in Venezuela instigated by Hugo Chávez, cultural policy posits reading and writing as tools for building a national community. The book is expected to register socio-historical reality and promote the recovery of local, regional, national and Latin American memory (Plataforma del Libro y la Lectura, 2007). This chapter examines how (auto)fictional writers counter this national narrative by asserting the place of the individual or the family (*El niño malo cuenta hasta cien y se retira* [Chirinos, 2010], *Todas las lunas* [Kozak Rovero, 2013] and *Rating* [Barrera Tyszka, 2011]), or exploring the complexities of national identity (*Círculo croata* [Zupcic, 2012] and *Transilvania unplugged* [Sánchez Rugeles, 2011a]). This trend mirrors the 'subjective turn' which characterised the texts written in opposition to the dictatorship of Marcos Pérez Jiménez (1948–1958).

Theory on the relationship between literature and the nation is extensive, exploring how writing has been used to bring disparate populations into order by instilling them with a sense of a shared national identity. To give just a few examples, Benedict Anderson (2006) proposes that the act of simultaneously reading the same texts cements 'imagined communities', by allowing people to identify with their fellow citizens who they will never meet in person, while the essays edited by Homi Bhabha in *Nation and Narration* (1990) maintain that the very concept of the nation is created through narrative. In other words, literature is used to mythologise roots and highlight the supposedly shared characteristics of all members of the nation. Within Venezuela, from the independence movement onwards, political leaders – whether democratic parties or dictators – have seen writing as a means of bringing together the disparate parts of the nation (Gomes, 1997, 838; Bermúdez and Sánchez, 2009, 543). Even during the Punto Fijo period, when writers had more freedom to be introspective or cosmopolitan, protecting and promoting national identity was still enshrined in cultural policy. With the resurgence of nationalism in Venezuela instigated by Hugo Chávez, the Bolivarian government built upon a long tradition of literary nationalism, with policies designed to facilitate the use of literature as a nation-building tool. As Richard Gott (2000, 198) writes, belief in 'a global renaissance of nationalism' was one of the President's defining characteristics. Chávez notably stated, 'I think we are living through a period in which nationalism is being reborn' (Gott, 2000, 198). Kenneth Roberts (2004, 67) equally describes Chávez as 'a throwback to Latin America's earlier populist tradition, which was characterised by strident nationalism'. This anachronism is what makes the Venezuelan case so interesting: in an age of globalisation, when borders between nations are becoming increasingly fluid, Venezuela is returning to nineteenth-century approaches to literature. In an instrumentalist reading of the development of world literature, Pascale Casanova (2004) argues that emerging nation states use literature to develop a sense of national unity among the disparate peoples they bring together. As nations mature, she maintains, literature tends to gain more autonomy, as it is no longer needed as a tool for creating a national identity, meaning that writers become freer to experiment and explore subjects other than the nation. This was visible in Venezuela during the Punto Fijo period. Many authors during this period challenged the idea of a national literary community by looking outside Venezuela for literary inspiration rather than following the nation-building model of their predecessors (Bencomo, 2006, 764). Rafael Castillo Zapata sees this as a consequence of the experience of a very insular dictatorship. He notes the obsession of Venezuelan intellectuals at the time with accessing a cosmopolitan contemporaneity, from which under Pérez Jiménez they felt cut off (Castillo Zapata, 1999, 77). While the literature of Punto Fijo focused on the alienation of the urban subject in a rapidly changing Venezuela, this introspective narrative, as well as a focus on aesthetic concerns, owed more to European and North American tradition than to any autochthonous literature.

Under the Bolivarian government, the perceived need to protect national identity against globalisation meant that Venezuela returned to being what Pascale Casanova (2004) calls a 'closed literary space'. Casanova (2004, 106) argues that 'The literary nations that are most closed in upon themselves, most concerned to equip themselves with an identity, endlessly reproduce their own norms in a sort of closed circuit, declaring them national and therefore necessary and sufficient within their own autarkic market.' Such declarations are made in the Organic Law of Culture (2005), which states the objective of the Bolivarian government not only to link culture with a sense of national identity, but to encourage citizens to value that national identity above all others. The preamble to the law describes 'nuestra actividad cultural como pieza fundamental de nuestra conciencia colectiva y como la más elocuente expresión de nuestro orgullo y soberanía nacional' [our cultural activity as a fundamental part of our collective consciousness and as the most eloquent expression of our national pride and sovereignty] (Comisión Permanente de Educación, 2005, 3). Equally, in accordance with Article 6, every citizen is legally obliged to honour and defend Venezuelan culture (Comisión Permanente de Educación, 2005, 5). In line with this law, in 2005, the Ministry of Communication and Information proposed the creation of a solid structure to strengthen national identity from within the heart of 'the people' (Bermúdez and Sánchez, 2009, 561). This became the Plataforma del Libro y la Lectura, launched in 2007. The representation of the national as 'necessary' as described by Casanova can be observed in the Platform's manifesto (2007), which stated the aim to promote 'el Libro Necesario que se escriba desde la esencia generosa del heroico pueblo venezolano' [the Necessary Book which is written from the generous essence of the heroic Venezuelan people]. The need for culture to express and reinforce identification with the nation was at the heart of the policies instigated by the Ministry of Popular Power for Culture, formed in 2005. In 2006, Francisco Sesto declared that the ministry would work to protect national culture from external influences and allow Venezuelans to articulate their national identity, citing 'una real necesidad de expresar lo que somos y no de caer de manera simplona en modelos prestados, de no caer en ramplona imitación' [a real need to express what we are and not naively fall into borrowed models, not to fall into vulgar imitation] (Wisotzki, 2006, 19). Sesto's reference to 'vulgar imitation' discredited the experimentation with foreign literary models by Venezuelan writers during Punto Fijo, which he saw as harmful to the national identity. He maintained that literature had no value if it was not an 'expresión profunda del alma colectiva' [a profound expression of the collective soul], adding, 'Si tú no eres de un lugar, si tú no respondes a tus orígenes, no eres nadie' [If you are not from a place, if you do not respond to your origins, you are no one] (Wisotzki, 2006, 19). This very pointed remark – the repetition of 'tú' emphasising that this message was targeted to specific individuals – expressed his condemnation of authors who chose to look beyond Venezuela for inspiration or to write about their disaffection with the country.

The kind of national identity that literature was expected to reflect and promote was not only bounded geographically but also rooted firmly in the past. Bermúdez and Sánchez (2009, 549) describe this as an idea of national identity based on the past, the land and common ancestors, stressing what is uniquely 'ours'. 'Misión Cultura', launched in 2005, had as its aim 'que todas las comunidades del país estén retomando la venezolanidad y reencontrándose con sus raíces, su historia, conociendo todo acerca de su ámbito y sus gentes' [that all the communities across the country take up Venezuelanness again and re-encounter their roots, their history, getting to know everything about their environment and their people] (Ministerio de Comunicación e Información, 2005, 19). This statement implied that, before this time, people had lost all idea of what it meant to be Venezuelan. The emphasis on the link between ancestors and the land oversimplified the complex mix of indigenous, colonial Spanish, African and later other European heritage which makes up the Venezuelan population. Furthermore, Eduardo Sánchez Rugeles (2011c) claimed that this 'empeño casi fanático' [almost fanatical insistence] on the purity of folklore and the authenticity of tradition clashed with the realities of globalisation which Venezuela was experiencing. Such an insistence on tradition, history and folklore is, according to Casanova (2004), typical of closed literary spaces.

The manifesto also stated that the Platform would work 'a favor de la construcción de una patria motorizada por el socialismo bolivariano' [towards the construction of a fatherland powered by Bolivarian socialism] (Plataforma del Libro y la Lectura, 2007). This outlook proposed writing as a form of democratic participation, where citizens would write to contribute towards the construction of a socialist nation. Their writing should both be rooted in and reinforce a sense of collective national identity. One way in which this was promoted was through the Misión Cultura storytelling workshops, where participants had to write their life story following the textbook *Trabajo con Autobiografía* [Working with Autobiography] (2006). Sujatha Fernandes (2017, 160) notes that these workshops 'encourage[d] participants to narrate their stories as subjects who move from humble beginnings to become model citizens capable of participation in civic life'. Writing their life story, often by following Chávez's story as a model, was meant to increase a sense of belonging and loyalty to the Bolivarian Revolution. These stories were intended to be collected and stored in a national archive, although this has not yet been carried out (Fernandes, 2017, 141). As for reading, the Plan Revolucionario de Lectura linked reading to the achievement of a socialist national community with a strong sense of identity. Reading was envisioned as a collective activity and associated with the military through the deployment of 'squadrons' of readers.[1]

---

1 See Brown, 2018 for a more detailed analysis of the Plan Revolucionario de la Lectura.

The authors analysed in this chapter respond to this insistence on the national with introspective writing which places emphasis on the individual and questions definitions of national belonging. The trend for introspective writing in Venezuela began with the 'subjective turn', which Raquel Rivas Rojas (2010) identified as a response by authors such as Andrés Mariño Palacio and Guillermo Meneses during the Pérez Jiménez dictatorship (1948–1958) to the official imaginary promoted by the strongly nationalist rulers. This 'subjective turn' produced 'relatos de intimidad que – en adelante – desafiarán la función redentorista y establecerán un territorio de introspección para la literatura y el arte locales, de donde serán expulsados los grandes relatos y los complejos proyectos políticos heredados de la tradición' [stories of intimacy which – from then on – would defy the redeeming role and would establish a space of introspection for local literature and art, from where the grand narratives and the complex political projects inherited from tradition would be excluded] (Rivas Rojas, 2010, 21). At the time, these books were the exception, as much of the literature of the Pérez Jiménez dictatorship continued in the nation-building tradition. However, these books led the way for increasingly inward-looking narratives during the Punto Fijo period (1958–1998). Disillusioned by the failure of revolutionary movements through the 1960s and 1970s, authors turned away from society and into themselves. The literature produced in these decades commonly featured characters who excluded themselves from all social or political participation, including politically committed writing (Casique, 2006, 605–606). Iraida Casique (2006, 606) argues that this in itself was a negative response to the situation of the time, critical of the present and denying any hope for the future. Casique's essay, 'Modelos de intelectualidad marginal en la narrativa de los sesenta y setenta' [Models of the Marginal Intellectual in the Narrative of the 1960s and 1970s] (2006), which includes close readings of the works of Renato Rodríguez, provides a valuable insight into how introspective narratives took hold of Venezuelan literature during this period:

> Al modelo espiritualista galleguiano de hombres que buscan la luz, se oponen esos 'pequeños seres' sin trazas de heroísmo, que ponen en evidencia la soledad y la incapacidad de vincularse con el 'otro' interno – desdoblamiento – y externo. (Casique, 2006, 621)

> [The Galleguian spiritualist model of men seeking enlightenment was countered by these 'small beings' without a trace of heroism, who display their solitude and an inability to relate to the internal 'other' – split personalities – and the external 'other'.]

In contrast to the literature of the 1920s and 1930s exemplified by Rómulo Gallegos, which promoted rationality and progress, the literature which flourished during Punto Fijo was characterised by the opposite of those values. The absurd, irrationality, irreverence, nihilism, ugliness and humour became key features of the literature of the time (Liscano, 1984, 121).

Absurd, nihilistic and irreverent are all characteristics of Juan Carlos Chirinos's novel *El niño malo cuenta hasta cien y se retira* (2010), particularly in relation to the protagonist, D.Jota. D.Jota's attraction to the absurd and irrational is demonstrated through his identification with the Surrealists. His best friend Madián had introduced him to the Surrealists and their experiments with writing:

> Madián me había enseñado a escribir cadáveres exquisitos, eso poemas surrealistas que Bretón y los demás hacían colaborando cada uno con un verso. Fueron muchas las noches en que imaginábamos, sin saber si fueron amigos y vivieron la misma época, a Bretón, Dalí, Buñuel, Jarry, Ionesco. (202–203)

> [Madián had taught me how to write exquisite cadavers, those surrealist poems that Bretón and the others made by each adding a verse. We spent many nights imagining Betón, Dalí, Buñuel, Jarry and Ionesco, without knowing that they were friends and alive at the same time.]

The two identify themselves with the Surrealists and are brought together through their shared love of these extravagant outsiders. This allows D.Jota to begin to explore the feelings he has for his friend without having to admit them openly. D.Jota's mention of the pair being thrown out of a café and told to find a gay club instead (205) gives some hint at what he is afraid of. Running away from the homosexual feelings which he cannot face (205), as well as his general dissatisfaction with life in Caracas, D.Jota heads north, drawn by his reading:

> Sólo las historias sobre el norte del mundo, los viajes de Roald Amundsen, las exploraciones de Jacques Cousteau, los documentales de animales extraños y las montañas emblanquecidas llamaban su atención. (16)

> [Only the stories of the North of the world, Roald Amundsen's journeys, Jacques Cousteau's explorations, documentaries about strange animals and white mountains caught his attention.]

D.Jota's personal transformation conforms to Trinh T. Minh-ha's (1994, 23) claim that 'traveling can turn out to be a process whereby the self loses its boundaries [which is] disturbing yet potentially empowering'. Away from his home, D.Jota stops straining against the moral boundaries imposed upon him by society, or that he imposed on himself to fit in, and embraces the 'evil' within him, what he calls 'la cápsula del mal' [the capsule of evil] (161). After leaving an injured Fanny and her flock of sheep in the snow to die, D.Jota's process of self-realisation is completed through reading. Rifling through the grandmother Derdriu's drawers, D.Jota finds an essay entitled 'Variaciones sobre el tema del maldito' [Variations on the Subject of Evil], which D.Jota calls 'un manuscrito que transformó la realidad' [a manuscript which transformed reality] (207). He is so struck by the essay that he transcribes large sections of it into a notebook he has stolen from Fanny (207–210). He does not know who wrote the essay, nor the 'tú' [you] to whom it is addressed – perhaps, he thinks, it is a response from the grandmother to her lover Eugenio – but he begins to feel that it has been written for him. He notes, 'Básicamente había allí un resumen de lo que, más o menos, sentía en ese momento [...]. Esas palabras brillan ahora en mí, todo lo que acontece y es en el mundo pareciera pasar a través de su sonido' [Basically it was a summary of what, more or less, I was feeling at that moment. Those words shine in me now, everything that happens and everything that exists in the world seems to pass through the sound of them] (210). D.Jota displays the kind of 'fan reading' characterised by 'an intensity of intellectual and emotional involvement' which Henry Jenkins describes as 'empowering' (Storey, 2003, 90). His reading, and his identification with what he reads, gives him the strength for self-realisation. The process is finally completed by writing his story in the stolen notebook as he escapes El Pueblo and rereading it to himself:

> Abro el cuaderno negro y comienzo a leer lo que he escrito, retazos de esos días, como quien se despierta y hace el esfuerzo de repetir, aún dormido, lo que acaba de soñar para que no se le pierda en la tectónica de la memoria. He agotado sus páginas, menos la final. Tal vez a mí no me sirva de nada. No pretendo sino hallar justo lo que me guíe para entender lo que ocurrió. (159)

> [I open the black book and begin to read what I have written, traces of those days, like someone who wakes up and tries to repeat, still half-asleep, what he has just dreamt so it doesn't get lost with the tectonics of memory. I've used up all but the final page. Perhaps it won't be of any use to me. I'm only trying to find just enough to guide me through what happened.]

Writing and rereading allows him to relive experiences, to keep thinking about them until he can make sense of them. At the end of the novel, having reread his story, D.Jota decides to abandon society altogether and follow his darkest impulses.

Todas las lunas (Kozak Rovero, 2013), is a much less nihilistic novel, which instead imagines an escape from the restrictive official concept of Venezuelan national identity through a celebration of emotional connections, set in a Utopia. As critic Roberto Lovera (2012) observes, the entire novel is constructed around affect. The protagonists, all from diverse ethnic and linguistic backgrounds, live together in Estefanía, a Utopia where immigrants from around the world coexist in harmony. Their love goes beyond familial bonds to romantic and sexual relations, upon which Loren's disappearance forces them to reflect. The tone of the novel is intimate and confessional, as the characters reassess their lives and the meaning of home. The utopic city-state Estefanía takes its name from a poem by Víctor Valera Mora (1935–1984) called 'Relación para un amor llamado amanecer' [List for a Love Called Daybreak], written in 1971. The poem includes the line

'Su capital es una ciudad resplandeciente llamada Estefanía' [Its capital is a dazzling city called Estefanía] (Valera Mora, 2015, 33). In Valera Mora's poem, Estefanía is a place 'Donde no hay academias militares ni policías ni cárceles' [Where there are no military academies or police or prisons], 'Donde somos sabios' [Where we are all wise]. In naming the city Estefanía, Kozak Rovero makes clear the kind of place in which she wants to live, one where wisdom is valued more than brute force. Valera Mora's collection *Amanecí de bala y otros poemas* [I Was Woken by a Bullet and other poems], in which this poem appears, was republished by El perro y la rana in 2015, with a presentation text referring to Valera Mora as 'una de las voces más representativas de nuestra poesía revolucionaria' [one of the most representative voices of our revolutionary poetry] (Valera Mora, 2015, 9), without addressing the tension between Valera Mora's pacifism and the militarism of the Bolivarian Revolution.

Verónica, one of the novel's protagonists, describes Estefanía in her memoirs, which open the novel:

> Estefanía, resguardada por sus montañas de toda inclemencia climática, pero con un brazo de mar que la deja abierta a las oleadas de inmigrantes que traen en su ligero equipaje un idioma, un libro, el bosquejo de un invento, una idea nueva, la voluntad preciosa de no mirar atrás. (18–19)

> [Estefanía, protected by her mountains from all inclement weather, but with a sea arm that leaves her open to the waves of immigrants who bring in their light luggage a language, a book, the sketch of an invention, a new idea, and the beautiful will not to look back.]

Belonging in Estefanía is not a matter of blood ties to the land nor of ancestors, but of choice. Books, however, are one of the few things considered useful for making of a new identity in Estefanía. Verónica notes that she lives not only in an 'espacio sin fronteras' [space without borders] but also in an 'época sin calendario' [era without a calendar] (125). The story takes place in no discernible time period – there are certain modern aspects, but neither the telephone nor the aeroplane has yet been invented. The official history of the nation, a key part of any construction of national identity, is absent, replaced with tales of immigration handed down through the makeshift family. Nonetheless, at one point, Kozak Rovero does link Estefanía to wider Latin American history, referring to Sor Juana Inés de la Cruz as the 'lejana inmigrante fundadora de Estefanía' [distant immigrant founder of Estefanía] (170). Sor Juana was a famous Mexican scholar of the seventeenth century. Self-taught, she became a nun in order to dedicate her life to study and to writing and advocated relentlessly for access to education for women. Kathleen Bartels (2008, 265) describes Sor Juana as 'the collective myth in which female students are asked to seek inspiration and group identity'. With Sor Juana as founder, Estefanía becomes a place where identity is not based on race, religion, language, or geography, but on shared passions and a thirst for art and knowledge. She also represents a desire for gender equality which Kozak Rovero implies is missing from the real world.

Verónica highlights the rootlessness which defines the group, explaining that her life, those of her family group and those of their children 'han sido flujo sin territorio, lenguaje sin patria, migración en cuerpo y alma' [have been a flow without a territory, a language without a fatherland, migration in body and soul] (20). In such a context, the group define themselves primarily through their personal relationships: familial, romantic and sexual. Having all lost their parents in a shipwreck, the eight orphans become a family, raised by the oldest among them, and rely on each other for emotional support. The driving force behind the novel is the need to keep this family together, as Loren's disappearance throws them into turmoil. Despite these familial relationships, the group maintain fluid sexual relations, in which sex is often more a sign of their affection for one another than of romantic love or passion. Both Verónica and Gabriela have a baby each with Robin, Hans and Jozef, which, added to Loren and Farrah's two offspring, makes eight children who are all raised together by the group. They pass their rejection of traditional ideas of belonging on to their children, as Jozef tells them, 'A todos les hemos dado ocho corazones, cuatro madres, cuatro padres, ocho idiomas, el saber todo, mil paisajes y ciudades' [We have given you all eight hearts, four mothers, four fathers, eight languages, all of knowledge, a thousand landscapes and cities] (198). It is clear that openness to different cultures, languages and people is seen as far superior to bounded and fixed ideas of belonging rooted in a place, a language and a history. Kozak Rovero (2015b) explained:

> El tema del soporte afectivo, sexual y cultural es clave en *Todas las lunas* y responde a una voluntad expresa de desafiar los límites crueles del estado nacional y conectar con lo que Bhabha llama la cultura y literatura internacional, entendida como los entremedios entre culturas, lenguas, raza, nación, género, clase, sexualidad.
>
> [The theme of affective, sexual and cultural support is key in *Todas las lunas* and responds to an explicit will to challenge the cruel limits of the nation-state and connect with that which Bhabha calls international culture and literature, understood as the intermediaries between cultures, languages, races, nations, genders, classes, and sexualities.]

Rather than identify with a limited, prescriptive national identity, Kozak Rovero invents a home where there are no limits to personal freedom. At the turn of the twenty-first century, Joséfina Ludmer (1994, 10) suggests, 'La literatura registra la desintegración y el estallido en mil pedazos del espacio unificante de la nación y la huida al espacio exterior' [Literature registers the disintegration and breaking into a thousand pieces of the unifying space of the nation and an escape to an exterior space]. In *Todas las lunas*, however, the escape is not a geographical one, but one afforded by openness to other cultures, celebrated through reading.

Reading not only provides knowledge of the world, but self-understanding, particularly in the case of Hans. In the first of three memoirs in which he reflects on his adolescence, and particularly on a formative voyage on the boat La Luna [The Moon], Hans states, 'Sólo el soneto de Lope de Vega que aprendí de memoria en mis años mozos puede describir aquel estado de alma enamorado y guerrero' [Only that Lope de Vega sonnet I memorised as a boy can describe my state of mind in love and at war] (77). He cites the whole sonnet, number 126, 'Desmayarse, atreverse, estar furioso' [To Falter, To Dare, To Be Furious], Lope de Vega's ode to the contradictions of love. The sonnet famously ends 'Esto es amor; quien lo probó, lo sabe' [This is love; whoever has tasted it knows], suggesting that the poem is not an abstract philosophising on the nature of love, but the expression of painful lived experience. The inclusion of the poem in full suggests that Hans's own words could not express his feelings as well as Lope de Vega does. Hans demonstrates 'fan reading' (Storey, 2003, 90), reading his own emotions into someone else's text as if it had been written for him. Just as for D.Jota in *El niño malo* (Chirinos, 2010), literary discussions become a way for Hans and Robin to realise their feelings for one another. Specifically, Hans recalls discussing the love between Achilles and Patroclus in Homer's *Iliad* (109). Roberto Lovera (2012) notes that *Todas las lunas* is the first novel openly to celebrate homosexuality in Venezuela, a country still plagued by systematic homophobia.[2] *Todas las lunas*, in Héctor Torres's opinion, is Kozak Rovero's response to, or perhaps escape from, the limits placed on identity under the Bolivarian Revolution. He writes that the absence of boundaries on creative or personal expression in the novel 'pertenece a la Gisela que hubiera querido vivir en otro universo sin cortapisas nacionales ni históricas' [belongs to the Gisela who would have liked to have lived in another universe without national or historical restrictions] (Torres, 2014). In the novel, reading, from Ancient Greek classics to Spanish poetry, gives the characters a means of processing and expressing their true feelings free from any limits.

As well as reading, writing is shown as an introspective practice in *Todas las lunas*, a way to think through personal issues or to come to terms with trauma. As Roberto Martínez Bachrich (2013) notes, Kozak Rovero eschews the grandiloquence of the third person for the intimate and domestic tones of self-writing. The novel is a patchwork of texts written in the wake of Loren's disappearance. Throughout the novel we see how writing helps the group not only to cope with Loren's absence, but also to process older traumas and to express or supress their emotions. The novel opens with memoirs by Verónica, which become a thread through the text, woven in with extracts

---

2 In a study by the Pew Research Center published in 2013, for example, 42 per cent of Venezuelans interviewed said that society should not accept homosexuality. The charity Acción Ciudadana Contra el SIDA (ACCSI, 2013, 19) recorded 99 anti-LGBTI hate crimes between 2009 and 2013, noting that many more go unreported.

CHALLENGING THE NATIONAL NARRATIVE   91

from Gabriela's diary, Farrah's letters, Robin's *crónicas* [non-fiction stories] and Hans's memoirs. Both Martínez Bachrich (2013) and Chacón (2009) stress that the characters in *Todas las lunas* are human, believable and often contradictory.

Verónica is a musician who had never considered writing before. In the opening paragraph, she states explicitly that she has only turned to writing now as a coping mechanism, as Loren's disappearance has stirred up painful memories, especially the death of her partner, Constanza:

> Comienzo a escribir estas memorias antes de cumplir cuarenta años, porque Loren ha desaparecido hace seis meses y su alejamiento, sin clara explicación, despertó el recuerdo de todas las ausencias terribles enfrentadas a través de mi existencia [...] Si no fuera por las lamentables e involuntarias separaciones, jamás hubiera sentido este impulso de guardarme en unas páginas. (17)
>
> [I'm starting to write these memoirs before turning 40, because Loren disappeared six months ago, and his distance, without any clear explanation, has awoken the memory of all the terrible absences I have faced in my life. If it weren't for these unfortunate and involuntary separations, I would never have felt the need to preserve myself in a few pages.]

On the surface, the idea of saving or preserving oneself on paper seems to chime with the Bolivarian idea of writing as a document of lived experience. Verónica does not intend for her memoirs to be shared though; they are instead a personal response to her overwhelming feelings of loss, a way to save her memories for herself before they fade. Her writing is not logical. She does not seek to understand nor explain, merely to capture essences (19). Verónica explains that the experience of loss has changed her understanding of writing. Previously, she had thought it sad that poets would write verses trying to recover a lost love, knowing that the loved one would never read them, and that writing would not bring them back. Now, she says she understands these poets, as 'Constanza nunca leerá estas páginas, pero yo sí lo haré una y otra vez' [Constanza will never read these pages, but I will, over and over again] (128). Even though writing cannot bring back Constanza, it remains the only way for Verónica to find any relief from her anguish. Writing down and rereading her memories allows her to relive them over and again. In state-sponsored story-telling workshops, Fernandes (2017, 146) notes, facilitators are told to avoid focusing on the emotions brought up by traumatic events, as this would 'deviate from the goals for which we are here'. *Todas las lunas* suggests such repression is psychologically unhealthy, and affirms the need to broach individual traumas, not just the collective.

Like Verónica, the younger members of the group, Farrah and Hans, equate writing with powerful emotions. Farrah only has recourse to writing when her emotions are running high, either extreme happiness or extreme anguish (30). Similarly, Hans turns to writing to cope with his emotions when he would otherwise express himself through violence. He admits, 'Esta desaparición me ha llevado a pensar en que la sangre podría volver a mi vida. Asustado ante esta idea, apelo a la escritura en nombre del varón de paz que siempre he intentado ser' [This disappearance has made me think that bloodshed could return to my life. Shocked by this idea, I am appealing to writing in the name of the peaceful man I have always tried to be] (77–78). In a Venezuela where violence is an everyday occurrence, such statements advocate for introspective writing practices as a potential solution.

Only one member of the group, Robin, is a professional writer, and his non-fiction stories about the group become a best-seller in the utopian world in which the novel is set. However, he seems uncomfortable with strangers knowing the intimate details of his life through his writing. He notes, 'Todo el mundo sabía de él, todo el mundo había leído mis crónicas. Sí, mis crónicas se leían, se traducían, se contaban, se copiaban, se chismeaban, se trastocaban, y todos nos conocían' [Everyone knew about him, everyone had read my stories. Yes, my stories were read, translated, recounted, copied, gossiped about, subverted, and everybody knew us] (205). Robin understands how stories travel from the page to oral retellings, becoming altered beyond the writer's control in the process. He displays an impossible urge to control his readership. Writing is his profession, yet he remains uncomfortable with the idea that once his texts are in the public domain, he can no longer restrict access to them nor dictate how they are interpreted. Although Robin is reluctant to write about Loren, the group encourages him to do so as part of a plot to get Loren back. In the end, he submits to the pressure to write a story about Loren, which becomes an instant phenomenon, against Robin's wishes. He describes, 'La crónica sobre la vida de Loren, historia viva capaz de hacer mover a miles de personas; nunca quise semejante cosa, solo quería mostrar la vida dejando huellas en los caminos' [The story of Loren's life, a lively story capable of moving thousands of people; I never wanted such a thing, I only wanted to show life leaving traces along the way] (224). Like Véronica, Robin writes to keep memories of loved ones alive and to celebrate the things that make them who they are. For Gisela Kozak Rovero, writing to remember intimacy and affect is vital in a context where the dominant narrative about life in Venezuela, spread particularly through the news media, is one of violence and suffering. In her prologue to *Siete sellos* [Seven Seals] (2017), a collection of *crónicas* exploring the increasingly difficult situation in Venezuela under Nicolás Maduro, Kozak Rovero stressed the importance of not forgetting what Venezuela gave to the world in terms of art, culture and innovation, nor the tastes, sounds and people which make up the country. Such a celebration of affect – of intimate memories, emotions and feelings – is subversive in a Venezuela where both the government and the opposition feed an atmosphere of tension leading to oppressive emotional climates. Kozak Rovero (2015b) explained that the harmony in Estefanía does not result from the absence of conflicts, but from the freedom for individuals to each hold and express divergent opinions and attitudes. In a politically polarised

Venezuela, there is little recognition of alternative viewpoints from either side, and political differences commonly divide families (Ponce, 2016). By giving equal recognition to a variety of voices, with divergent opinions yet united by affect, *Todas las lunas* argues for greater acceptance.

Miguel Gomes (2010, 853) observes in the fiction of both Gisela Kozak Rovero and Alberto Barrera Tyszka a mistrust of 'la retórica mesiánica, heroica, didáctica que domina la vida pública' [the messianic, heroic, didactic rhetoric that dominates public life]. Like Kozak Rovero, in *Rating* (2011), Barrera Tyszka turns to self-writing – in this case, the memoirs of veteran screenwriter Manuel Izquierdo – to craft an intimate portrait of a flawed, contradictory and very human character. For Manuel, before the events narrated in the novel, writing was only his way of earning a living; he had always sworn that he would never write anything other than a television script (26–27). However, following his fiftieth birthday, Manuel becomes increasingly preoccupied with his own mortality, and finds himself doing what he always swore he would never do (27), writing his life story. Over the course of *Rating*, writing becomes a means for Manuel both to remember and critically to reassess his life so far. His memoirs begin as a record of his life should he be struck with dementia:

> La simple sospecha de perder la memoria me aterra. Por eso abrí este archivo y comencé a escribir. Porque quiero tener mi memoria fuera de la cabeza, al alcance de la mano. Quiero poder leer mi vida si algún día amanezco [...] con la mente casi en blanco. (27)
>
> [The very possibility of losing my memory terrifies me. That's why I opened this file and started to write. Because I want to have my memory outside of my head, within reach. I want to be able to read my life if one day I wake up with an almost blank mind.]

This autobiographical writing is for him a pragmatic task without any literary pretensions, as he assures himself, 'Esto no es literatura, esto sólo es profilaxis' [This isn't literature, this is prophylaxis] (27). However, as he writes, he begins to reflect on his life, and finds, like the protagonists of *Todas las lunas* (Kozak Rovero, 2013), that the process offers him relief from painful emotions and a way to find some kind of meaning (28). His writing is not designed to be shared, but as a vehicle for introspection. He notes, 'Ahora me doy cuenta de que ya no puedo cambiar nada de lo que fui. Ahora sólo puedo escribirlo. Quizás la escritura es la única oportunidad que tengo de ser distinto' [Now I realise that I can no longer change anything about what I have been. Now I can only write about it. Perhaps writing is the only opportunity I have to be different] (34). Manuel's writing has a personal, intimate value, but it is not entirely removed from society. Brockmeier (2015, 171) describes autobiography as 'narrative self-making', a process 'driven not by cognitive mechanisms but by affective motives and concerns, by emotional entanglements rooted as much in individual lives as in the social and cultural worlds in which these lives are lived'. For Manuel, the emotional entanglements that drive his autobiographical writing are his bond with his mother, his failed marriage to Patricia, and his botched relationship with the actress Beatriz Centeno.

Writing, in terms of his job as a scriptwriter, is intrinsically linked to Manuel's relationship with his mother, given that she was diagnosed with leukaemia when he had just started working in television. Writing his memoirs allows Manuel to relive the many hours he spent talking to his mother while she was in hospital. He describes his mother watching his *telenovela* as she is dying, noting 'Creo que sentía orgullo, o quizás tan sólo deseaba que yo sintiera que ella estaba orgullosa de mí' [I think she was proud of me, or maybe she only wanted me to think that she was proud of me] (112). As he is currently in a moment of crisis, thinking that his work in television has been a waste of his life, recalling his mother's pride provides some positive reinforcement. Manuel's mother is also linked to writing symbolically, as he keeps her pacemaker on his bookshelf (158). Like his mother, his books are a source of emotional support and wisdom.

In contrast to his strong bond with his mother, Manuel's romantic relationships with women had been wholly unsuccessful. Looking back on his life through his autobiographical writing makes him reflect on where he went wrong. He had thought his marriage to Patricia when they were both students was doomed to failure, as her parents objected not only to the marriage in itself but to him in particular (180). However, in writing the story, he admits that he was not prepared for a family, a home and a settled life (180). His memoirs become a kind of confession, admitting and accepting his guilt for the failure of this marriage to which he was not ready to commit. Writing the memoirs also forces Manuel to face his painful memories of his relationship with Beatriz, which he would otherwise hide from. Waking up in the middle of the night thinking of her, he writes, 'Me levanté de la cama y vine directamente a la computadora. Sin pasar por el baño, sin hacer café, vine directamente a escribirla. Si no es así, quizás no la pronuncio. Beatriz' [I got out of bed and went straight to the computer. Without going to the bathroom, without making coffee, I went straight to writing about her. Otherwise, I wouldn't pronounce her name. Beatriz] (174). This relationship was conditioned by his scriptwriting from the beginning, as they became a couple when Beatriz starred in a *telenovela* that Manuel was writing, *La ley del corazón* [The Law of the Heart] (102). At this point, Manuel's life was so saturated with *telenovelas* that he began to understand events through the lens of a *telenovela* plot (204). When Beatriz told him that she was pregnant while they were being taken from a drug-fuelled party in a police van, Manuel thought his life was a poorly written, clichéd plot. He responded, 'Tú no vas a convertir mi vida en una telenovela' [You are not going to turn my life into a *telenovela*] (204). These were the last words he had said to her and, at the point when he begins writing his memoirs, he has never seen his son. Writing, remembering and reassessing makes Manuel realise how stupid this was. Writing becomes the catalyst for Manuel to change his life; he gives up television and reunites with his former lover and his son.

The intimate, confessional tone of both *Todas las lunas* and Manuel's memoirs in *Rating*, as well as the characters' willingness to change and to have their beliefs tested, provides a contrast to the epic national narrative presented by the Bolivarian Revolution. As Miguel Gomes (2010, 835) argues, this indeterminacy and acceptance of different viewpoints in both authors' work suggests 'un proyecto nacional que se traduzca antes en diálogo o matizada búsqueda de sentido que en maniqueísmo, división y contienda' [a national project that translates to dialogue and a nuanced search for meaning rather than Manichaeism, division and contention].

Literature of *desarraigo*

In much of the narrative of the Punto Fijo period, the most common protagonist was rootless and directionless (Britto García, 1999, 40). In her analysis of the fiction of Renato Rodríguez, Iraida Casique (2006, 614) describes his characters as subjects adrift, who cut themselves from a society which disgusts them. Rodríguez's first and most famous work, *Al sur del Equanil* [South of the Equanil] (1963), challenges the pressure to belong to society. Presenting a protagonist who has no family, wandering through Paris, *Al sur del Equanil* is a novel characterised by isolation and confusion in which identity is presented as something lacking (Casique, 2006, 608). In this way, identity is seen 'no como ilusión, sino como estrepitosa y aniquilante desilusión' [not as an illusion, but as a resounding and crushing disillusionment] (Casique, 2006, 615). The characters want to believe in the national identity promoted so forcefully both by the Pérez Jiménez dictatorship and by the subsequent governments of the Punto Fijo period, yet find it fundamentally unattainable. This ambivalence towards identity has continued into literature written during the Bolivarian Revolution, a period, as we have seen, characterised by fervent nationalism.

The literature of *desarraigo* [rootlessness or uprooting] is, according to Raquel Rivas Rojas (2012), an expanding archetype. In an essay entitled '¿Irse o quedarse?' [To Stay or To Go?], Luz Marina Rivas (2011) explores the tendency, in recent literature, to include discussion about why to emigrate or why to stay as part of the characters' discourse or reflection. Although there are no official figures kept by the National Institute for Statistics, emigration since 1999 has been estimated at between 1 million and 2.5 million, out of a population of around 30 million. Rivas Rojas (2014, 228) argues that, faced with official rhetoric that ignores or denigrates those who leave the country, a growing body of literature aims to make visible those who are trying to make sense of their belonging.

Círculo croata (Zupcic, 2012) and *Transilvania unplugged* (Sánchez Rugeles, 2011a) are examples of this literature of *desarraigo*. Both Zlatica from *Círculo croata* and José Antonio from *Transilvania unplugged* are torn between societal and personal pressures to feel a sense of belonging to the nation and their own feelings of rootlessness, made more complicated by the fact that both are second-generation immigrants. Both young men write to work out who they are, where they come from and where they belong. In her pioneering doctoral thesis on the figure of the immigrant in contemporary Venezuelan literature, Naida Saavedra (2012, 150) notes that this is a subject that has yet to receive much scholarly attention. As a first step towards remedying this shortfall, her study considers the portrayal of Portuguese, Italian, Spanish and Colombian immigrants in eight novels from 1961 to 2008, focusing on how their socio-economic status, language/accent and personal relationships affect the way that they are viewed by native Venezuelans. She concludes that native Venezuelans are generally accepting of the immigrants who have formed part of their daily existence since the mid-twentieth century and therefore contribute to the ever-evolving Venezuelan national identity (Saavedra, 2012, 151). However, Saavedra's study does not consider how immigrants and their descendants identify themselves and view their own place within Venezuelan society, which is problematic, as the novels discussed in this section demonstrate. The protagonists of *Círculo croata* and *Transilvania unplugged* share an ambivalence towards Venezuela. While both were born and raised in the country, neither feels that they completely belong there. Gina Saraceni (2000) attributes this common sentiment among second-generation immigrants in any country to an inherited uprooting or alienation (*desarraigo*):

> Desarraigo de segunda mano, ese desarraigo geográfico, cultural, lingüístico que los hijos heredan de los padres, está relacionado con una identidad conflictiva que se construye en el cruce de dos o más imaginarios culturales que fracturan al sujeto sometiéndolo a una tensión constante entre el allá que hereda y el aquí que habita. (Saraceni, 2000, 199–200)

> [Second-hand alienation, a geographical, cultural and linguistic alienation which children inherit from their parents, is related to a conflictive identity constructed at the meeting point of two or more cultural imaginaries, which fracture the individual, subjecting them to a constant tension between the there which (s)he inherits and the here which (s)he inhabits.]

Given that the family is often used as a metaphor for the nation, Víctor Carreño (2013, 97–98) argues that the recurrent theme of missing father figures in contemporary Venezuelan literature represents the characters' conflictive relationships with their roots. He gives examples of hatred for fathers in novels by Gustavo Valle and Juan Carlos Méndez Guédez, suggesting that this symbolises a rejection of Venezuela's patriarchal culture and militarism. In *Círculo croata* and *Transilvania unplugged*, the protagonists do not hate their fathers, but they do not acknowledge them as part of their identity.

For the two young protagonists, writing becomes a way to release this tension, providing them with a space to explore questions of national identity and to tease out how different aspects of both their inherited culture and Venezuelan culture relate to their own personal situations. Saraceni (2000, 200) argues that 'explorar el rastro del origen escarbando en las ruinas del pasado paterno es la herencia que el hijo recibe, una herencia-carencia' [exploring the traces of their origins by rummaging through the ruins of the paternal past is the inheritance that the child receives, an inherited lack]. It is the pretence of needing material for their writing that allows these two aspiring authors to 'rummage through the ruins of the past'. An important part of this process is reading letters written in languages that they do not speak, Romanian for José Antonio and Croatian for Zlatica. Both are sure that the key to their identity is contained in those letters, if only they could read them. The impossibility of reading is additionally frustrating for both as reading, like writing, is a key part of their identities. Reading and writing alleviates the pressure to define themselves as one or another nationality by providing them with new 'master statuses' as 'readers' and 'writers'. Statuses, in sociological theory, 'are socially defined positions which people occupy' (Tischler, 2007, 121). All individuals have many distinct 'statuses' defined by characteristics like nationality, race, gender or occupation. In different settings, one of these characteristics comes to the fore as a 'master status', meaning that this is the major focus when either defining one's own identity or making a judgement of others. These two protagonists push their status as 'reader' or 'writer' to the fore in an attempt to escape the pain and confusion of not feeling like they belong anywhere.

Círculo croata (Zupcic, 2012), we are told on the first page, is a novel 15 years in the making (85), the product of young writer Zlatica Didič's obsession with writing the story of the father he has never met, a Croatian immigrant to Venezuela. With the help of the Croatian writer Salvador Prasel,[3] Zlatica reconstructs the story from a photo album and a pile of letters in Serbo-Croatian that he will never be able to read. Zlatica is an 'author–narrator' (Cazzato, 1995, 31), alternating extracts from the various versions of the novel that he is writing with first-person narration of the writing process. Janet Hendrickson (2014, 177) remarks that 'Reading, rather than a concern about readers, begins young Zlatica's writing career'. His first story, *Pedro Mecaretombe*, is about a boy who learns to read at the age of 18 months thanks to a hormone called 'leerona' (86), suggesting that, to him, the ability to read makes someone more gifted or powerful, like a superhero. Writing is also evidently a key part of Zlatica's identity, as he frequently refers to his literary studies and ambitions and affirms that he has already participated in two literary workshops (85). In contrast to the writing workshops coordinated

---

3 Prasel is a real-life Croatian writer who emigrated to Venezuela following the Second World War, and published three novels there in the 1970s. In *Círculo croata*, Prasel is portrayed as a former member of the Croatian government in exile during the war, along with Zlatica's father. See Chapter 4 for further analysis of Salvador Prasel as a character in *Círculo croata*.

by state institutions, which aim for mass participation, the workshops which Zlatica attends are for aspiring literary elites, a mark of distinction and used by him to indicate that he is truly committed to literature. Zlatica makes clear from the start that his intention is to write a novel, originally called *Círculo Croata de Venezuela* (88). The motivation behind his writing is an awareness of the disconnect between himself and his Croatian background, worsened by the pain of growing up without a father:

> Recordando esas palabras [*hvala, dovidjenja*] sobre una sábana con dibujos de Popeye, así fue cómo mis manos comenzaron a construir la historia de mi padre, Zlatica Didič, a quien nunca en vida había visto y de quien me había acostumbrado a decir cuando alguna anciana indiscreta o un compañero del colegio preguntaba por él que sencillamente había desaparecido, que su ausencia en el patio del colegio no tenía nada que ver con la guerra ni con la cicatriz que le surcaba la mejilla izquierda, sino que había desaparecido, así no más, desaparecido, a pesar de lo difícil que resultara entender: de-sa-pa-re-ci-do. (94)

> [Remembering these words over a Popeye sheet, that was how my hands started to construct the story of my father, Zlatica Didič, whom I had never seen in my life and about whom I had become used to saying, when some indiscreet old lady or a classmate asked about him, that he had simply disappeared, that his absence at the school gate had nothing to do with the war or the scar on his left cheek, but that he had disappeared, nothing more, disappeared, as difficult as it may be to understand: dis-ap-pear-ed.]

Zlatica's rant seems more directed at himself than other people, trying to convince himself to accept that there is no logic in his father's absence. In Zlatica's case, national identity is intrinsically linked to the deeply personal issue of his father's absence. Without his father around to model what being Croatian means, nor to explain aspects of the culture that Zlatica does not understand, his distance from a Croatian national identity is the result of far more than just the physical remoteness of the country. At the same time, his lack of understanding about his paternal culture only increases the pain he feels about having been deprived of a father and not being able to understand why. Like the protagonists of *Todas las lunas* (Kozak Rovero, 2013), Zlatica turns to writing to make sense of a traumatic absence. In his case, dealing with this absence is necessary for him to be able to formulate an idea of his own identity. It is not surprising that it takes him such a long time to complete the novel. Although he affirms repeatedly that he wants a finished product to further his writing career, it is the process of writing which he really needs and therefore cannot allow to end. After three years, he still has not finished the novel, but has filled dozens of notebooks. He explains, 'En un ejercicio de ficción [esos cuadernos] intentaban descifrar el laberinto en el que las cartas de mi padre habían terminado convirtiendo mi vida' [In an exercise of fiction these notebooks tried to work out the labyrinth that my father's letters had turned my life into] (96–97). His obsession with solving the mystery of his father's story belies his own urgent need to understand where he comes from and who he is. He confesses that the novel 'me perseguía, me obsesionaba' [followed me, I was obsessed with it] (97).

Towards the end of the novel, the story Zlatica is writing changes dramatically. From an adventure romp, in which Zlatica Senior and Salvador Prasel travel to Italy to bring the remains of a saint back to Croatia, it suddenly becomes the story of a boy travelling to Croatia to find his father:

> Aunque te haya perdido y cualquier intento de palabra simule tu hallazgo, nunca, nunca comprendió que debía buscarte y encontrarte no fue la pulsión que lo arrastró [...] hasta la impronunciable Krk. (181)

> [Even though he has lost you and any attempt at words only pretends to find you, he never, never understood that he had to search for you and finding you was not the force that pulled him to that unpronounceable Krk.]

The use of pronouns in this final section is striking. While Zlatica had been writing a third-person description of his father's youthful adventure, he switches to referring to his father as 'tú' [you], as if he were writing only for him. Abandoning the conventions of commercial fiction, Zlatica's writing becomes an extremely personal exercise, reflecting his increasing preoccupation with working out his own identity. At the same time, he refers to himself in this final text as 'él' [he] rather than 'yo' [I], perhaps to gain some critical distance with which to attempt to make sense of his own confused identity. This grammatical change coincides with Zlatica's impending reunion with his father, which is ultimately disappointing. Having placed so much emphasis on trying to find his roots throughout years of writing, Zlatica is left utterly disillusioned by the reality of his situation. The meeting with his father is not a new beginning, but an unsatisfying ending, leaving Zlatica with the impression that they will not meet again (195). In the end, Zlatica's father leaves him again, for good:

> Dejando como única huella la promesa cumplida de un paquete de cartas, diarios y documentos escritos ya no en serbocroata sino en una mezcla entre inglés, francés y español que llegó a la casa a los cinco días y con el que yo nuevamente me propuse escribir una, quizás otra, novela. (195–196)

> [Leaving as his only trace the kept promise of a packet of letters, diaries and documents, no longer written in Serbo-Croatian but in a mixture of English, French and Spanish, which arrived at the house five days later and with which I resolved to write a(nother) novel.]

That novel is *Círculo croata*, the one we have just finished reading. Unable to identify with a national identity, Zlatica has thrown himself into his writing as an easier way to define himself.

Transilvania unplugged shows even greater disillusionment with the concept of national identity. The presence of Emil Cioran can be felt throughout *Transilvania unplugged*, made explicit through an epigraph from the philosopher (147) and reference to protagonist Emilio walking down Emil Cioran Avenue, 'con lucidez similar a la del poeta del desengaño' [with a similar lucidity to the poet of disillusionment] (99). Even the name Emilio seems to come from Emil. Cioran, who was born in Romania but who made his name in France, was a great influence on Sánchez Rugeles, who wrote a thesis on him and refers to Cioran as his Virgil (Sánchez Rugeles, 2015). Indeed, Sánchez Rugeles's decision to visit Sibiu while travelling through Europe was because Cioran was born there (Sánchez Rugeles, 2015). Cioran (2010, 4) notably wrote that fanaticism is a 'lyrical leprosy by which [man] contaminates souls, subdues them, crushes or exalts them'. In *A Short History of Decay*, written in the shadow of the Second World War, Cioran posits the need to believe – in religion, in ideology, in the supremacy of one race – as the most dangerous force on Earth. Throughout *Transilvania unplugged*, Sánchez Rugeles demonstrates a similar wariness of totalising beliefs, particularly the belief in nationalism.

Like Zlatica in *Círculo croata* (Zupcic, 2012), José Antonio Galleti is an aspiring writer and second-generation immigrant. José Antonio, or Iosep Antonescu Lacatusu Calinescu, is the son of Romanians, born in Venezuela and raised by an Italian stepfather (17). Saraceni's (2000, 200) theory of an inherited lack certainly applies to José Antonio, who knows nothing about his Romanian heritage as his mother, Irina de Lacatusu, refuses to speak of her homeland. José Antonio's step-father, Nino Galleti, explains to him that Irina denied any kind of link with her past (38). José Antonio therefore travels to Romania and writes about this journey as a way to explore his national identity. When José Antonio affirms 'Vine a ver quién soy, necesito encontrarme' [I came to see who I am, I need to find myself] (85), his friend Emilio makes fun of this literary commonplace, drawing attention to the fact that José joins a long line of literary wanderers who have used travel to 'discover who they really are'. These identity-seeking travellers are often people, like José, who have failed to make significant connections in their home countries (Sarup, 1994).

Throughout the novel, however, it becomes clear that not just writing this story but writing in general has always been a way for José Antonio to define himself. Much like Zlatica, José Antonio compensates for the fragmentary national identity which is painful to him by creating for himself the master status of 'writer'. Emilio notes that José had wanted to be a writer since he was young (48). As a child, José Antonio had suffered from being different and felt shame at his Spanish tainted with a Romanian accent and his lack of vocabulary. Emilio remembers:

> Desde sus primeros días en las escuelas caraqueñas José Antonio sabía que su castellano no era normal. Hablaba con vergüenza, censuraba palabras

esdrújulas y, consecuentemente, trataba de disfrazar el canto ineludible de las segundas lenguas. (48)

[From his first days in Caracas schools José Antonio knew that his Castilian was not normal. He was embarrassed when he spoke, he censored long words and, consequently, tried to disguise the inescapable song of second languages.]

In her study of how immigrants have been treated in Venezuela, Saavedra (2012, 118) highlights that accents indicate a person's nationality for the listener. She concludes that while language is a marker of difference, this difference does not adversely affect the way immigrants are treated (Saavedra, 2012, 123). However, this conclusion does not take into account how the immigrant himself feels. Regardless of whether other people show him less respect or not because of his accent (we are not told if they do), to José Antonio it is a permanent reminder of his status as an outsider. This is an example of reactive identity formation, 'the process of forging a reactive ethnicity in the face of perceived threats, persecution, and exclusion' (Portes and Rumbaut, 2001, 148). In writing, José's perceived flaws become strengths. Free from the problems of pronunciation, José Antonio could be more experimental with language. As Emilio observes, 'Esa lengua disímil, propia pero extraña, permitió a José, a través de la escritura, explorar un espacio con el que no podía hacerse a través de lo dicho' [This unusual language, his own but strange, allowed José, through writing, to explore a space which he could not through speech] (49).

Having found in writing a way to assert his own identity, José Antonio began to want more, that is, for writing to lead him to fame, fortune and critical acclaim. This would give him the sense of acceptance and belonging which he sorely lacked during his childhood. To this end, as Emilio notes disparagingly, José Antonio began to change his writing style to suit popular taste, leaving behind the exploration of his identity which had fuelled his earlier writing (49). This move, however, does not bring José Antonio the success he craves:

Escribir en Caracas fue imposible. Internet y la prensa le echaban en cara su falta de colegiatura para no contratarlo. Publicaba, en ocasiones, una columna en un periódico alternativo que casi nunca pagaba. Sus novelas, idealistas y, en su mayoría, de tesis, habían sido ignoradas en todos los concursos. (45–46)

[Writing in Caracas was impossible. The internet and the press threw his lack of degree back in his face as an excuse not to hire him. He occasionally published a column in an alternative paper which almost never paid. His novels, idealistic and mostly arguing a thesis, had been ignored in all the competitions.]

Set in 2007, the year in which the Plataforma del Libro y la Lectura was launched, the novel suggests that Bolivarian plans to improve inclusivity had not managed to dislodge ideas about literary quality held by the rich and educated circles who ran literary competitions and wrote literary criticism. Presumably José Antonio could have published through the state-run Cada día un libro scheme launched in 2005,[4] but instead he seeks validation from those imbued with more cultural capital, the educated, elite literary critics who remain the literary gatekeepers despite the state's dominance in publishing.

Consequently, as well as his desire to 'find himself', another key motivation behind José Antonio's journey to Romania is the search for the story which will finally win him approval, hopefully in the form of an international literary prize (46). In that respect, his journey to Romania begins fruitfully. Having met his uncle Lucien and heard tall tales about shady characters supposedly responsible for the fall of Ceaușescu, José Antonio comforted himself in the thought that 'al menos para sus aspiraciones literarias, tenía elementos suficientes para contar una historia pintoresca' [at least for his literary aspirations, he had enough elements to tell a colourful story] (40). Nonetheless, as his journey progresses, José Antonio develops a new self-awareness and begins to doubt the belief in his own literary talent which had for so long sustained his sense of self: 'Dudaba [...] de su talento como escritor. Perdía el hilo de su crónica y la inminencia del premio. Sus fracasos, recopilados desde Caracas, pedían la palabra y de manera violenta denunciaban su compromiso con la estupidez' [He doubted his talent as a writer. He lost the thread of his story and the imminence of the prize. His failures, collected since Caracas, took the floor and violently denounced his commitment to stupidity] (69). As he wanders through Bucharest, he feels inspired to write, but then rereads his work and throws it away, realising that 'su utopía literaria [...] no podría realizarse' [his literary Utopia could not come true] (166). He must accept that writing will not be the way for him to gain a sense of self-worth, as he does not have the requisite talent or skill.

As José Antonio realises that his vision of himself as a famous writer is unattainable, he also loses faith in any set notion of national identity. On arrival in Romania, he had been remarkably self-assured: 'Decía, además, orgulloso, que el ser rumano de nacimiento podía condicionarlo estéticamente a comprender las realidades del Este' [He added, proud of himself, that being Romanian by birth could condition him aesthetically for understanding the realities of the East] (19). He subsequently loses this bravado when it becomes clear that he cannot speak Romanian, nor understand the culture. He concedes, 'Vine a Rumania a ver si, todavía, más allá de mi apellido,

---

4 Building on the idea of 'unstated background', in which elements are taken to be true in the story-world despite not being mentioned, because they are true in the real world and the narrative has not contradicted them (Davies, 2007, 53–69), I imagine that Cada día un libro and similar state publishing initiatives exist in the story-world, given that the setting which Sánchez Rugeles depicts is recognisably Venezuela under Chávez.

tengo algo de Rumania [...] No tengo nada. No entiendo el idioma, no conozco la geografía, no entiendo nada, no sé nada' [I came to Romania to see whether, beyond my surname, I still have any Romania in me. I don't have anything. I don't understand the language, I don't know the geography, I don't understand anything, I don't know anything] (143). The repeated negative here emphasises just how despondent José Antonio has become. The migrant characters in the stories told by the Venezuelan diaspora, including those of Eduardo Sánchez Rugeles, typically do not settle in new homes and put down new roots (Rivas Rojas, 2011, 10). José Antonio does not feel rooted either in the Venezuela he leaves or in the Romania he travels to. In this way, *Transilvania unplugged* puts into doubt both the idea of a rooted national identity and the literary convention of travel as the path to discovering one's identity (see Duncan and Gregory, 1999; Blanton, 2002; Conroy, 2003).

However, although Emilio and José Antonio do not miss Venezuela, they cannot disassociate themselves from the country. Laura Chirinos Castellanos (2014) notes that the characters 'sufren el eterno castigo de herir eso que llaman identidad nacional' [suffer the eternal punishment of inheriting what is known as national identity] (162). They try to repress the collective past, displaying an attitude which Chirinos, with reference to Espinoza, labels 'presentism' (163), but it comes back. For example, while he is physically in Romania, Emilio's mind is often in Caracas with his on-again off-again girlfriend María Gabriela. Chirinos describes national identity as a 'shadow' in Jung's terms, something that an individual does not want but from which they cannot escape (165). In Romania, both José Antonio and Emilio are forced into the master role of 'Venezuelan' and all the stereotypes that come with it by Romanians whose only knowledge of Venezuela comes from dubbed *telenovelas*. Both are frequently referred to as 'venezolano', as if that were their defining characteristic, making them seem interchangeable. In fact, it is a case of mistaken identity between José Antonio and Emilio, based on generalisations of Venezuelans by Romanian officials, that is the direct cause of José Antonio's perdition. José insists that he is not proud of Venezuela, yet he maintains an affective link with the country, as his language is Venezuelan, and his loved ones are there (123). This ambiguous feeling towards Venezuela – a mixture of disdain and nostalgia – is particularly evident towards the end of the novel when José considers a return to Caracas: 'Pensó en Caracas e, imaginando sus calles desahuciadas, se sintió feliz. Sintió nostalgia por aquellos fracasos. Aquella miseria, al menos, la entiendo' [He thought about Caracas, and imagining its hopeless streets, he felt happy, He felt a strange nostalgia for those failures. At least I understand that misery] (220). Patricia Valladares-Ruiz (2013, 127–128) argues that a distinctive feature of Sánchez Rugeles's trilogy of *desarraigo* is the focus on characters' affective link with the country they have left behind, rather than creating links with their new country, to the point that we cannot speak of a country of welcome or reception. Nonetheless, whereas the Spanish language literature of migration has tended to promote the ideal of a return to the motherland, in Sánchez Rugeles's novels this return is rejected. Valladares-Ruiz (2013, 128) maintains, 'La constante evocación de la venezolanía no es impulsada por el anhelo de lo perdido, sino por la necesidad de ajustar cuentas con una dinámica nacional que los excluye y rechaza' [The constant of evocation of Venezuelanness is not driven by the desire for what has been lost but by the necessity to settle the score with a national dynamic which excludes and rejects them]. Sánchez Rugeles himself stated in an interview that he is not opposed to Venezuela as a country, but to the excessive patriotism of its government: 'No destruyo la venezolanidad o aquello que nos hace ser un colectivo, sino eso que podemos llamar patrioterismo. Ese falso canto a una bandera, a un rasgarse las vestiduras. Eso que es lo que pretendo atacar' [I'm not destroying Venezuelanness or that which makes us a country, but that which we can call patriotism. That false song to the flag, that indignation. That's what I'm trying to attack] (Fermín, 2012).

All the books discussed in this chapter display a tension in terms of the national. They do not identify with the nationalism of the Bolivarian Revolution and its image of the 'heroico pueblo venezolano' [heroic Venezuelan people] (Plataforma del Libro y la Lectura, 2007), but they cannot avoid questions about national politics and society. Miguel Gomes (2012) describes the difficulty of leaving behind the national, asserting that experiences of globalisation and mobility are a key part of contemporary Venezuelan existence and intrinsically linked with developments in national politics. Read in the context of official nationalism, the novels in this chapter demonstrate a desire to break away from restrictive notions of national identity. *El niño malo* channels the nihilism and irreverence of Punto Fijo literature as D.Jota embraces his evil side; in *Todas las lunas* and *Rating*, self-writing offers an alternative to a divisive national discourse; and in *Círculo croata* and *Transilvania unplugged* travel writing leads the protagonists to question the definitions of national identity.

CHAPTER 4

Making Literary Connections

As well as (auto)fictional writers, there is a notable presence of real-life writers as characters in contemporary Venezuelan fiction. In the context of Bolivarian cultural policy, which posited that enthusiasm was the only necessary criterion for writing, offered limited access to international literary developments and disregarded Venezuelan literary tradition, the novels discussed in this chapter put emphasis on individual literary talent and assert the value of literary tradition, placing their own work as a continuation of this tradition. As discussed in the previous chapter, Venezuela under the Bolivarian Revolution became a 'closed literary space' in Pascale Casanova's (2004, 106) terms. On the one hand, this meant difficult access to developments in the wider literary world, as, in addition to geographical distance from the major publishing centres – Paris, London, New York, Barcelona – protectionist policies limited the books which were imported to Venezuela, promoting instead the idea that autochthonous writing was all that was necessary (Valery, 2009a; Lionetti, 2012). On the other hand, a lack of engagement in world literary space stemming from Venezuelan authors not needing to look beyond the state for publishing opportunities in the past meant that Venezuelan literary tradition remained largely unknown beyond national borders. Moreover, even within this closed literary space, Bolivarian cultural policy did little to encourage the reading of works by earlier generations of Venezuelan writers, unless they could be used to propagate revolutionary ideology. This chapter explores how the interrelated issues of literary isolation and disregard for Venezuelan literary tradition have been explored and challenged in contemporary fiction, suggesting that the writers analysed here assert a continuity of tradition. This chapter begins with analysis of how the consequences of literary isolation are satirised in *Chulapos Mambo* by Juan Carlos Méndez Guédez (2011) through the use of both intertextual references and cameos from famous Latin American writers to tie the novel into a wider literary field. The second half of the chapter then considers two cases of real Venezuelan writers as protagonists in contemporary novels – Eugenio Montejo in *El niño malo cuenta hasta cien y se retira* by Juan Carlos Chirinos (2010) and Salvador Prasel in *Círculo croata* by Slavko Zupcic (2012). Through these characters, the authors both celebrate Venezuelan literary tradition and attempt to incorporate their own writing into this tradition.

The nationalist and protectionist nature of Bolivarian cultural policy outlined in Chapter 3 was evident in the difficulty of importing foreign fiction to Venezuela. The Bolivarian government put in place laws and policies – particularly related to currency exchange and exports – designed to promote autochthonous literature and fortify national identity at the expense of access to literature from other countries. Article 38 of the 2005 Organic Law of Culture asserted the duty of the state to protect national culture from international competition: 'Se declara de interés público el fomento, promoción, protección y defensa de las industrias culturales nacionales' [It is considered in the public interest to foster, promote, protect and defend our national cultural industries] (Comisión Permanente de Educación, 2005, 10). As a result, according to Ana Teresa Torres (2006, 912), while books by Venezuelan writers piled up in bookshops, it was increasingly difficult to get hold of new releases from abroad. The situation worsened since she made this comment in 2006, as, through strict currency controls, the government made it financially unviable to import books. *El País* reported in 2009 that, to qualify for the preferential exchange rate for dollars to pay for imports, publishers first had to send a list of the titles they wanted to import to the Ministry for Industry and Commerce, proving that there were no books by Venezuelan authors on the same subject (Primera, 2009). This policy affirmed that what was produced nationally was sufficient and disregarded the benefits of local ideas entering into dialogue with international developments. These currency regulations also impeded the import of books written by Venezuelan writers but published abroad (Silva-Ferrer, 2014, 136–137). Consequently, according to booksellers Roger Michelena and Rodnei Cáceres, books came late or not at all, and many distributors left Venezuela (Fermín, 2011). The result was a marked literary isolation: Venezuelan readers and writers were increasingly cut off from the new trends and developments in foreign writing. While the internet helped somewhat to alleviate literary isolation, Venezuelan readers could generally only access what was freely available online, as the currency controls limited their ability to purchase anything online from abroad.

Chulapos Mambo (Méndez Guédez, 2011) demonstrates the stifling effect on a writer of the limited flow of books both between Latin American countries and across the rest of the world. *Chulapos Mambo*'s protagonist, Henry, grows up unaware of Modernist literary developments and therefore assumes he is being radical and original when he experiments with different writing styles. After recreating the style of James Joyce accidentally, for example, 'con voz firme aclaró que acababa de inventar una nueva técnica literaria' [in a resolute voice he affirmed that he had just invented a new literary technique] (37). According to Linda Hutcheon (1995, 91), irony of this type is based on an 'assumption of shared previous knowledge' among discursive communities. Ironic discourse creates included and excluded groups, giving those included a 'sense of superior intellect' as part of the 'knowing minority' (Hutcheon, 1995, 94). Méndez Guédez assumes that his readers, unlike Henry, will recognise the literary techniques he believes he is inventing as those of the Modernists and therefore feel superior to Henry. According to Hutcheon's theory, the resulting ego boost would make readers more interested in and receptive to the novel. This raises the question of who these readers are. As the novel was published by Casa de Cartón in Madrid, many are likely to be Spanish. Consequently, Méndez Guédez draws attention to the disparity between the readers' own literary advantages and the limited exposure to literary developments faced by readers and writers in his native Venezuela. Henry admits that isolation is a problem for his writing:

> Se dio cuenta de que su problema era el aislamiento. Vivir en aquella ciudad lejana, aplastada por el sol, arrasada por las lluvias, oyendo el canto de los grillos y las historias interminables sobre ese incendio del depósito de maíz, aniquilaría su feroz, su inabarcable talento. Debo salvarme, debo huir. (39)

> [He realised that his problem was isolation. Living in that far off city, blasted by the sun, flattened by the rains, listening to the crickets sing and the interminable stories about the fire in the corn store, would destroy his ferocious, vast talent. I've got to save myself, I've got to escape.]

Living in a small city far from Caracas means for Henry, above all, a lack of subject matter. Short on imagination, Henry finds little worth writing about in his mundane surroundings. At the same time, this remoteness has resulted in a literary isolation, as very few books, especially imported ones, reach his city: 'En su casa solo tenían una enciclopedia repleta de cagarrutas de mosca; y un par de libros de tapas color hueso' [In his house there was only an encyclopaedia covered in fly droppings; and a couple of bone-coloured books] (36). Dull and dirty, the few books found in Henry's house are far from appealing. Henry's deluded opinion of himself as a prodigious talent results in part from his lack of access to other works of fiction against which to judge his own meagre output. The only access Henry has to foreign literature is through books being passed from person to person. It is the far better read Saúl Junco who provides Henry with 'montones de novelas' [mountains of novels], including copies of the Boom texts which are to have an enormous impact on Henry's definition of literature and on his own writing (39). Years later, upon returning one of the books to Saúl, Henry declares, 'Ya me lo aprendí de memoria. Te lo juro. Me los sé de memoria' [I've learned it off by heart. I swear. I know them off by heart] (62). Henry is impressed by the Boom texts, in spite of, or indeed because of, his inability to understand them fully: 'En esos días, nuestro personaje recitó en alta voz aquellas narraciones que le resultaban oscuras pero que poseían ese resplandor genial que palpita en todo lo que no se comprende a plenitud' [In those days, our protagonist recited aloud those narratives which were obscure to him but which possessed that fantastic splendour that beats in everything that one does not fully understand] (39). Because of this formative reading experience, Henry values the Boom authors far more than their Venezuelan counterparts. When Henry bumps into Saúl Junco in Madrid, he asks Saúl to send him a spare copy of his latest novel if he has one, explaining 'Yo pensaba adquirirla, pero aquí la venden muy cara, cuesta lo mismo que la última de Vargas Llosa, así que no pude comprar ambas' [I thought about buying it, but it's very expensive here, it costs almost as much as the latest Vargas Llosa novel, so I couldn't buy both] (62). Why is Henry surprised that a Venezuelan novel should cost the same amount as one by Vargas Llosa? On one level, this comment highlights the perceived inferiority of Venezuelan literature among certain Venezuelan readers, the 'ugly duckling syndrome' (Fraile, 2012b), according to which Venezuelan literature must not be as good as Mexican or Argentinian literature because it has had less international recognition. At the same time, the comment alludes to how, within Venezuela, state published books are sold at a fraction of the cost of those produced by independent publishers or imported, leading to an expectation among readers that books by Venezuelan authors should be much cheaper than foreign ones (Kozak Rovero, 2007b, 114).

Henry's estimation of the Boom texts above all other writing is evident in his plagiarism of *Cien años de soledad*:

> Encendió el ordenador. Apretó sus manos, miró hacia el techo como buscando una iluminación súbita y tecleó:
> Muchos años después frente al pelotón de fusilamiento ...
> Respiró hondo, contempló la frase con tierno orgullo y se dispuso a seguir escribiendo. (11)
>
> [He turned on his computer. He clenched his hands, looked up to the ceiling as if searching for a sudden illumination, and typed:
> Many years later, as he faced the firing squad ...
> He took a deep breath, contemplated the phrase with tender pride and readied himself to continue writing.]

There are layers of intertextuality here. As well as the iconic opening lines of García Márquez's famous novel, there are echoes of Borges's Pierre Menard in this writer recreating word for word an exemplary text. On the final page, significantly headed 'Aclaratoria cuya lectura puede omitirse' [Clarification which it is not necessary to read], Méndez Guédez explains that the short texts that Henry writes and then destroys over the course of the novel belong to Gabriel García Márquez, Julio Cortázar and Carlos Fuentes (285). The title suggests an assumption that his readers will be familiar with these texts already and therefore do not need to be told who wrote them. This both reveals the kind of reader that Méndez Guédez imagines for his work and his desire to please 'the erudite reader [who] would delight in recognising citations' (Worton and Still, 1990, 21). In addition, by suggesting that readers are already familiar with these citations, Méndez Guédez asserts the existence of a Latin American canon to be respected. At the same time, by incorporating references to these works in his own, he places himself in this company.

On other occasions within the novel, Méndez Guédez makes his debt to earlier writers even more explicit. We are told that while reading *Madame Bovary*, for example, Henry 'estudió con papel y lápiz cada línea, cada manera que tenía el narrador de aparecer en la historia' [studied with a pencil and paper every line, every way in which the narrator appeared in the story] (36). Cloyd and Bates (1964, 122) affirm, 'People quote another author for complex reasons – to confer meaning, authority or depth upon a statement, to demonstrate familiarity with other work in the same field, and to avoid appearance of plagiarising even ideas conceived independently'. By citing or otherwise referencing the work of authors from Flaubert to Borges, Méndez Guédez not only displays his vast literary knowledge, but also places himself within the field of writers within which he would like his own work to be considered.

Chulapos Mambo has been referred to as a novel of homages (Sánchez Aparicio, 2012). Méndez Guédez outlined his diverse sources of inspiration in an interview with *El Nacional*, including English comedies in the tradition of Waugh, Sharpe and Hornby, the picaresque, the films of Billy Wilder and Luis García Berlanga, and the jokes told in his family (Sánchez Aparicio, 2012). As well as through citations and stylistic borrowings, Méndez Guédez pays homage to fellow writers by giving them cameo appearances in the novel. In his desire to become a famous writer, Henry becomes hyper-aware of the current stars of world literary space, as evidenced by repeated references to them. One notable scene reads like a *Who's Who?* of the Hispanic literary community in Madrid, as Jorge Eduardo Benavides, José María Merino, Eduardo Mendoza, Blanca Riestra, Fernando Iwasaki, Andrés Neuman and Manuel Longares all make an appearance (248). Méndez Guédez explained in an interview:

> En esta historia he hecho un pequeño homenaje a autores en lengua española a los que tengo mucho aprecio y cariño. Les he invitado a pasear por la novela, aunque ellos aún no lo saben y, salvo Iwasaki, no tienen relación con este tipo de texto. Los autores con los que compartes tu tiempo se convierten en una suerte de familia. (Volpini, 2011)

> [In this story I've paid a small homage to Spanish language authors who I have a lot of affection and respect for. I've invited them to stroll through the novel, even though they don't know about it and, except for Iwasaki, don't have any link to this kind of text. The authors with whom you spend time become a kind of family.]

Of the many authors who appear in the novel, two in particular deserve further analysis, Mario Vargas Llosa and Alfredo Bryce Echenique, both authors known for writing themselves into their texts. Méndez Guédez listed *Conversación en la catedral* [Conversation in the Cathedral] by Vargas Llosa and *La vida exagerada de Martín Romaña* [The Exaggerated Life of Martín Romaña] by Bryce Echenique as two of his five essential books (*Prodavinci*, 2012). Building on Bourdieu's (1993, 138), argument that citations function as both recognition of and annexation to another author, I maintain that by incorporating these figures into his narrative, Méndez Guédez both signposts his debt to their metafictional works and attempts to equate himself with these highly successful authors.

Critics have referred to Méndez Guédez as an heir to Bryce Echenique (*Prodavinci*, 2012) and Bryce himself has expressed his appreciation of Méndez Guédez (*El Periódico de Catalunya*, 1999). Through casting himself as an author–narrator–character in his novels, Bryce Echenique explores the nature of self-representation in fiction (Bustillo, 1997, 132; 191–192), a theme which also permeates *Chulapos Mambo*. Henry cites Bryce Echenique, who Simao has pointed out to him in a restaurant, as an author he aspires to: 'Bryce Echenique, el gran novelista, el primer gran novelista que tropezaba desde que llegó a Madrid. Un escritor de verdad, un escritor con muchos libros, con maravillosos libros, y que no debía sobrevivir escribiendo manuales de sexualidad para una colección patriótica' [Bryce Echenique, the great novelist, the first great novelist he had bumped into since he arrived in Madrid. A real writer, a writer with many books, with wonderful books, and who didn't have to survive writing sexuality manuals for a patriotic collection] (116). Although Henry sees him as a success to emulate, in his own novel, *Tantas veces Pedro* [So Many Times Pedro] (1977), Bryce Echenique's self-inspired protagonist Pedro Balbuena is portrayed as a failed author, an author with nothing to write. Bustillo (1997, 132) observes that Bryce caricatures himself in his writer's block, using hyperbole to present himself as a pseudo-writer. Henry, who defines himself as a writer and yet is tortured by his inability to write anything, mirrors Bryce's protagonist Pedro Balbuena, and by naming Bryce in the novel, Méndez Guédez both acknowledges that source of inspiration and equates himself with Bryce in the minds of readers. Henry asks himself:

> ¿Bryce Echenique es un escritor reaccionario? ¿Yo leo a Bryce Echenique frente a mis amigos del Ministerio o no lo leo? Recordó haber revisado unos ensayos en los que se afirmaba que era un novelista conservador, burgués. (116)

> [Is Bryce Echenique a reactionary writer? Do I read Bryce Echenique in front of my friends from the Ministry or not? He remembered having looked over some essays which affirmed that he was a conservative, bourgeois novelist.]

A descendant of English aristocracy and the great-grandson of former president José Rufino Echenique, Bryce Echenique would be considered an 'oligarch' in Bolivarian terminology, even though his debut novel, *Un mundo para Julius* [A World for Julius] (1970), challenges social inequality through a scathing portrayal of the hypocrisy of a high-class family in Lima. Henry later admits that Bryce Echenique challenged the bourgeoisie from inside. He finally decides that it is acceptable to like the Peruvian author, because he is eating vegetables, a 'popular' food. Henry ends the chapter throwing a copy of his own book into Bryce Echenique's moving taxi. Having equated himself with Bryce Echenique through making use of similar literary techniques and narrative themes, Méndez Guédez here criticises how supporters of the Bolivarian Revolution judge not only Bryce Echenique's writing but Méndez Guédez's own work not on its literary quality but on the author's background. Reference to Bryce Echenique is also significant in terms of the novel's relationship with citation or plagiarism. The awarding of the Premio FIL at Guadalajara in 2012 to Bryce Echenique sparked a polemic because in 2009 he had been charged with plagiarising 16 articles by 15 authors (*El País*, 2009). Méndez Guédez was one of 110 intellectuals to sign a letter in support of Alfredo Bryce Echenique (*Laberinto*, 2012). By featuring Bryce Echenique in the novel, Méndez Guédez excuses his own creative use of excerpts from other texts.

As with Bryce Echenique, Mario Vargas Llosa's appearance in *Chulapos Mambo* signposts the similarities between his work and that of Méndez Guédez. Vargas Llosa is another writer–character–narrator (Bustillo, 1997, 55), who raises questions about the boundaries between reality and fiction and the power of the writer as a creator through his self-representation in his novels, especially *Tía Julia y el escribidor* [Aunt Julia and the Scriptwriter] (1977). The choice of Vargas Llosa rather than any other Boom author is significant not only for his use of metafiction, but also for his ideological positioning. De Castro and Birns (2010, 6) suggest that Vargas Llosa is 'unusual' among Latin American intellectuals in his affiliation with the liberal Right. As Philip Swanson (1995, 77) notes, 'Vargas Llosa has always been scrupulously honest and courageous in expressing his changing political outlook', even when his views have been 'unfashionable'. Like Bryce Echinique, Vargas Llosa is described as 'el detestado Mario que Henry también leía a escondidas de sus amigos del ministerio' [the detested Mario whom Henry also read behind the backs of his ministry friends] (133). Henry cannot be seen to like Vargas Llosa, because his politics are in opposition to those of the Bolivarian government. Vargas Llosa has been critical of Chávez, calling him 'un dictador clásico que sigue el modelo cubano' [a classic dictator in the Cuban model], and expressing his relief that the Chávez-backed candidate Ollanta Humala did not win the Peruvian presidency in 2006 (Norberg, 2010). Moreover, Vargas Llosa has long believed in literature as a challenge to any dominant power, as expressed in 'La literatura es fuego' [Literature is Fire], his acceptance speech for the Rómulo Gallegos Prize in 1967:

> Dentro de la nueva sociedad, y por el camino que nos precipiten nuestros fantasmas y demonios personales, tendremos que seguir, como ayer, como ahora, diciendo no, rebelándonos, exigiendo que se reconozca nuestro

derecho a disentir, mostrando, de esa manera viviente y mágica como sólo la literatura puede hacerlo, que el dogma, la censura, la arbitrariedad son también enemigos mortales del progreso y de la dignidad humana. (Vargas Llosa, 1967)

[Within the new society, and along the path that our own personal ghosts and demons push us down, we must continue, like yesterday, like today, to say no, to rebel, to insist that our right to dissent is recognised, showing, in this lively and magical way of which only literature is capable, that dogma, censorship, and unfairness are the mortal enemies of progress and human dignity.]

Vargas Llosa's attitude is one that Méndez Guédez clearly shares. Even though Henry knows he is not supposed to read Vargas Llosa's work, he cannot help but admire the celebrated Peruvian's literary talent and crave his approval. In a scene of pure slapstick comedy, having spotted Vargas Llosa at a literary event, Henry chases him and his wife through the hotel, brandishing a copy of his own book, 'y él, Mario, Marito, tratando de atrapar el codo del peruano, no te vayas sin mi libro, ellos alejándose, saltando una pared …' [and him, Mario, Mario buddy, trying to grab the Peruvian's elbow, don't go without my book, them moving away, jumping over a wall] (134). The scene reflects the absurdity of judging literature by authors such as Vargas Llosa on ideological criteria alone. Emilio Quintana (2010) describes the 'demonisation' of Vargas Llosa following the announcement that he had won the Nobel Prize for Literature in 2010. Quintana cites journalist America Vera-Zavala, who called Vargas Llosa, among other slurs, vindictive, antidemocratic, ignorant and coup-mongering. Swedish author Johan Norberg (2010) highlights the hypocrisy of this outcry against Vargas Llosa:

People who never voiced any concerns about the politics of other Nobel Prize winners – like Wisława Szymborska, who wrote poetic celebrations of Lenin and Stalin; Günter Grass, who praised Cuba's dictatorship; Harold Pinter, who supported Slobodan Milošević; José Saramago, who purged anti-Stalinists from the revolutionary newspaper he edited – thought that the Swedish Academy had finally crossed a line. Mario Vargas Llosa's politics apparently should have disqualified him from any prize considerations.

In *Chulapos Mambo*, Méndez Guédez parodies this hypocrisy, suggesting that neither Vargas Llosa, nor he, nor any other writer should be judged on their politics instead of the quality of their writing. He insists on recognition of writers including Bryce Echenique and Vargas Llosa as part of a tradition to be celebrated and continued through his own writing.

While Juan Carlos Méndez Guédez establishes links with other Latin American writers, Juan Carlos Chirinos and Slavko Zupcic pay homage to earlier Venezuelan writers in their novels, in response to a lack of recognition both within and outside Venezuela. As discussed in the introduction, when many writers across Latin American were reaching out to international audiences in the 1960s and 1970s, those authors posited as the leading Venezuelan voices of the 1960s and 1970s – Renato Rodríguez (Fraile, 2012a; 2012b), José Balza (Colmenares Gil, 2012), Guillermo Meneses and Salvador Garmendia (Gomes, 1997) – were writing highly experimental works influenced by the rapid urbanisation and modernisation of Caracas and not written to appeal to mass international audiences. This was made possible by the state, during Punto Fijo, funding the publishing of works by the intellectual elite of the time. As Ana Teresa Torres (2006, 919) explains, the state did not just finance literature but organised it, bringing writers together and promoting their work. Because of these state-funded publishing houses and the promotional activities of state-run institutions such as the Consejo Nacional de la Cultura [National Council for Culture], for 40 years Venezuelan writing took place almost entirely outside of the market (Torres, 2006, 920). Then in the Bolivarian period, the government's vision for literature as a nation-building tool meant that, when it came to distribution, the focus was much more on reaching readers within Venezuela than investing in international distribution or exposure. Meanwhile, the insistence on a radical break with the Punto Fijo regime also meant that authors who were published by the state during that period were not celebrated by the Bolivarian government, especially if their work challenged the nationalist or socialist ideologies promoted by the government.

Juan Carlos Chirinos engages with a wide range of international literary references in his fiction. *El niño malo cuenta hasta cien y se retira* (2010) is full of intertexts, or, in the words of Elda Stanco (2013a), 'enigmatic literary innuendos', which the reader must recognise to get the most out of the novel. As well as referring to his profession in radio, D.Jota's name marks him as a tropical Don Juan. Derdriu is the tragic heroine of Celtic myth, Svevo the storyteller is named after Italo Svevo, the playwright and novelist famously championed by James Joyce, and Fanny's dog, which D.Jota hates, is called Don Camilo after Camilo José Cela.[1] Each of these references demonstrates the influence of European literary traditions on Chirinos's writing, despite efforts by successive governments from the Punto Fijo period to the Bolivarian Revolution to ground Venezuelan literature firmly in the national. Nonetheless, his biggest influences are closer to home. Chirinos describes his first novel as 'justísimo homenaje a los poetas venezolanos' [a well-deserved homage to Venezuelan poets] (223), particularly Ana Enriqueta Terán (1918–2017) and Eugenio Montejo (1938–2008). The title is taken from

---

[1] Chirinos explains the reason he hates Cela: 'Vendió su pluma al dictador venezolano Marcos Pérez Jiménez para escribir una novela (*La Catira*) que fuera respuesta a la maravillosa *Doña Bárbara*, de Rómulo Gallegos' [He sold his pen to the Venezuelan dictator Marcos Pérez Jiménez to write a novel (*La Catira*) which was a response to Rómulo Gallegos's wonderful *Doña Bárbara*] (EFE, 2010).

Terán's 1967 poem 'La poetisa cuenta hasta cien y se retira' [The Poetess Counts to 100 and Bows Out]. Terán was not only from Chirinos's native city of Valera, but a descendant of the city's founders. She formed a close bond with Chirinos, as he was born on the same day as her son. As for Montejo, Chirinos first read his poetry when he had recently moved to Salamanca, Spain, and wanted to share this work through the novel he began writing at that time (Chirinos, 2018).

As well as integrating fragments of Montejo's poems into the narrative, Chirinos turns one of Venezuela's greatest poets into one of the main characters of his story, although he is keen to point out that the real Montejo was a gentleman whereas his character is a more flawed, literary invention (Chirinos, 2018). The poet becomes a dockworker, a loyal friend, an exotic lover, an absent grandfather, and finally the star of folk stories told in the local pub. Through the figure of Montejo – only ever named as Eugenio – Chirinos both argues for a greater recognition of Venezuelan literary tradition and reflects on his own condition as a Venezuelan writer in exile. Montejo's work demonstrates a strong ambivalence towards Venezuelan identity and certainly does not form part of the Bolivarian canon. Montejo's poem 'Los árboles' was the inspiration for *El niño malo*, while Chirinos's second novel, *Nochebosque* [Nightwood] (2012), is also inspired by a collection of poetry by Montejo called *Terredad* [Earthliness] (1978), particularly the opening poem 'En el bosque' [In the Woods].

Eugenio Montejo was, according to Nick Roberts (2009, 1), 'one of the most notable individual literary voices to emerge not just from Venezuela but from Latin America generally in the twentieth century'. Antonio López Ortega (2012) agrees that Montejo was possibly the most influential and widely read of recent Venezuelan poets. Montejo, whose real name was Eugenio Hernández Alvarez, wrote ten collections of poetry and three essay collections between 1959 and 2006, for which he was awarded the National Prize for Literature in 1998 and the Octavio Paz International Prize in 2004. As Roberts (2009, 1) describes, Montejo 'consistently underscored the importance of understanding the traditions within which one writes', which for him meant not only the immediate Venezuelan context but also other Latin American and European traditions. Chirinos follows Montejo's example, weaving together everything from the stories of native Venezuelan tribes to Jules Verne and the Brothers Grimm.

The first reference to Eugenio appears early on in the book, when the grandmother, Derdriu, is introduced as an 'amante de un oscuro extranjero que alguna vez residió allí' [lover of a gloomy foreigner who once lived there] (25). Before we are told any more about this character, we get to know him through the poems that he left behind. Chirinos includes lengthy extracts of Montejo's poetry within the novel, as the legacy which Eugenio left to his family. One afternoon, Fanny finds a leather-bound volume, on the first page of which is Montejo's poem 'Los árboles' [The Trees]. Chirinos reproduces the entire second half of the poem (nine lines), which begins with Montejo musing, 'Es difícil llenar un breve libro | Con pensamientos de árboles' [It is difficult to fill a short book | With the thoughts of trees]. The poem is one of the most significant of Montejo's oeuvre, exemplifying his preoccupation with nature and the impossibility of capturing it in words. The grandmother explains to Fanny that the poems, which have captured her attention, are 'parte de la herencia que Eugenio, su abuelo tropical [...] le dejó antes de marcharse en busca de nuevos espacios' [part of the inheritance that Eugenio, her tropical grandfather, left her before going in search of new places] (38). Later in the novel, Chirinos includes a long extract from Montejo's poem 'Caracas' (127), in which Montejo explores how his native city had changed and been separated from nature, beginning, 'Tan altos son los edificios | que ya no se ve nada de mi infancia' [The buildings are so tall | that nothing from my childhood can be seen now].[2] By quoting extensively from the poem, Chirinos gives readers who might not have heard of Montejo an opportunity to experience his writing.

Despite certain international renown following the Octavio Paz Prize, and Sean Penn reciting a verse of his poem 'La tierra giró para acercarnos' [The Earth Turned to Bring Us Together] in the film *21 Grams* (González Iñárritu, 2003), Montejo has not achieved anything like the fame that Chirinos feels he deserves. Like others of his generation – Salvador Garmendia, Renato Rodríguez – Montejo was ignored by the Bolivarian government, which, as Gisela Kozak Rovero (2008) argued, systematically discredited all that did not fit with their 'revolutionary' ideology. Neither Montejo's final book of poetry *Fábula del escribe* [A Scrivener's Tale] (2006) nor his Complete Works were published in Venezuela, although they have been published in Spain and Mexico (*Letralia*, 2008). Montejo himself claimed shortly before his death that there was 'una censura velada' [a veiled censorship] within Venezuelan media and an unfavourable situation for intellectuals in the country (*Letralia*, 2008). He denounced Chávez's propagandistic use of literature and the lack of support for anyone who did not follow official ideology. The divide between Montejo and the Bolivarian government was evident on his death, according to Antonio López Ortega (2012), who highlighted that no official obituary was published, and no condolences sent to his mourners. In such a context, Chirinos reaffirms the value of Montejo's writing through his own fiction. Chirinos's admiration of Montejo's mastery of words is expressed through

---

2 An extract from *Caracas* appears again towards the end of the novel, when D.Jota finds the poem among Derdriu's private possessions as he raids the house. He finds Montejo's poem stupid, remarking, 'Caracas no es eso, Caracas es el desorden, la divina disposición del caos. Este abuelo Eugenio, tan poeta y tan singón' [Caracas isn't this. Caracas is disorder, the divine will of chaos. That grandfather Eugenio, such a poet and such a philanderer] (212). Given that D.Jota is not a likeable character at the best of times, and is at that moment masturbating over the thought of Fanny dying in the snow, the reader is not encouraged to agree with his criticism of Montejo. Through D.Jota, Chirinos criticises those who do not recognise this poetic tradition.

Fanny. For her, 'Nada tenía verdadero sentido si no guardaba de alguna manera relación con el libro. Fanny comprendió así por qué los hombres – tan violentos siempre – se matan a causa de las palabras de algunos libros' [Nothing really made sense if it wasn't in some way related to the book. Fanny understand now why some men – who are always so violent – kill because of the words in some books] (43). While this statement emphasises just how important Montejo's words become for Fanny, it also draws attention to how writing can be a powerful political tool. We can think, for example, of El Libro Azul [the Blue Book], the book of Chávez's thoughts, inspired by Simón Bolívar, Simón Rodríguez and Ezequiel Zamora, which became obligatory reading for Venezuelan citizens.

This awe at the power of words is further expressed through the impact that the fictionalised Eugenio has on Svevo. The two first meet at one of the nightly gatherings of dockworkers in the bar to swap stories (108). Eugenio 'parecía acostumbrado a que una muchedumbre escuchara sus palabras' [seemed used to a crowd listening to his words] (108). The words Chirinos puts into Eugenio's mouth contrast the beauty of his poetry. Defending Svevo in a bar fight, which began with a disagreement about the famous bears of El Pueblo, Eugenio tells a burly Irishman:

> El rugido de uno solo de esos osos sería suficiente para cerrarte esa bocota, irlandés; y el pálido miembro que forzosamente te cuelga entre las piernas no volvería a levantarse, no sé si alguna vez lo ha hecho, si tuvieras la suerte de verlos copulando, y sobrevivir. (109)

> [The roar of just one of these bears would be enough to shut that mouth of yours, Irishman; and the pale member which inevitably hangs between your legs would never rise again, if it ever has done before, if you were lucky enough to see the bears copulating and survive.]

The stunned silence among the boisterous group introduces Svevo to the power of words. Under Eugenio's tutelage, Svevo then develops a great skill for storytelling (114–116), a recognition of how Montejo's poetry has been an inspiration for Chirinos and other Venezuelan writers of his generation. Through Svevo, Chirinos also acknowledges that Montejo is not always an easy read. When the lovesick Eugenio recites poems he has written for the prostitute Laurencia, Svevo does not understand and feels 'dolido, frustrado' [hurt, frustrated] (113), suggesting that a certain level of literacy is necessary to engage with Montejo. Chirinos includes fragments of the poem that Eugenio is writing: 'Como guerrero que vuelve, | mi corazón ha recogido su carcaj, | para llenarlo de nuevo | como guerrero que va' (113) [Like a warrior who returns, | My heart has picked up its quiver, | To fill it again |Like a warrior who leaves]. We are led to believe that this is another poem written by Montejo, as all the excerpts thus far have been, but it is not. Here, Chirinos blurs the boundaries between the real writer and the fictional one, between Montejo and himself. By creating this link between himself and

Montejo, Chirinos not only pays homage to Montejo but also associates his own work to the great poet symbolically.

In addition to direct quotations, *El niño malo* is replete with Montejian motifs, which only readers familiar with Montejo's work would appreciate. The novel thereby becomes a puzzle to be solved by following the clues back to Montejo's poetry and associating their meanings with Chirinos's story. A key example of this is the setting of *El niño malo*: a frozen, bear-infested wasteland north of Caracas, it could perhaps be Canada or the northern United States, except everyone speaks Spanish. When read as a reference to snow as a 'leitmotiv' for Montejo (Roberts, 2009, 36), however, new layers of meaning become apparent. In Montejo's poems, set primarily in the Venezuelan tropics, snow is frequently referred to as something missing, to the extent that the absence of snow acts like snow, covering the landscape. Roberts (2009, 102) explains, 'Montejo uses the lack of snow in Venezuela and the tropics not just as a cipher for the process of loss, of time-passing and leaving people behind forever, but, as the title of 'Hombres sin nieve' [Men without Snow] indicates, to define both the region and its people'. The snow of El Pueblo marks the mythical no-place as fundamentally different from Caracas, the home of both Eugenio and D.Jota, and a place where they cannot belong. The association between snow and loss or leaving people behind makes D.Jota's self-imposed exile from his forbidden love in Caracas all the more poignant. *El niño malo* is in a symbiotic relationship with Montejo's work; if Chirinos's novel succeeds in leading readers to Montejo's poetry, they can return to the novel with renewed understanding.

Beyond his admiration for Montejo's skill as a poet, Montejo's ambivalent relationship with Venezuela draws Chirinos to him. Through the character of Eugenio, and the associations with Montejo's poetry, Chirinos can explore within the narrative his own condition as a Venezuelan writer abroad. Although Chirinos no longer resides in Venezuela, having left for doctoral study in Salamanca in 1997, he remains an ardent promoter of his native literature. However, he has been criticised by his compatriots for having left the country. In his contribution to *Pasajes de ida* [One-Way Tickets], a collection of essays by Venezuelan writers about their experiences of living abroad, he admits that he has faced reproach for having left Venezuela and living abroad, being told 'ya no era uno de ellos' [I was no longer one of them] (Chirinos, 2013b, 52). Marta Eugenia Martínez (2006, 27), for example, claimed in an article that Chirinos had no right to complain about the lack of reading public in Venezuela having left the country instead of staying and trying to foster an audience there himself. The sense of being torn between Venezuela and Spain, of missing Venezuela but not wanting to go back, is something Chirinos shares with Montejo. In many of his poems, Montejo presents himself as fragmented. In 'El ángel indeciso' [The Indecisive Angel], for example, Montejo talks of how 'Procura estar a un tiempo en dos ciudades | En dos continentes' [He tries to be in two cities at once | On two continents] (Montejo, 1978, 66), while in 'Mudanzas' [Moving], he describes breaking in two, 'Separándonos siempre para que alguien se quede | Y algún otro se vaya' [Separating ourselves forever so that someone can stay | And someone else can leave] (Montejo, 1978, 12). This is the Eugenio we meet in *El niño malo*; torn between his love for Derdriu, which keeps him in El Pueblo, and his longing for his homeland, Eugenio spends long, melancholy hours staring out of the window contemplating the snow and thinking of the sands of his home. The scene recalls his poem 'En el norte' [In the North], in which he contemplates the distance from his Atlantic home as he watches the Thames flow in London (Montejo, 1978, 31–32). Derdriu explains to her granddaughter, 'No tuve valor para detenerlo, la fuerza que me amarraba a mí aquí era la misma que lo hacía a él irse, en busca de su lugar' [I didn't have the courage to keep him here, the force which held me here was the same which made him leave, looking for his place] (64). However, there is a tension in Montejo's poetry between longing for Venezuela and yearning to explore foreign lands. A notable example is 'Partida' [Leaving], in which he imagines himself leaving for Rotterdam with every boat at the port (Montejo, 1978, 27–28). Chirinos presents this side of Eugenio too, particularly in the flashbacks to his life on the docks. The fictional Eugenio of *El niño malo* affirms, 'Un viajante sabe cuándo llega, pero no cuándo se va' [A traveller knows when he arrives, but not when he is leaving] (111).[3] In these words, there is a sense of the transient nature of his existence; he cannot spend much time in one place before he starts longing for somewhere new. Roberts (2009, 165–166) maintains that Montejo was so nomadic because he did not feel at home in his 'homeland'; he lacked a sense of belonging, and so continued to travel in search of what his homeland could not provide. This 'experiencing of the homeland as foreign', Roberts (2009, 166) adds, is shown in Montejo's poetry as a permanent and enduring characteristic of the Venezuelan people. This experiencing home as an outsider is expressed by many of the contributors to the collection of essays *Pasajes de ida* (2013), who write that since the Bolivarian Revolution their country has become a foreign land. Chirinos (2013, 51) himself conveys this feeling in his essay, stating that when he returned in 2001, after four years away, 'encontré un país que ya no se parecía al que había dejado, pero que conservaba muchos de los afectos y los espacios intactos' [I found a country that did not resemble the one I had left, but which kept many of the attachments and spaces intact].

In the context of the nationalism of the Bolivarian government, which, according to Chirinos and many of his fellow writers, has irrevocably changed Venezuela, it is not the official symbols nor the heroes that make up the nation in the imaginary of those who have left, but personal connections. Building on Montejo's preoccupation with the meaning of home, Chirinos gives voice

---

3 Chirinos (2015) explained to me that this line is a small homage to Paul Bowles, who emphasises the difference between tourists and travellers in his 1949 novel *The Sheltering Sky*.

to his own ideas about identity and belonging through the character of Eugenio, stating:

> Alguien me dijo una vez que el mapa de una ciudad es en realidad el de los sitios donde encontramos a nuestros amigos, que lo que conocemos de la ciudad donde vivimos es el afecto que hemos prodigado en diferentes rincones; todo lo demás desaparece. (150)
>
> [Someone once told me that the map of a city is in reality one of the sites where we find our friends, that what we know of the city in which we live is the affection we have bestowed in different corners; everything else disappears.]

This someone was José Balza, another Venezuelan author who Chirinos (2015) admires greatly. It is in this situation that words and language take on utmost significance. Throughout the novel, linguistic differences are shown to separate people, as exemplified by Fanny and Derdriu's inability to understand words such as *tordo* [thrush] in Eugenio's poems. This linguistic barrier reflects Chirinos's own experience of living in Spain, where small linguistic differences mark him out as foreign. Chirinos (2013b, 50) notes the 'pequeñas diferencias que te van alejando poco a poco de tus raíces, pero que al mismo tiempo las subrayan' [small differences which slowly take you away from your roots, but also underline them]. He affirms that the hybrid language he now speaks – a mixture of peninsular Spanish and the dialect of his native Valera – is at the centre of his identity, stating, 'La anormalidad lingüística es el sello de mi mundo y de lo que escribo desde hace años' [Linguistic abnormality has been the signature of my world and what I write for years now] (Chirinos, 2013b, 54). If language becomes the defining feature of someone's identity, it also becomes a way for people to connect with one another. For writers in exile, words are a way of remaining connected to the people and places left behind. Eugenio therefore advises Derdriu, 'No me busques en los mapas, en la morgue ni en las estaciones de policía: escudriña mis palabras y da conmigo' [Don't look for me in maps, in the morgue or in police stations: study my words and find me there] (36). With this statement, Chirinos affirms what for him is the value of writing and therefore the need to allow and support the flow of literature beyond national borders.

When I told Chirinos that his novels had inspired a love of Montejo in me, he replied, 'No puedo imaginar un mejor fin para mis novelas: Difundir el amor por la poesía de Eugenio Montejo. ¡Un lujo!' [I can't imagine a better end for my novels: Spreading love for Eugenio Montejo's poetry, what a luxury!] (Chirinos, 2014). Chirinos's 'humble indebtedness' to other writers, Stanco (2013a, 149) suggests, is one of the main attractions of the novel. Nonetheless, she adds, 'When he emotes "I am grateful to all", he gently inserts himself into the pantheon of his personal literary icons' (Stanco, 2013a, 149). Equating himself with Montejo not only allows him to express his fragmentary identity and ambivalence towards Venezuela, but also reveals a desire to be appreciated for his writing in the same way that he appreciates Montejo.

Such indebtedness to other writers is one of the main themes of Slavko Zupcic's novel *Círculo croata* (2010). In her analysis of 'Amor que a otro puerto perteneces' [Love who Belongs to Another Port], Zupcic's short story that was the basis for *Círculo croata*, Janet Hendrickson (2014, 176) observes that 'its protagonist tries to write his way through his literary and personal past in the context of an internationalised body of writing'. In other words, narrator–protagonist Zlatica's exploration of his own identity, which is the foundation of his writing, is intertwined with literary references, particularly to two key figures: Salvador Prasel and William Faulkner. Zlatica's identity is shown to be intrinsically linked with that of the absent father with whom he shares a name, and the first mention of this father comes at the end of an anecdote about Faulkner and Prasel:

> [Mi tía] había logrado que William Faulkner los firmara [*Pylon* y *Mientras agonizo*] luego de esperarlo durante por lo menos cinco horas en las puertas del Ateneo de Valencia [...] Pudo verlo descender de una camioneta por puestos en compañía de Salvador Prasel, un escritor yugoslavo que había arribado a Valencia en 1951, el mismo año en que lo hiciera mi padre, Zlatica Didič. (87)

> [My aunt had managed to get William Faulkner to sign *Pylon* and *As I Lay Dying* after waiting for him for at least five hours at the doors of the Ateneo de Valencia cultural centre. She caught him descending from the bus in the company of Salvador Prasel, a Yugoslavian writer who had arrived in Valencia in 1951, the same year as my father, Zlatica Didič.]

It is easy to see why Salvador Prasel, a writer from Croatia who migrated to Venezuela following the Second World War, is of particular interest to both Slavko Zupcic and his fictional alter-ego Zlatica Didič. In the essay 'El viaje secreto de Salvador Prasel' [The Secret Journey of Salvador Prasel], published before *Círculo croata*, Zupcic (2005) pays homage to the 'escritor invisible' [invisible writer] who did not belong anywhere: 'Venezolano en Mostar y "yugoslavo" en Caracas, no era de ninguna parte. Nadie lo conoció y sus novelas a veces se consiguen en los remates' [Venezuelan in Mostar and 'Yugoslavian' in Caracas, he was not from anywhere. Nobody knew him and his novels can sometimes be found in bargain bins] (Zupcic, 2005, 26). Prasel, to whom, among others, *Círculo croata* is dedicated, is treated in the novel in much the same way as Eugenio Montejo in *El niño malo* (Chirinos, 2010). *Círculo croata* is both a tribute to Prasel, which introduces new audiences to him, and an attempt by Zupcic to identify himself with the writer he so admires. This admiration is clear from 'El viaje secreto de Salvador Prasel', in which Zupcic (2005, 24) remarks that, once in Venezuela, Prasel did not miss an opportunity to enter a literary competition: 'Enviaba y ganaba. Así publicó sus libros: *Apartamento 22* (1969), *Adiós Hogar* (1971), *Mitin* (1973), *Máxima culpa* (1975)' [He entered and he won. That's how he published his books: *Apartment 22, Goodbye Home, Meeting, Maximum Sin*]. Similarly, in *Círculo croata*, Zlatica is impressed by Prasel's position within the Venezuelan literary community, noting that, after settling in Caracas, 'se hizo muy amigo de José Ignacio Cabrujas y de Salvador Garmendia' [he became very good friends with José Ignacio Cabrujas and Salvador Garmendia] (100), two leading figures in Venezuelan culture in the 1970s.

According to the family legend, Salvador Prasel and Zlatica Didič Sr were both Croatian ministers who arrived in Venezuela on the same boat. Zlatica Jr,[4] however, is never really sure whether the story that, according to his aunt, his father would tell about his relationship with Prasel was true or just 'otra demostración de la fantasía familiar' [another demonstration of the family fantasy] (172). Prasel becomes a main character of Zupcic's novel *Círculo croata*, as Zlatica develops a relationship with him after asking him to translate the letters that his father had left behind from Serbo-Croatian to Spanish. Prasel never translates the letters as he is too ill to meet Zlatica in person, but continues talking to him for years over the phone, and Zlatica admits that he started to feel affection for him (103). When the day finally arrives for them to meet in person, Zlatica is informed by Prasel's granddaughter that he has just died (174), exactly as happened to Slavko Zupcic in real life (Zupcic, 2005, 26). Zupcic (2005, 26) laments that his death was not reported in any newspapers, a sign that his prize-winning works and supposed connections were not enough to guarantee him national recognition. The novel thus becomes a long overdue eulogy.

Prasel is also a protagonist of Zlatica Didič's *Círculo croata de Venezuela*, the novel within the novel, in which Zlatica Sr and Salvador Prasel embark on a bizarre mission to Italy to bring back the bones of San Desiderio for the Prince of Spoleto. In Zlatica's story, there are small intertextual references to Prasel's writing. Prasel and Didič being offered a mission to deliver a batch of condoms to Vienna (93), for example, refers to one of Max Balbek's jobs in *Máxima culpa*:

> ¿Sabe que en Eslovaquia había prohibido la venta de condones, pero su gobierno fomentaba la producción para luego exportar tan pecaminosa mercancía? Nuestro amigo el padre Procopio se ayudaba en Viena – porque los compatriotas le daban muy poco – con la venta de medias de seda italianas y preservativos eslovacos. Yo se los iba colocando en los burdeles. (Prasel, 1975, 15–16)

> [Do you know that Slovakia has banned the sale of condoms, but the government supports their production to then export such sinful merchandise? Our friend Father Procopio helped himself out in Vienna – because

---

4 Future mentions of Zlatica refer to Zlatica Jr.

his compatriots gave him very little – by selling Italian stockings and Slovakian condoms. I used to deliver them to the brothels for him.]

This is a small example of the damning indictment of the Catholic Church and of political hypocrisy that is the narrative thread of Prasel's novel. In Zlatica's novel, by contrast, all social commentary has been removed; delivering condoms to Vienna is just another funny anecdote in the humorous narrative. In addition, Zlatica names his father and Prasel as members of Ante Pavelich's exile government with pride (92), whereas Prasel made clear in his own writing that Pavelich's party was the Ustache, Fascists and Nazi-collaborators, whose members were welcome neither in Croatia nor many other countries after the Second World War. While Zlatica's tale sees his father and Prasel end up in Venezuela because a church there wants to buy the religious relics under their care, in *Máxima culpa* it is explained that Venezuela was the only country willing to take ex-Ustache, who were living in refugee camps. The fact that Venezuela was willing to take him in does not stop the narrator-protagonist Max Balbek from criticising Venezuela throughout the confessions which form *Máxima culpa*. He observes, 'Qué magníficas leyes tenemos en Venezuela: el artículo treinta y uno de la Ley del Trabajo por el cual te dan un puntapié y tú tienes que darles las gracias por no cobrarte nada' [What magnificent laws we have in Venezuela: Article 31 of the Law of Work by which they kick you and you have to thank them for not charging you] (Prasel, 1975, 11). It is little wonder that Venezuelan officials would not want to celebrate Prasel's memory, if they were aware of his writing at all. No such criticism is displayed in *Círculo croata*: both Zupcic's novel and Zlatica's novel-within-the-novel are personal, not political. Likewise, in Zupcic's desire to eulogise Prasel, he does not engage with aspects of Prasel's writing that readers may find uncomfortable. In *Máxima culpa*, for example, Balbek describes in detail his sexual abuse of other boys as a child. Nor are the hopelessness and nihilism so evident in *Máxima culpa* – encapsulated in Balbek's final lament, 'Ay, padre, después vienen ustedes y nos dicen que la tierra no es un infierno' [Oh, Father, then you come and tell us that the Earth isn't a Hell] (Prasel, 1975, 236) – reflected in *Círculo croata*. In the main body of the novel, Prasel is a kindly mentor figure, and in Zlatica's fiction, he is a serious young man, frustrated by Zlatica Sr's recklessness. Zupcic, and his fictional alter-ego Zlatica, identify with Prasel as a person, because of their shared ethnic heritage and later personal connection, and admire and aspire to his literary output, yet their writing style has not been influenced greatly by Prasel.

Rather than incorporating elements of Prasel's writing in his own novel, Zupcic refers to books he has written as Prasel's, equating himself with Prasel in readers' minds. Zlatica reports having bought one of Prasel's books, *Pésame mucho* [I'm So Sorry for Your Loss], at the Librería Cultural (99). *Pésame mucho* is not a book by Prasel, but in fact one of Zupcic's novels, published as part of the collection *Tres novelas*, along with *Círculo croata* and *Barbie* in 2006. Zupcic even draws attention to his masquerading as Prasel by criticising Prasel for doing the same thing with esteemed Venezuelan intellectuals:

> En la única travesura literaria que le había conocido después de *Adiós Hogar*, impostaba la voz de José Balza, Caupolicán Ovalles, Juan Sánchez Pelaez, Ramón Palomares, Eduardo Liendo, Jacobo Borges, Guillermo Sucre, Mario Abreu, Oswaldo Vigas, Luis Alberto Crespo, Miguel Von Dangel, Salvador Garmendia e incluso Henry Charrière, y aceptaba sin mayores preámbulos que éstos escribiesen de su obra las maravillas que nunca realmente pensaron. Ese era el contenido de *Mienten los demógrafos*. (145)
>
> [In his only known literary hijinks after *Goodbye Home*, he imitated the voices of José Balza [...] and even Henry Charrière and accepted without further ado that they would write wonders about his work that they had never really thought. That was the content of *The Demographers Lie*.]

Mienten los demógrafos does not exist. However, this fictional intertext allows Zupcic to admit to his own games within his novel, to point readers towards many other Venezuelan novelists, poets, and even painters with whom they may not be familiar, and, above all, to acknowledge the debt that his writing owes to previous generations of Venezuelans, establishing a continuity.

Like Juan Carlos Chirinos in *El niño malo*, Zupcic also masquerades briefly as Eugenio Montejo. The catalyst for Zlatica's writing, and his introduction to Salvador Prasel, is a book that he had found in a remainders shop earlier that day:

> La copia de uno de los primeros poemarios de Eugenio Montejo, *Soledades*, cuyos espacios habían sido rellenados por la letra diminuta y metódica de un hombre que se hacía llamar Salvador Prasel y pretendía recuperar un álbum de fotos que había perdido en extrañas circunstancias. (87)
>
> [The copy of one of Eugenio Montejo's first poetry collections, *Lonliness*, whose gaps had been filled with the tiny and methodological handwriting of a man calling himself Salvador Prasel who was attempting to recover a photo album that had been lost in strange circumstances.]

Montejo never wrote a collection called *Soledades* and the poems cited by Zlatica as part of the collection – 'Sentimental', 'La revolución es un sueño que ganó el premio nacional de literatura'[5] [The Revolution is a Dream that Won the National Prize for Literature] – are fabrications. As with Chirinos, Zupcic's impersonation of Montejo both pays homage to the great poet and suggests a desire to be considered as part of the same literary tradition.

---

5 This may be a reference to Andrés Rivera's *La revolución es un sueño eterno* [The Revolution is an Eternal Dream] which won the Argentinian National Prize for Literature in 1992.

Zlatica imitates Salvador Prasel further through the letters from Prasel to William Faulkner that Zlatica imagines in his novel (135, 159). In one extract, for example, Prasel informs Faulkner that he has just purchased ten copies of *As I Lay Dying* in Italy to send to him (135). Through this impersonating of Prasel – depicted as an ardent promoter of Faulkner, working to bring him to Croatia (92) – Zlatica displays his own high regard for the Southern author. Zlatica is so determined to associate himself with Faulkner that the author photo that he sends to a newspaper to be printed alongside his prize-winning story shows him at a barber's where there is a clipping on the wall of an interview with Faulkner from when he had his hair cut by the same barber 30 years before (138).

This focus on Faulkner is significant for multiple reasons. First, as Hendrickson (2014, 177) notes, reading Faulkner 'places [Zlatica] in the company of the Boom writers influenced by the American'. Moreover, it acknowledges Faulkner's influence in the development of Latin American literature not only in aesthetic terms but especially in bringing Latin American authors into world literary space (Cohn, 2004). While much has been made of Faulkner's role in what was to become the Boom, the specific importance of Venezuela is often overlooked. As part of his position as a goodwill ambassador for the United States, Faulkner first visited Venezuela in 1954, and returned in April 1961 for a two-week stay, during which time he dined with Arturo Uslar Pietri and his wife (Brodsky, 1987, 226). According to Deborah Cohn (2004), 'he was warmly welcomed by intellectuals who, though often anti-American, were receptive to his work and had themselves been influenced by him'. The visit was declared 'one of the most successful of all cultural approaches by the United States to Venezuela' (Cohn, 2004). As well as improving the image of the United States in Latin America, Faulkner's visit awakened his sympathies for Latin American authors who struggled to publish in their own countries and inspired him to set up the Ibero-American Novel Project. The project aimed to 'use the prestige associated with Faulkner's name to convince publishers to take the risk of translating and publishing the award-winning novels from a region whose literature was only beginning to gain recognition in the U.S. in the early 1960s' (Cohn, 2004). Although others of the 14 winners of the Ibero-American Prize – José Donoso (Chile), Juan Carlos Onetti (Uruguay), Augusto Roa Bastos (Paraguay) and Miguel Ángel Asturias (Guatemala) – went on to achieve far greater international success, it was in fact the Venezuelan novel *Cumboto* by Rámon Díaz Sánchez which was voted by a jury at University of Virginia as 'the most outstanding novel' and the only one of the 14 winners to be published in English through the project (Cohn, 2004). This publication took years to complete, however, as U.S. readers and publishers disliked the regionalism of Díaz Sánchez's work, and the novel remains largely unknown.

While writing his novel, Zlatica recalls Faulkner's trip to Venezuela: 'Recordé el instante en que William Faulkner, aprovechando su visita a Venezuela luego de la concesión del Nobel, presentó a los dos Salvadores,

Prasel y Garmendia' [I remembered the instant in which William Faulkner, taking advantage of his visist to Venezuela after being awarded the Nobel, introduced the two Salvadors, Prasel and Garmendia] (136). By referencing Faulkner's visit to Venezuela in this period, Zupcic encourages readers to explore Faulkner's praise for Venezuelan literature and how Faulkner's time in the country sparked his interest in Latin American literature, thereby placing Venezuela within the history of the Boom and challenging the narrative of Venezuelan literature as inferior to that of its Latin American neighbours. As Hendrickson (2014, 177) observes, 'While the father places the narrator in an internationalised space by birth, the narrator's predilection for imported and translated books places him in an international literary culture'. In *Círculo croata*, Salvador Prasel functions as a model of a writer caught between two cultures, while William Faulkner serves as a symbol of Venezuela's unfairly peripheral place in world literary space.

The three novels discussed in this chapter all attest to David Lodge's (1995, 146) claim that 'you cannot begin to write novels without […] defining yourself in relationships of apprenticeship, discipleship, rivalry and antagonism with precursors and peers'. Méndez Guédez, Chirinos and Zupcic are readerly writers who demonstrate their wide reading and their indebtedness to other writers through their fiction. Cloyd and Bates (1964, 122) maintain that imagined readers of these quotations 'are supposed to have some knowledge of the work quoted', arguing that otherwise there would be no point in quoting. However, Méndez Guédez, Chirinos and Zupcic make their reference to other authors explicit not only through quotation but through making other authors appear as characters in their novels. The novels explored in this chapter were all written in the digital age, where it is much easier to search for the source of a reference while reading. As J. Andrew Brown (2015, 78) argues in 'Googling McOndo', the ability to look up quotes or references online has led to 'a model of reading in which reader, print text and internet form new kinds of networked reading'. Following this model, intertextual references can lead readers first to search online for, then read the referenced text, returning to the original text with a greater understanding. Quotation, along with naming other texts or writers, therefore not only speaks to those who have prior knowledge of the intertexts, but can also introduce readers to texts that these authors consider worthy of greater attention. Through their use of writers as characters, these authors establish a continuity of tradition, looking back with respect and taking aspects of this tradition forward in their own work. In a context where authors do not receive the recognition they feel they deserve from the state, 'self-valorising annexation' (Bourdieu, 1993, 138) – that is, linking their own writing to that of an author they admire through quotation, allusion or reference – is a form of protest. The writers who appear in each of these novels allow the authors to explore issues of particular importance to them. Through Alfredo Bryce Echenique and Mario Vargas Llosa, Méndez

Guédez can criticise the Bolivarian habit of dismissing writers as elites or oligarchs and putting political concerns over the literary; through Eugenio Montejo, Chirinos can demonstrate the value of literature and explore issues of being a writer abroad; and through Salvador Prasel and William Faulkner, Zupcic can open up the closed literary space of Venezuela.

CHAPTER 5

Form and Popular Culture

The incorporation of aspects of popular culture into literary texts is not new, but it takes on new significance in the context of the distinction between the popular as 'lo nuestro' [ours] and the elite as 'apatriado' [unpatriotic] in Bolivarian rhetoric. Moreover, the 'popular' as celebrated by the Bolivarian Revolution is defined by the national and often the indigenous, while popular culture in terms of globalised media is condemned as neo-imperialist. This chapter examines how a selection of novels – *Bajo las hojas* (Centeno, 2010), *Chulapos Mambo* (Méndez Guédez, 2011), *Transilvania unplugged* (Sánchez Rugeles, 2011) and *El niño malo cuenta hasta cien y se retira* (Chirinos, 2010) – involve aspects of popular culture, building on the spirit of aesthetic renovation that characterised the Punto Fijo period. 'Popular' is understood here in a variety of ways: as genres such as the gothic, comedy and detective fiction with mass appeal; as experienced by multitudes (global media and the internet); and as folk or indigenous. Using a combination of these aspects of popular culture allows these authors both to fulfil their literary aims, such as storytelling, building suspense or giving free rein to their imagination, and to comment on the socio-political realities of Venezuela under Chávez.

During the Punto Fijo period, the political and economic stability brought about with the transition to democracy led to aesthetic renovation (Barrera Linares, 2005), characterised by a diversity of styles and themes. Free from political obligations, authors could write about whatever subjects interested them, and did not have to fear censorship or punishment if they criticised the government (Porras, 2006, 626–627). Nonetheless, writers were discouraged from political radicalism through financial incentives from a state eager to maintain order, while, according to Ángel Rama (1982, 174), increased oil wealth had also created a middle class unwilling to jeopardise their new social position by supporting revolutionary movements. In this context, aesthetic concerns became the primary focus for many writers. Luis Britto García (1999, 50) suggests that, having lost hope in the possibility of improving society, writers began to strive for aesthetic perfection instead. At the same time, the state's use of oil revenue to fund publishing gave writers the economic freedom to be creative. Without state funding, publishing in

Venezuela would not have been financially viable, given that the reading public in Venezuela was very small and there was little private industry. Instead, the state was happy to indulge writers in their stylistic experimentation without fear that alienating potential readers would limit profits. As Ana Teresa Torres (1999, 61) noted, 'Puesto que el Estado era y sigue siendo el gran editor ¿qué importaba que los libros se vendieran?' [Given that the state was and is our great publisher, what does it matter if books sell?] Funding literary production became not only a way to ensure the support of intellectuals, but also a way for the nascent democratic Venezuela to improve its international standing, gaining cultural capital from the reputation for literary quality won by Monte Ávila throughout Latin America.

Without pressure to reach mass markets, literature became 'distinguida, inaccesible, inconsumible' [distinguished, inaccessible, inconsumable] (Torres, 1999, 59). Literature became the preserve of educated elites, partly because they were the only ones who could understand the complicated, experimental texts being produced, but also because the majority of the population was more interested in popular culture and mass media than literature. Consequently, authors began to condition their writing to cater to an audience which read more for analytical ends than for enjoyment (Barrera Linares, 2006a, 808). As a result of this focus on academic audiences, as well as the economic freedoms and the move away from political commitment, the literature of the 1980s came to be defined by a preoccupation with the aesthetic. Experimentation with new forms increased, which led to a period of great diversity, in terms of both theme and style, towards the turn of the century. Luis Barrera Linares (2006a, 809) notes the introduction of crime fiction, adventure stories, horror and Sci-Fi, combined with narratives of exile and a cynicism towards the revolutionary fervour of the 1960s. Punto Fijo writers also incorporated other forms of popular culture into their narratives, such as José Balza who in *D* (1977) explores Venezuelan rock music and radio advertising alongside references to Barthes, Kristeva and Proust (Barragán, 2005).

It is an interesting paradox, although certainly not one limited to Venezuela, that popular culture was used by these authors to create elite, exclusive texts. In what has become known as the 'new novel', authors such as Manuel Puig, Mario Vargas Llosa and Alejo Carpentier incorporated aspects of popular culture into texts aimed at an elite, educated audience (Swanson, 1995). As well as a desire for aesthetic renovation, this experimentation with genre and popular culture therefore tied the Venezuelan authors of Punto Fijo into wider Latin American literary developments. In his study of the 'new novel', Philip Swanson (1995, 11) asks:

> Does not the discussion of the gap between High Culture and Popular Culture undermine the very popular quality of popular culture and generate a new form of elitism? Does not the urge to situate popular culture in a 'new novel' framework imply the hierarchical superiority of the framework over the popular element contained within it?

While the incorporation of popular genres in 'new novels' has been considered radical, Swanson (1995, 75) makes it clear that these are not texts aimed at a mass audience, but rather texts which appropriate elements of popular culture to provide 'a sophisticated entertainment for a literate reading public'. This point of view is shared by Donald L. Shaw (1998, 20), who argues that, in works by Puig, Vargas Llosa and Carlos Fuentes, 'a "low" or "popular" fictional genre is adapted to serve a different (but always in the end "higher") literary purpose'. Such arguments, however, deny the possibility of the authors as readers and fans of popular genres. The authors discussed in this chapter show great fondness for genres such as comedy, fantasy or crime, in contrast to the snobbishness sometimes shown to popular genres in literary criticism, which dismisses them as kitsch and escapist. They embrace the storytelling possibilities offered by genres whose conventions offer 'frameworks for constructing meaning and value' (Frow, 2006, 72).

In the context of Bolivarian Venezuela, where the popular was valued by the state to the point where officials spoke of 'eliminating' elite culture, authors appropriating the popular as their Latin American predecessors did becomes an act of defiance. The Bolivarian period has been characterised by conflict and polarisation (Buxton, 2011), and the literary field is no exception. Ana Teresa Torres (2006, 915) claimed that hostility towards intellectuals, artists and writers prevailed since Chávez announced his 'cultural revolution' in 2001, a 'declaration of war' which sought the kind of polarisation seen in other areas. Chávez himself reinforced this image of war during his *Aló, Presidente* television broadcast on 2 December 2009, declaring, 'Estamos en medio de una lucha histórica [...] y no hay reconciliación posible' [We are in the middle of a historic fight and there is no reconciliation possible] (Silva-Ferrer, 2014, 105). Following Chávez's lead, in his speeches as Minister for Culture, Francisco Sesto divided culture into two, discrediting 'elite' culture and affirming that 'la nuestra es la cultura' [ours is the culture] (Kozak Rovero, 2007b, 105). In a 2011 speech to the National Assembly, Sesto listed 'la eliminación de las élites de la cultura' [the elimination of cultural elites] among his achievements as Minister for Culture (Falcón, 2011). This division is even enshrined in Article 36 of the Organic Law of Culture (2005), which divides the population into those for and those against 'national' culture: 'El Estado fomentará, protegerá y conservará el Patrimonio Cultural de la Nación, especialmente frente a los intereses pecuniarios e ideológicos que continuamente amenazan su existencia' [The state will promote, protect and conserve the Cultural Heritage of the Nation, especially when faced with the financial and ideological interests that continually threaten its existence] (Comisión Permanente de Educación, 2005, 10).[1]

---

[1] It is very interesting to note that this distinction between 'popular' and 'elite', so prevalent in the literary field, has not been made for music. Venezuela's famous programme of youth orchestras, El Sistema, often plays classical, mainly European, music, which would usually be considered 'high culture'.

Those authors who prioritised aesthetic values and viewed literature as a profession were made to feel excluded, denounced by Sesto as 'los vetustos y decadentes que defienden a ultranza el pasado' [those outdated and decadent ones who defend the past at any cost] (Wisotzki, 2006, 28). Disregarding the literary tradition of the Punto Fijo period was necessary for the image of a radical break that the Bolivarian regime wished to portray.[2] However, as discussed in the previous chapter, the authors analysed in this book believe that this tradition deserves respect and position themselves as a continuation thereof.

As well as being made to feel excluded, another concern voiced by critics of the Bolivarian approach to literature was that within Francisco Sesto's denunciation of 'la cultura exquisita de las élites' [the exquisite culture of the elites] was an implicit assumption that 'the people' need easy to understand texts and should not be challenged by literature. Kozak Rovero (2007b, 114), for example, complained that the Bolivarian understanding of the democratisation of culture did not mean making the most varied cultural offering available to the widest range of people. In this way, the Bolivarian approach to literature differed from the Cuban one, which aimed to raise the levels of understanding of all Cubans. In his 'Palabras a los intelectuales' [Words to the Intellectuals], Castro (1961) proclaimed, 'Hay que esforzarse en todas las manifestaciones por llegar al pueblo, pero a su vez hay que hacer todo lo que esté al alcance de nuestras manos para que el pueblo pueda comprender cada vez más y mejor' [We must make an effort in every way to reach the people, but at the same time we must do everything in our reach so that the people can understand ever more and ever better]. Castro's policy, building on José Martí's famous affirmation that 'El único modo de ser libre es de ser culto' [The only way to be free is to be educated], focused on raising literacy skills. We can observe a contradiction in Bolivarian policy. On the one hand, the Bolivarian Revolution prided itself on literacy, with cultural officials even declaring Venezuela a 'Territorio Libre de Analfabetismo' [Land Free from Illiteracy] in 2005 (Colectivos de trabajadores, 2012, 10), an achievement recognised by the United Nations, which praised the country's leading role in the fight against illiteracy in Latin America (Castillo E., 2011, 127). On the other hand, the scepticism shown towards more complicated narratives suggests only a limited level of literacy was expected to have been reached.

At this point, it is necessary to clarify that 'lo popular' in Bolivarian rhetoric fits William Beezley and Linda Curcio-Nagy's (2012, 1) definition of popular culture as 'a set of behavioural practices with pervasive, ordinary character' and 'the set of images, practices, and interactions that distinguishes a community and often serves as a synonym for national identity'. This is a romantic approach to popular culture as an expression of the essential, pure

---

2 See Brown, 2018 for the importance of the idea of a radical break with the past in Bolivarian cultural policy.

spirit of a people, which must be defended against capitalism and universalising cultural industries. While 'cinema, television and the Internet have reconfigured the face of cultural production on the continent' (Kantaris and O'Bryen, 2013, 2), the Bolivarian definition of popular refers to the national, specifically the folkloric, not to globalised mass media such as Hollywood film or imported pop music, which are seen as weapons of cultural imperialism.[3] According to Gisela Kozak Rovero, the Bolivarian government saw U.S. mass culture as an enemy to be combatted through education programmes (Chacón, 2009, 41).

The discrediting of 'elite' culture, together with cultural nationalism, translated to a distrust of formal and linguistic experimentation, and a recourse to realism in Bolivarian cultural policy. In earlier periods of Venezuelan literary history, as Miguel Gomes (1997, 839) notes, 'dominant meditation about national problems and identity' led to the predominance of realism and naturalism. Pascale Casanova (2004, 197) observes 'a genuine hegemony of realism' in those places where literature is highly politicised:

> In literary spaces that are closely monitored by political authorities, formalism is considered for the most part a luxury to be indulged by countries in the centre, which no longer have to concern themselves with either the national question or political commitment. (Casanova, 2004, 198)

According to this theory, concentrating on aesthetic concerns would detract from the political content of writing. Writing should be as plain and easy to understand as possible, to get the message to the widest range of people. This position was argued by the prominent literary critic José Antonio Portuondo in Cuba in the 1960s, who advocated for socialist realism, but was vehemently rejected by Ernesto 'Che' Guevara (Kumaraswami, 2007, 73). In Bolivarian Venezuela, the manifesto of the Plataforma del Libro y la Lectura (2007) states, 'El libro debe contribuir indefectiblemente a la masificación del conocimiento' [The book should contribute without fail to the spreading of knowledge], as well as recording socio-historical reality and local, regional, national and Latin American memory. As discussed in Chapter 3, books were thought of as a means of documenting supposedly national characteristics, essential for the process of building a national, socialist community. However, while this rhetoric suggests a preference for realism, in practice, genre fiction was also published by the state. Let us think again of *La segunda oportunidad* by Maritza Avilez (2007), the *telenovela*-esque romance between genetically engineered, telepathic Nazi hunters published by El perro y la rana, who, as explored in Chapter 1, marketed the book as the story of how determination and teamwork brings good things to a hard-working Venezuelan mother. The

---

3 See Emanuelsson, 2010 for a report on the Villa del Cine and Chávez's promise to 'romper la dictadura de Hollywood' [end Hollywood's dictatorship].

criticisms by the authors discussed in this book therefore seem to respond more to the speeches and mission statements of the Bolivarian cultural officials than to publishing practice.

The authors analysed in this chapter have recourse to a range of popular genres – the gothic, comedy, fantasy and detective fiction – and references to globalised media to meet their literary concerns of storytelling, gripping the reader and crafting narrative worlds. This does not, however, mean that their writing is apolitical. Through their uses of popular culture, the writers studied here comment on contemporary Venezuelan socio-political issues, from a critique of Bolivarian authoritarianism in *Bajo las hojas* (Centeno, 2010) to the polarisation of Venezuelan society in *Chulapos Mambo* (Méndez Guédez, 2011).

Israel Centeno's 400-page novel *Bajo las hojas* (2010) is a prime example of an attempt to choose the audience, as it demands an educated, committed reader. The first 40 or so pages are a relatively straightforward, if self-reflexive, account of a middle-aged Venezuelan novelist who seizes the opportunity to run off to London with his young and beautiful mistress. From then on, the novel becomes increasingly difficult to follow. Julio becomes a pawn in a grander scheme involving his mistress, his son, his old revolutionary colleagues turned police officers, an Italian dancer, and a death-worshipping cult of psychologists. The narration constantly switches between these disparate but linked characters and a mysterious omniscient power, so the reader must continually ask who is speaking, or, more specifically, who is writing. *Bajo las hojas* is a polyphonic novel, in which 'we find not an objective, authorial voice presenting the relations and dialogues between characters but a world in which all characters and even the narrator him or herself are possessed of their own discursive consciousness' (Allen, 2000, 23). As David Lodge (1995, 157) argues, 'as soon as you allow a variety of discourses into a textual space [...] you establish a resistance to the dominance of any one discourse'. The different narratorial voices of *Bajo las hojas* often contradict one another, challenging the dominant discourse. As well as this polyphony, *Bajo las hojas* displays features of Bakhtinian carnivalesque, including sacrilegious behaviour, bizarre rituals, disguise and depravity, all of which encourages the subversion of political order (Bakhtin, 1984).

Bajo las hojas requires constant concentration and perseverance to follow the story and the web of intrigues it spins. The novel is further complicated by a wealth of erudite references to British history, Latin American poetry and more. In the name of the cult at the heart of the novel alone, 'Los Argonautas Junguianos de los Últimos Días' [The Latter-Day Jungian Argonauts] (59), Centeno crams in references to Ancient Greek mythology, psychoanalytical theory and Mormonism. As a result, while its characters ponder the nature and power of literature, the novel itself seems to be a protest against both a 'dumbing-down' of literature and the use of narrative as a tool for building a socialist national community, fighting instead for writing and reading as artistic and intellectually stimulating endeavours. While the style may put off readers looking for an easy read, Centeno aims to attract a complicit reader, willing to put in the effort to follow his work. As Silda Cordoliani (2011) observed in her presentation of the novel, Israel Centeno 'no es autor que ceda un ápice de Literatura (Literatura con mayúscula) en procura de público' [is not an author who will relinquish an ounce of Literature (with a capital L) in search of an audience].

To create this complex narrative, Centeno merges elements of fantasy, mystery, eroticism and the gothic. María Negroni (2009, 9) suggests that what has been referred to as Latin American fantasy derives from the gothic, as both share the same 'nocturno y afiebrado' [nocturnal and feverish] quality, and the same obsessions. The gothic, she argues, is by nature unruly and chaotic (Negroni, 2009, 9), labels which certainly apply to *Bajo las hojas*. As Jesús Suárez (2014) highlights, in *Bajo las hojas*, the gothic does not just allow Centeno to present a gallery of supernatural characters, spooky castles and mysterious assassinations, but also becomes an allegory for a decadent society. *Bajo las hojas* bears many of the hallmarks of classic gothic fiction. The novel opens with a description of the creaking floorboards of the 'viejo y quejumbroso' [old and complaining] hotel where Julio and his lover are staying in Camden Town (11), setting the ominous tone which will run through the story. Throughout we find the uncanny in María Inmaculada, as the doppelgänger of Julio's lover Victoria. María Inmaculada is first introduced as part of the cult, but is also controlled by the *relatores*, the invisible force controlling the story, who say they did what was necessary for her to be in the right place at the right time (74). She is said to be pretending to be a nameless friend, while that friend imitates her (74–75). Over the course of the book, we are led to believe – although it is never made explicit – that the real María Inmaculada is alive and well in London with Julio while her friend has died in her place in Caracas. Coming from German folklore, the doppelgänger was considered a bad omen, usually signifying death (Serrano, 2010, 902). Moreover, in gothic fiction, the doppelgänger can be read as a symbol of social disparities, demonstrating the divergent outcomes that can befall the same character in different circumstances (Hughes, 2013, 86). Through these double women, Centeno suggests that migration is a route to safety compared with the dangers of Caracas. Another key gothic element of the book are vampires and graveyards, as Julio is attacked by, and later befriends, old Bill the vampire hunter, who has 'el deber divino de mantener a esta tierra santa de Highgate limpia de los espectros que chupan sangre' [the divine duty to keep this holy land of Highgate clean from blood-sucking spectres] (121–122). Julio's first encounter with Bill is when the vampire hunter, thinking him undead, hits our protagonist over the head with a rock. Being seen as a vampire symbolises Julio's feeling of being in limbo, surviving through a government contract while his literary career is dead. Julio later describes himself playing at Van Helsing, the famous vampire hunter from Bram Stoker's *Dracula* (1897). In that way, he joined 'las corrientes esotéricas que liberaban a la humanidad de la lógica opresora, del relato omnisciente que sujeta al personaje y le roba la libertad' [the esoteric currents which freed humanity from oppressive logic, from the omniscient story which holds the character and robs them of their freedom] (362). Pretending to be the gothic hero, Centeno suggests, brings relief to a subject otherwise utterly helpless in the face of a powerful and oppressive regime. According to Carmen Serrano (2010), vampires can be seen as symbols for dictators, as both control their victims absolutely and are very difficult to get rid of. Perhaps Julio pretends to fight vampires because he is incapable of fighting against the increasingly authoritarian government in Venezuela.

The doppelgängers and vampire hunters are coupled with the persecution and paranoia that David Punter and Glennis Byron (2003, 273) see as key ingredients of the gothic, through which 'the self experiences itself as at the mercy of forces beyond its control'. After his night in Highgate cemetery, Julio:

> Había quedado vacío, una brasa intangible lo había quemado, le ardía el esófago, el estómago, la planta de los pies. No fue el licor de Dora, la homeless, ni el golpe de Bill, el cazavampiros, Caracas lo presionaba, eso le decíamos, hay presión, hay urgencia, debes moverte, no puedes parar y él buscaba un tema para volver a escribir, un volumen o tres folios, no debes parar. (246–247)

> [Had been left empty, an intangible ember had burned him, his oesophagus burned, his stomach, the soles of his feet. It wasn't homeless Dora's liquor, nor the whack from Bill, the vampire hunter, Caracas was putting pressure on him, that's what we told him, there's pressure, there's urgency, you have to move, you cannot stop and he looked for a topic to get back to writing, a volume or three sheets, you must not stop.]

Far scarier than vampires are the mysterious, mind-reading Inteligencia Móvil [Mobile Intelligence], who can make Julio suffer unless he does what they want. Like the thought police from George Orwell's *Nineteen Eighty-Four* (1948), Inteligencia Móvil represents the ultimate authority of a totalitarian government powerful enough to know what its citizens are thinking. The presence of Inteligencia Móvil mixes the gothic traits of fear and suspense with fantasy, as their powers are beyond the humanly possible. As Jacqueline Rose (1996, 8) claims in *States of Fantasy*, such fantasy is useful for understanding contemporary politics, given that 'the modern state's authority passes straight off the edge of the graspable, immediately knowable world'. Centeno (2015b) argues as much in his description of *Bajo las hojas*, stating that perhaps the most important aspect of his work is 'la posibilidad que le ofrece al lector para entender, ontológica y psicológicamente, cómo podemos dialogar con aquello que no vemos de la realidad' [the possibility it offers the reader to understand, ontologically and psychologically, how we can dialogue with that which we cannot see in reality]. The telepathic *relatores* offer a way of speaking back to the power which is omnipresent but intangible.

For Juan Carlos Méndez Guédez, the blending of literary and popular genres is a way to undermine the insistence on national narratives which has been part of official attitudes to literature in Venezuela not only under the Bolivarian Revolution, but throughout the Punto Fijo period and the preceding dictatorships. When asked about the mix of styles in *Chulapos Mambo*, he responded:

> Frente a ese proyecto que nos enseñaban en el colegio como parte obligatoria de una supuesta venezolanidad pura y que ahora es el credo de la siniestra cursilería chavista, las calles, la existencia cotidiana mostraban la necesidad continua de expandirnos, de probar otros sabores, otros modos, otras formas de entreverar códigos diferentes, sonoridades antagónicas. (Sánchez Aparicio, 2012)

> [Faced with this project which we were taught in school as an obligatory part of the supposed Venezuelan essence and which is now the creed of the sinister *chavista* vulgarity, the streets and everyday existence demonstrate the need to continue to expand our horizons, to try other tastes, other methods, other ways to combine different codes, opposing sounds.]

In *Chulapos Mambo* (2011), Méndez Guédez combines multiple nods to Hispanic literary tradition with comedy and action to create what Elda Stanco (2013b, 164) describes as 'a literary version of a Guy Ritchie movie script'. Méndez Guédez explains that he wanted to write an English-style comedy because the genre was underappreciated in Spanish-language literature (Volpini, 2011). The comedic elements greatly add to the pleasure of reading the novel. Stanco (2013b, 166) describes *Chulapos Mambo* and Méndez Guédez's other recent works as 'boisterous and fetching novels that bring a very welcome – and much needed – breath of fresh air and straightforward fun to Spanish language novels'. This fun or pleasure from reading can have great benefits, according to Méndez Guédez, who believes that humour can help readers to relax:

> Y ya se sabe, la gente relajada siente de inmediato el deseo de comer bien, de beber jugos de parchita o buenos vinos, de hacer el amor, de bailar, de reunirse con los amigos. Y cuando la gente hace todas estas cosas suele alegrar el mundo y no hacer daño a los otros. (Sánchez Aparicio, 2012)

> [And, you know, relaxed people immediately feel the need to eat well, to drink passion fruit juice or some good wines, to make love, to dance, to meet friends. And when people do all these things they tend to make the world a happier place and not cause harm to others.]

While providing some much-needed levity, the comedy in *Chulapos Mambo* also allows for social and political commentary. Méndez Guédez maintains that sometimes the story he is telling requires a comedic or 'esperpéntico' voice, as was the case with *Chulapos Mambo* (Sánchez Aparicio, 2012). The 'esperpéntico', a term coined by Spanish dramatist Ramón Maria del Valle

Inclán, describes a genre in which the exaggeratedly grotesque serves as a form of social criticism. Much of the humour of the story derives from the caricatured protagonists – Alejandro, the womanising businessman, Simao, the scrounger, and Henry, the deluded wannabe writer – and the farcical situations in which they find themselves, as they devise an absurd scheme for Henry to seduce Alejandro's wife so that he can be free to enjoy his mistress. The narration switches between the three characters, often retelling events from different characters' points of view with humorous contrasts which suggest that readers should not take any one point of view too seriously. Juan Manuel Romero (2013, 146) argues that the idiosyncrasy of the three protagonists makes them subversive of the idea of a pure identity and the need for strict control.

From the opening descriptions of beer-bellied Henry 'arrojando litros de un líquido viscoso' [spewing litres of viscous liquid] off the balcony (13), the novel uses grotesque comedy to censure the Bolivarian Revolution. *Chulapos Mambo* supports Jésus Suárez's (2014) claim that humour and sarcasm in contemporary Venezuelan novels offer a desacralising space that was missing from the very serious, nihilistic Punto Fijo novels. Desacralisation of the Bolivarian Revolution through humour is a key aspect of *Chulapos Mambo*. Desecrating the Christ-like image of Hugo Chávez as the saviour of Venezuela (Michelutti, 2016), Henry gives his support to the Bolivarian Revolution simply because Chávez's election brings his militarist father and his socialist mother together: 'Henry se implicó paulatinamente con el Movimiento y el Proceso [p]orque algo que era capaz de hacer que sus padres se desnudaran para copular tenía que ser algo bueno' [Henry slowly became involved with the Movement and the Process because anything that was capable of making his parents get naked to copulate had to be something good] (188). Following Bakhtin's (1984, 92–93) theory of the carnivalesque, according to which 'laughing truth, expressed in curses and abusive words, degrade[s] power', Méndez Guédez challenges the almost religious power that the Bolivarian Revolution exerts over its followers. *Chulapos Mambo* mocks the militarism, extreme nationalism and corruption that have characterised the Bolivarian Revolution. When the president returns to power following the brief coup in 2002, for example, Méndez Guédez describes a rather pathetic figure, 'la figura regordeta del militar que en ese momento anunciaba que para festejar su regreso al poder grabaría un CD con rancheras que se repartiría en todas las oficinas públicas' [the chubby figure of a soldier who at that moment was announcing that to celebrate his return to power he would record an album of country music to be distributed in all public offices] (165). Although this seems absurd, in 2008 the Venezuelan Socialist Party did indeed release an album called 'Música para la batalla' [Music for the Battle], featuring Chávez singing 'El corrido de caballería' [The Ballad of the Cavalry] (PSUV, 2008). Eschewing historical accuracy, Méndez Guédez pulls together events from different time periods (here 2002 and 2008) for maximum comedic effect, encouraging readers to laugh at the real-life practices of the Bolivarian leaders. Similarly, humorous examples of corruption abound, such as the following exchange:

> [Simao:] ¿Qué puede tener de malo una conferencia?
> [Henry:] Pues como no hubo público en las conferencias de una universidad dominicana, organizamos otra en el propio hotel. Llamamos a varias muchachas que podían tener interés en nuestra cultura. Ellas no fueron por el dinero. Querían que les hablásemos de poesía actual. Luego Silvio decidió ayudarles con alguna cantidad para que pudiesen pagar el taxi de regreso a la discoteca en la que vivían durante la noche, pero al parecer varias estaban fichadas por la policía y él colocó como gastos de producción al abogado que debió sacarlas de la cárcel. (89)

> [(Simao:) What can be bad about a conference?
> (Henry:) Well as no one was going to the conferences at a Dominican university, we organised one in our hotel. We called various girls who might be interested in our culture. They didn't come for the money. They wanted us to talk to them about contemporary poetry. Later Silvio decided to help them out with the taxi fare to the nightclub where they lived, but it seems they were caught by the police and he claimed on expenses for a lawyer to get them out of jail.]

The deadpan way in which Henry recounts this story, as if he has no idea why such behaviour might be construed as improper or corrupt, adds to the irony of the scene. By emphasising the absurdity of aspects of the Bolivarian regime to humorous effect, anecdotes such as these throughout *Chulapos Mambo* open a space for more serious critical reflection.

Nonetheless, the novel is not only critical of the Bolivarian Revolution. Comedy, Méndez Guédez proposes, can break down divides in a polarised society. The *emigré* opposition are not shown in a particularly flattering light either, presented as ineffectual and apathetic. Their only idea is to have a mass against the Comandante:

> —¿Y una misa para rogar que los militares vuelvan a derrocar al Comandante y no lo regresen al poder a las pocas horas?
> —Eso también lo hicimos esta mañana.
> Durante otros veinte minutos nadie habló. (178–179)

> ['And what about a mass to pray that the military otherthrow the Comandante again and don't let him come back to power within a few hours?'
> 'We already did that this morning.'
> No one said anything for the next twenty minutes.]

With scenes such as this, Méndez Guédez suggests that the opposition need to recognise their own flaws as well as those of the government.

Moreover, none of the characters is immune from Méndez Guédez's derision. Simao, the privileged underachiever, and Alejandro, the greedy

Spanish businessmen, are presented as equally flawed through humorous caricature. Simao is the son of a Portuguese immigrant to Venezuela, who set up a shop and made enough money to give Simao a comfortable upbringing and a good education. Simao squandered these opportunities and threw his family into poverty by accidentally sparking riots and looting through not thinking before he spoke: 'Subrayé que una protesta verdadera debía golpear directamente al Capital, a los explotadores, a los que con sus fortunas impedían el bienestar del pueblo' [I pointed out that a real protest had to be a direct strike on the Capital, on the exploiters, on those whose fortunes impeded the welfare of the people] (72). Like Henry, Simao has a totally warped sense of reality. Reflecting on what happened to his family, he states, 'Me deprimí, incluso sentí algo de culpa' [I became depressed, I even felt a little guilty' (73), when the fault is entirely his own. He is a caricature of the Venezuelan middle class that has lost its privilege and now does not know how to cope. Alejandro, meanwhile, is introduced to us as a man who owns a Barceló, a Tapiès and a Brancusi because they are luxury items, rather than from any cultural sensibility (13). Indeed, Méndez Guédez ridicules Alejandro's lack of cultural knowledge throughout the novel. He is shown, for example, not to know *Don Quijote*, the most famous book ever written in his country: 'Tiempo atrás, Candelaria había leído un libro de esos que vienen repletos de mentiras [...] algo de un caballo y un señor gordo que acompañaba a otro' [Some time ago, Canderlaria had read one of those books full of lies [...] something about a horse and a fat man who accompanied another man' (170). Calling it 'one of those books full of lies' suggests that Alejandro does not even really understand what fiction is. Alejandro is also an embodiment of European xenophobia (Romero, 2013, 146), who presents an exaggeratedly negative view of Latin Americans:

> Son horribles esas personas, Candelarita, son todos polígamos, no se bañan, lapidan a las esposas infieles, se drogan y no respetan el quinto ni el séptimo mandamiento, todo el día matan y roban y luego bailan unas músicas horribles y además odian las paellas y los toros. (156)
>
> [They are horrible people, Candelarita, they're all polygamous, they don't wash, they stone unfaithful wives, they take drugs and they don't respect the fifth or the seventh commandment, all day they're killing and stealing and then they dance to horrible music and on top of that they hate paellas and bullfighting.]

Through Alejandro, Méndez Guédez parodies the divisive, xenophobic rhetoric of certain Spanish media outlets and political campaigns, which present immigrants as a threat to both public safety and national identity. It is therefore significant that Alejandro has been portrayed throughout the book as devoid of education, as it suggests that people who espouse such ideas are ignorant and should not be taken seriously. Méndez Guédez affirmed in an interview that while the comic novel exaggerates and caricatures, we all have a monstrous potential (Volpini, 2011). He suggests that his writing 'ilumina las heridas' [shines a light on the wounds], encouraging readers to laugh at ourselves and our flaws.

In *Transilvania unplugged* (2011a), Eduardo Sánchez Rugeles draws on diverse sources of inspiration, from Emil Cioran and Jorge Volpi to Colombian popstar Carlos Vives, weaving together travel writing, the gothic, detective fiction and dark humour. Ricardo Ramírez Requena (2012) calls *Transvilania unplugged* and Sánchez Rugeles's collection of *crónicas*, *Los Desterrados*, 'obras de un Poe que combina marihuana con ácido' [works by a Poe who mixed marijuana with acid]. For Sánchez Rugeles, 'elite' literature and popular culture are on the same level, equally open to appropriation for his story. Even the title of the novel evidences this mixture of influences, referencing both Bram Stoker's 1897 novel *Dracula* and the MTV series of live concerts. Throughout *Transilvania unplugged*, Romanian characters reference *Dracula* as an example of both the appropriation of Romania by the West and Romanian efforts to become part of the West (73, 90, 129). Unplugged, meanwhile, demonstrates from the outset that this is not a Venezuelan nation-building story, but the story of young people who define themselves through global media. Unplugged also suggests that the story is unfiltered, raw, or authentic, but this is counteracted by the explicit use of genre tropes throughout.

Given the Romanian setting of the story, its gothic elements, such as monstrous or vampiric characters, deserted towns and shadowy corners, are unsurprising. Although these monsters have a scientific explanation – they are people suffering from elephantiasis and hydrocephalus – they nonetheless make José Antonio feel increasingly wary as his surreal journey to find Luzny Hervasy takes him further in to rural Romania. The story provides an allegory for *desarriago* [rootlessness or uprootings], exemplifying the fear and disorientation that result from leaving behind the familiar and finding oneself in a country where the language, customs and people are unknown. Furthermore, Belkis Barrios (2011, 126) argues that Sánchez Rugeles employs gloomy images and repeated reference to 'tinieblas' [shadows] to evoke the horror and confusion experienced by young people in 'decadent' societies. She maintains that both Venezuela and Romania are decadent societies, places plagued by shortages, corruption and a lack of opportunities.

When thinking about Eduardo Sánchez Rugeles and detective fiction, the most obvious choice of novel to consider is *Jezabel* (2013), which was written to order for Ediciones B's crime fiction collection, Vértigo. In fact, *Qué Leer* magazine (2013a) referred to *Jezabel* as Sánchez Rugeles's first foray into the crime fiction genre. Critic and publisher Luis Yslas, however, called *Transilvania unplugged* 'la novela negra del destierro venezolano del siglo XXI' [the crime novel of the Venezuelan rootlessness of the twenty-first century] (Sánchez Rugeles, 2011b). Sánchez Rugeles himself has confessed his fondness for the genre (*Qué Leer*, 2013a), which shines through in this first novel. Although it differs considerably from a traditional detective story,

Transilvania unplugged presents José Antonio as a kind of detective, following clues and gathering testimony to find the 'criminal', Luzny Hervasy. José Antonio himself recognises the similarities between the bizarre situation he finds himself in and a detective story, stating, 'Si soy capaz de llevar estas sensaciones, estas experiencias, estas miradas, estas irreverencias reales a palabras escritas ganaré, sin duda, el Premio Nobel de Literatura o, al menos, algún concurso de novela negra' [If I'm able to carry these real sensations, experiences, viewpoints and irreverence to the written page I'll undoubtedly win the Nobel Prize for Literature, or at least a crime fiction competition] (220). While foreign detective fiction became very popular in Latin America in the mid-twentieth century, autochthonous detective fiction traditionally enjoyed limited success, due largely to its supposed incompatibility with the widespread corruption and ineffectual justice systems seen to characterise the continent (Simpson, 1990, 21). In an article about the lack of Latin American crime fiction, Mexican writer Carlos Monsiváis (1973) notably claimed, 'Una policía juzgada corrupta de modo unánime no es susceptible de crédito alguno' [No one can believe in the police when they are unanimously judged as corrupt]. However, home-grown detective fiction has seen a sharp increase in popularity since the 1970s, particularly among Post-Boom writers in Cuba, Argentina and Mexico (see Lockhart, 2004; Craig-Odders, 2006). This Latin American detective fiction tends to differ from European and North American models in its distrust of the legal system, often narrating crime from alternative perspectives than the police. As Amelia Simpson (1990, 139) maintains, those who make the format their own create novels which are ideal vehicles for socio-political concerns.

In *Transilvania unplugged*, the merging of a mystery plot with the everyday realities of migrants to and from Venezuela serves to impress upon the reader the impossibility of establishing a secure national identity and allows for criticism of Venezuela's supposed 'twenty-first-century socialism'. Conforming to Laura Marcus's (2003, 255) concept of the 'mirrored selves of detective and criminal', through retracing Luzny's steps, speaking to those who knew him and trying to fit together the pieces of his life, José Antonio identifies with the mysterious character, and begins to question how his own life fits together. On his quest, José Antonio is asked repeatedly who he is and why he is in Romania, which makes him question himself. When Viorica, his Romanian guide, asks him outright whether he is Venezuelan or Romanian, he replies, '¡Qué sé yo!, supongo que venezolano. A veces tengo la impresión de que no pertenezco a ninguna parte' [What do I know! Venezuelan, I suppose. I sometimes feel like I don't belong anywhere] (123). Maieke Krajenbrink and Kate Quinn (2009, 8) argue that, in crime fiction, 'investigations illustrate the fragmentary and illusive nature of identity'. Just as his investigations into Luzny only give subjective, contradictory glimpses into an unrealistic character who bears little resemblance to the real man, in trying to discover his own identity, José Antonio becomes increasingly confused about who he is and where he belongs. *Transilvania unplugged* thus elucidates the breakdown of belief in a stable, definable identity, undermining the official assertion that literature can and should serve as a tool for building a national identity. Sánchez Rugeles further increases this sense of confusion and loss of certainties by employing the typical detective fiction device of withholding, letting the reader know that he is keeping information from them. In the testimonies about Luzny translated from Romanian to Spanish, the phrase 'fragmento sin traducir' [untranslated fragment] appears three times (80, 146, 203). Their translator, Viorica, explains, 'Faltan algunos párrafos. Hay cosas que no me atrevo a traducir' [There are some paragraphs missing. There are things I can't bring myself to translate] (122). This is not a technical problem of words or concepts that have no equivalent in the other language, but an ethical one; she does not dare to translate what she has read. Viorica is concerned about the possible consequences both to herself and to her reader, José Antonio, raising questions about the ethics of intervening in a volatile situation through writing.

As Kate Quinn (2009, 296) maintains, in Latin American detective fiction, 'investigations into the identities of absent individuals [shed] light on contemporary issues'. The investigations into Luzny Hervasy allow comments on both the history of Romania under Nicolae Ceaușescu (1965–1989) and Romania today, which in turn serve as comments on contemporary Venezuelan politics and society. The novel is punctuated with letters that uncover frequently contradictory fragments of Luzny's life and identity: 'El mesero del Palace, el gaviero de Tulcea, el barbero de Brazov y el traductor de Cluj aparecían, de manera jocosa, como los testigos inmediatos de la traición de Luzny' [The waiter from the Palace, the lookout from Tulcea, the barber from Brazov and the translator from Cluj appeared, facetiously, as the witnesses to Luzny's downfall] (39). In her analysis of *¿Quién mató a Cristián Kustermann?* [Who Killed Cristián Kustermann?] by Chilean novelist Roberto Ampuero (1993), Quinn (2009, 302) notes that witness testimony 'says as much about the history of communism during the life of the victim as it does about Kustermann himself'. The same occurs in *Transilvania unplugged*. Through the written testimonies, as well as the conversations that José Antonio has with various witnesses during his investigations, we glimpse the history of Romania under Ceaușescu, a history in which socialism left the people poor and miserable, where crime and corruption reined. It is revealed, for example, that the ministerial elite in Romania got rich through the dealings of the local crime boss, Dracos (139). Given that Romania has been established as a mirror to Venezuela,[4] these references provide a criticism of socialism

---

4 At first, the only obvious link between the two countries is the twinning of Valencia in Venezuela with Sibiu in Romania, described in the first few pages of the novel: 'Se firmaron acuerdos culturales y económicos. El gobierno de Caldera permitió, de manera espuria, sentar lazos amables con los países del bloque soviético' [Cultural and economic treaties were signed. Caldera's government, spuriously, allowed friendly links to be established with the Soviet bloc] (24). However, similarities between the two countries become apparent throughout the novel, from a geographical

in contemporary Venezuela, of its inefficiency, its corruption and the rise of the *boliburguesía* – those who got rich through supporting the Bolivarian Revolution (see Valery, 2009b). Equally, the reference to the 'socialismo personalista del conducatore' [personalist socialism of the *conducatore*] (92) calls to mind the personality cult which characterised the *chavista* regime. Although Chávez himself is never explicitly named, the parallels are so clear that these accounts of Romania under Ceaușescu read as a warning against Bolivarian socialism. When a witness claims, 'El conducatore gobernó para sí, su socialismo era individual yególatra' [The *conducatore* governed for himself, his socialism was individual and egocentric] (53), for example, it is also a criticism of Chávez's style of governing. In this way, *Transilvania unplugged* refutes the myth of 'twenty-first-century socialism', according to which the socialism of the Bolivarian Revolution is different from what came before. The novel insinuates that, rather than innovative, *chavista* socialism is a repetition of previous, corrupt regimes.

In detective fiction, techniques that involve the reader in the story can enhance the effectiveness of the underlying message. This reader identification with the 'detective' is one of the central stylistic features of classic detective fiction according to Marcus (2003, 245), who highlights the similarities between detection and reading. As Linda Hutcheon (1984, 73) explains, 'the logical deductions demanded of the reader place him in the shoes of the detective himself'. In *Transilvania unplugged*, the central role of the question 'Who is Luzny Hervasy?' is made clear from the very opening, as in the prologue, '"Decir" todo lo que sepa de Luzny Hervasy' ['To say' all you know about Luzny Hervasy] is stated as one of the conditions for help to find José Antonio (12),[5] suggesting that the puzzling character plays a key part in his eventual disappearance. The question is asked again and again throughout the novel, leading readers to join José Antonio in his quest for answers, piecing together information alongside him. Accordingly, readers are primed to search for deeper meanings in what is written, not only to solve the mystery, but to understand the political content of the novel. As Sánchez Rugeles (2011c, 142–143) made clear in his acceptance speech for the 2010 Uslar Pietri Prize, he believes writing should have both socio-political and aesthetic value. By using tropes of detective fiction in criticism of the Bolivarian Revolution, he demonstrates the literary value of a genre that he has always enjoyed and is able to make a political stand without sacrificing storytelling to political content.

As well as incorporating aspects of the gothic and detective fiction, the form of *Transilvania unplugged* is conditioned by both the overwhelming array of popular culture referents – films, television, music – available simultaneously, and the prevalence of the internet and social media. In this

resemblance between Bucharest and Caracas (16) to the peripheral position of both countries (Romania in the European Union and Venezuela in Latin America) and mass youth emigration.
5 The question comes from a foreign reporter who speaks only a rudimentary Spanish.

FORM AND POPULAR CULTURE   143

respect, Sánchez Rugeles's work can be compared to the 'post-nationalist' McOndo writers, such as Alberto Fuguet and Edmundo Paz Soldán, whose novels revolved around popular culture and technology as a way to place Latin Americans in global society as opposed to the exotic 'Other' (Fuguet and Gómez, 1996). In his study of the effects of globalisation and connectivity on culture, *The Barbarians*, Alessandro Barricco (2006, 68) suggests that 'the barbarians' – his ironic term for young producers and consumers of culture – use books to complete sequences of meaning that begin elsewhere. A book has value in so far as it relates to meanings created elsewhere. Barricco (2006, 92) argues that the internet, especially Google, has led to 'a collective mutation' whereby sense is made through links between different sources of information, breaking down geographical and chronological borders. In addition, the advent of multitasking has led to 'constellations of meaning' (Barricco, 2006, 98), as the different activities carried out simultaneously affect how each one is understood. *Transilvania unplugged* is full of references to the media and the internet; one particularly striking example is when Emilio reads the news online, checks his emails and talks to José Antonio on MSN messenger all at the same time. Sánchez Rugeles recreates the sounds and sights of this online multitasking for the reader:

> Emilio (*Conectado*). José Antonio Galleti «iosepagalleti@hotmail.com» (*Ausente*) Rectángulo naranja. Sonido analógico. Emilio dice: ¿Estás? Melodía bufa. Emilio dice: ¿Dónde estás? *José Antonio está ausente y es posible que no conteste.* www.globovision.com: Lluvias fuertes, ciudad colapsada. Correo electrónico (1) Recibido: Promoción de Timberland. Sonido analógico. José Antonio dice: ¡Emilio! (193)

> [Emilio (*Connected*). José Antonio Galleti «iosepagalleti@hotmail.com» (*Offline*). Orange rectangle. Analogue sound. Emilio says: Are you there? Comical sound. Emilo says: Where are you? *José Antonio may not reply because his or her status is set to Away.* www.globovision.com: Heavy rains, city collapsed. (1) new email: Timberland Sale. Analogue sound. José Antonio says: Emilio!]

This continues over three pages, becoming further confused as María Gabriela begins to talk to Emilio at the same time. As Belkis Barrios highlights (2011, 124), after María Gabriela and José Antonio both type messages, it is unclear to which person Emilio's response of 'No me jodas' [Don't fuck with me] is directed. Emilio's distraction from the conversation foreshadows how his lack of interest in José Antonio's adventures will lead to the latter's disappearance. In this digital age, Geoffrey Kantaris and Rory O'Bryen (2013, 18) argue, 'network rather than nation' is 'the final referent'. Emilio is not completely cut off from Venezuela, as shown by his browsing the Venezuelan news website. Indeed, having access to news from home when halfway across the world is evidently changing the experience of emigration. However, the nation is just one part of a network of interests and associations with make up his daily experience. The global flow of culture, information and capital as presented through the intermedial form of *Transilvania unplugged* establishes the idea of separating the national from the international as anachronistic.

El niño malo cuenta hasta cien y se retira (Chirinos, 2010), by contrast, engages with the kind of popular culture celebrated by the Bolivarian Revolution, namely the indigenous traditions that are considered part of national heritage. Various indigenous groups in what is now Venezuela used oral storytelling to express their vision of the world and to remember their history, but because this part of the Empire was largely ignored by the Spanish colonialists, and the peoples in this area were small nomadic communities who did not produce the body of literature of the Mayans or Incas, it was not until the 1920s and 1930s that this storytelling tradition began to be recognised (Dinneen, 2001, 10). In *El niño malo* (2010), Juan Carlos Chirinos pays homage to this oral storytelling tradition and the indigenous beliefs it expressed. The stories in *El niño malo* suggest that these traditions can coexist with international avant-garde culture, rejecting the separation between the popular and the elite in Bolivarian rhetoric.

El niño malo is notable in stylistic terms for its incorporation of oral intertexts. These complement the reflections on oral storytelling that become a major narrative theme through the character of Svevo, the local storyteller. The novel explores how to tell a good story, the importance of storytelling to communities, and how storytelling is used to keep traditions alive. A.N. Doane (1991, 78) suggests an oral text has 'generic features understood and recognised by both speakers and hearers, and markers at the beginning and ending that separate it from the aural flow around it'. In *El niño malo* there are two key examples of oral texts: Chapter 15, the story of Rufiño the woodcutter and Yamankabe the ant (67–74); and Chapter 18, in which Eugenio fights a giant ant to rescue the dog Abatón (85–89). The didactic tone of both marks them as oral texts, which start by setting the scene, in the imperfect tense, and work up to a revelation. They are foundational stories told by Svevo to the local community, recounting the origins of Derdriu, the grandmother, and Don Camilo, the dog, respectively. Svevo repeats or reworks these foundational myths night after night in the bar (67), exemplifying how oral storytelling is used to preserve tradition by constantly recreating it. According to Doane (1991, 82), 'the oral performance is in its essence a pattern of indefinite regression to an originary event that can never be imagined outside of the present action/telling'. Everything that is known about Derdriu is known through the stories about her shared in the bar. As the oldest resident of El Pueblo – highlighted by the fact that everyone refers to her only as 'la abuela' [grandmother] – her history has become the local mythology. The most common stories are about how the *abuela*, together with a *duende* (like an elf or an imp, but especially linked to imaginative creation), invented the whole history of the world: 'La historia era más o menos larga y siempre dependía de los conocimientos que el narrador, leñador o granjero, poseyera' [The story was more or less long and always depended on the knowledge that the narrator, woodcutter or farmer, possessed] (54). Oral storytelling is celebrated in *El niño malo* as a sharing of knowledge, both on a practical level (passing down skills or trades) and on a more ontological level, knowledge of how the world came to be.

These stories contain within them intertexts that link them to two very different traditions: indigenous culture and European avant-gardes. In the first story, Rufiño the woodcutter is about to chop down a tree when an ant named Yamankabe appears from inside it and asks him not to, as it is home to the ants who provide food for the humans. They agree instead that the ants will vacate a tree each time Rufiño needs one. This compromise works until, one day, Rufiño follows Yamankabe to an enormous tree full of food. Overwhelmed by greed, Rufiño chops down the tree and food rains on the village. Yamankabe chastises Rufiño for his ignorance, as the tree was the source of the food the ants brought to the villagers and now they have nothing left to bring them. Yet Yamankabe sticks to her word and continues vacating trees to provide wood. Eventually, Rufiño learns that his wife is pregnant and goes to tell Yamankabe the good news; the ant replies by giving the child her name, Derdriu. The story draws on part of the creation myth of the Ye'kuana, an indigenous people of the Orinoco:

> En el principio del mundo los hombres no tenían comida, no había árboles en la tierra, no se sabía cómo hacer un conuco, tampoco había agua. La gente sólo sabía comer tierra [...] La diosa Yamankabe, guardiana de la yuca y dueña de la comida vivía en lo alto del cielo. De vez en cuando Yamankabe enviaba a la tierra a Damodede, un mensajero que traía casabe para los Ye'kuana. [...] Lo mismo hacía la gran hormiga Yak [quien] bajaba agua del cielo para los Ye'kuana. (Velásquez, 1993, 43)

> [When the world began, people did not have food, there were no trees on Earth, they didn't know how to make a plot of land, nor was there water. People only knew to eat earth. The Goddess Yamankabe, guardian of the yuca and keeper of the food, lived high in the heavens. From time to time Yamankabe would send to Earth a messenger, Damodede, who brought cassava bread for the Ye'kuana. So did the giant ant Yak, who would bring water down from the heavens for the Ye'Kuana.]

Other aspects of the myth are present in Svevo's story too, such as a human following the messenger to the tree in which all the food is kept, and the chopping down of the tree. The incorporation of these indigenous myths into the novel asserts that they are still of value today. The story's message to beware of short-term gain at long term expense, for example, seems pertinent to the context of spending oil wealth in populist measures.

Not only are folklore and narratives of origin at the heart of Bolivarian ideas of culture and national identity, but the Bolivarian government has also promoted itself as a defender of indigenous peoples and their cultures.[6] Indigenous communities are portrayed as under threat from capitalism, transculturation and globalisation, and only the Bolivarian Revolution can save them (Becerra Jiménez, 2010). Anthropologist and historian Ronny Velásquez, for example, maintained, 'Casi quedan extintos de no haber surgido un líder como el presidente Chávez, quien es de esa ascendencia, él asumió la negritud y la indianidad como banderas de lucha' [They would be almost extinct had a leader like President Chávez not emerged, who is of the same ancestry, adopting blackness and Amerindianness as banners of struggle] (Becerra Jiménez, 2010). By integrating indigenous stories into *El niño malo*, Juan Carlos Chirinos claims that indigenous culture should not be a political tool for the Bolivarian Revolution but part of the cultural inheritance of all Venezuelans.

As well as indigenous beliefs, the presence of ants in the stories calls to mind Surrealism, particularly given the reference to Surrealist poets later in the book (202–203). The use of ants is a common characteristic in Salvador Dalí's work specifically. Kritsky, Mader and Smith (2013) list 50 works by Dalí featuring ants, including some of his most famous creations, *Un chien andalou* (1928), *The Great Masturbator* (1930), and *The Persistence of Memory* (1931). Ants, Mikhail Iampolski suggests (1998, 173), 'unify the themes of death and eros', as they both symbolise putrefaction and 'function erotically, being associated persistently with pubic hair'. Antonin Artaud, André Breton and Philippe Soupault also used red ants in their work as a symbol for blood, signifying both death and passion (Iampolski, 1998, 174). In *El niño malo*, Chirinos takes ants as a symbol for the meeting of death and eros, which is one of the main themes of the novel. Ants crawl over a sleeping D.Jota as he dreams of seducing Fanny, foreshadowing the disturbing climax of the novel in which D.Jota and Fanny have intercourse among the entrails of Fanny's beloved slaughtered sheep shortly before he leaves her to freeze to death. Kritsky et al. (2013) add that Dalí's ants represent self-loathing and guilt caused by carnal thoughts, feelings experienced by D.Jota in the novel. As foreign, rich elites who made purposefully difficult to understand work, the Surrealists are precisely the kind of influences that the Bolivarian officials would wish to eliminate. By combining these references with aspects of indigenous culture, Chirinos not only demonstrates his appreciation of both, but also makes a stand against the assumption in Bolivarian cultural policy that these two fields should be kept separate.

Popular culture is an amorphous term, which can be interpreted as mass media, as cultural production experienced by multitudes or as the representative behaviours and practices of nations. When representatives of the

---

6 See Mansutti Rodríguez, 2011 for a detailed list of the constitutional articles, laws and policies introduced by the Bolivarian government in relation to indigenous culture.

Bolivarian Revolution claimed to represent and support 'lo popular', they defined this both in opposition to cultural elites and to globalised mass media. The novels analysed in this chapter challenge these categories. Like their 'new novel' and Punto Fijo predecessors, the authors in this study embrace popular genres – the gothic in *Bajo las hojas*, comedy in *Chulapos Mambo* and detective fiction in *Transilvania unplugged* – while *El niño malo* blends indigenous traditions with European cultural references. They celebrate the ability of such genres and traditions to engross readers, to create suspense and to provide a framework of meaning within which to place their story. These novels cross geographical and temporal borders in their influences and intertexts. They reject the limit to the national inherent in the Bolivarian idea of the popular, but often return to national preoccupations – particularly national politics – through these genres, making the national one strand of a network of meanings.

CHAPTER 6

Fiction and Reality

Fiction drawing attention to itself as a fabrication is one of the defining characteristics of metafiction (Cazzato, 1995; Currie, 1995; Waugh, 1995). Through both style and content, the novels discussed in this chapter foreground their own fictionality. Drawing readers' attention to the text as a creation allows authors to assert that writing is an activity which requires special skill in contrast to the Bolivarian vision for a nation of writers, exemplified by Francisco Sesto's comments that 'todos pueden manejar bien la palabra' [everyone can use words well] (Wisotzki, 2006, 38). More than just a reaction against the delegitimisation of the author as an individual talent, however, fiction that highlights its own constructed nature also challenges the official narratives of the Bolivarian Revolution. With the breakdown of grand narratives throughout the twentieth century, the possibility of a mimetic literature has also been questioned across global literary trends, leading to literature that examines perceptions of reality and how they are formed. In the Latin American case, for example, Philip Swanson (1995, 3) observes in the development of the 'new novel' since the mid-1900s how:

> Regional issues give way to a universal epistemological or ontological scepticism and the ordered narrative form which reflected an ordered world view gives way to a fragmented, distorted or fantastic narrative form which reflects a perception of a contradictory, ambiguous or even chaotic reality.

Fiction that highlights its own constructed nature encourages readers to question official narratives. By highlighting the ways in which a reality is created within fiction, the novels examined in this chapter reveal how narrative techniques can be and are used by the Bolivarian government through the media, speeches and official history to create a perception of reality which allows them to maintain their control. In this way, the metafictional trend in these novels – above all, the process of creating reality through oral, written and audio-visual narrative as a key theme in *El niño malo cuenta hasta cien y se retira* (Chirinos, 2010), *Bajo las hojas* (Centeno, 2010) and *Rating* (Barrera Tyszka, 2011) – challenges the Bolivarian Revolution and its ideals.

According to Peter Widdowson (1999, 5), '"Literature" identifies itself quite self-consciously as belonging to the artificial discursive realm of "creative" or "imaginative" writing as opposed to other, more quotidian forms of written communication'. Through the opinions voiced by their characters and their stylistic choices, the authors considered in this chapter express their belief in the value of literature as a creative, imaginative activity. Such literature requires talent and skills, which are negated by the Bolivarian regime's insistence that everyone can write and that all are equally deserving of publication. Defined by 'a self-consciousness of the artificiality of its construction' (Currie, 1995, 2), metafiction gives these authors a way to remind readers of the creative skill required to construct their narratives. One way in which this is achieved is through the figure of the 'author–narrator' or the 'author-in-the-text', who disrupts the narrative to discuss his or her own role in creating the book that we are reading and what it means to be an author (Cazzato, 1995). The most extreme example of this among the corpus featured in this book is the autofictional narrator of *La fama, o es venérea, o no es fama* (Castañeda, 2012), who announces from the very beginning that he is the author of the book that we are reading and that the subject of the book will be the process of its creation. As discussed in Chapter 2, the central concern of *La fama* is how difficult it is to craft a narrative, how many different decisions must be made, and how competing demands are placed upon the author. Equally, among the ever-shifting narratorial voices of *Bajo las hojas* (Centeno, 2010), an authorial voice first outlines what Julio is thinking and then asserts, 'Él, como personaje, no nos interesa, a nosotros nos interesa la historia' [We are not interested in him as a character, what we are interested in is the story] (102), before continuing to tell the story from an impersonal viewpoint. As Silda Cordoliani (2011) highlighted in her presentation of *Bajo las hojas*, on one level the whole novel can be read as an exploration of the work of an author, demonstrating what it takes to craft a novel. More often, the 'author–narrator' is a conventional narrator who 'at his will drops his narratorial mask, letting the reader see the person of the author with a pen in his hand' (Cazzato, 1995, 31). *Chulapos Mambo* (Méndez Guédez, 2011) is a good example of this. For the majority of the novel, the narrator is invisible, immersing readers in the story, only occasionally to remind us that we are reading a piece of fiction which has been created for us. After Henry faints, for example, the narrator states, 'Necesario es aclarar a los lectores que el desmayo de Henry no tuvo consecuencias graves' [It is necessary to clarify to readers that Henry's fainting did not have serious consequences] (33), drawing attention to the author imagining readers for his work. Similarly, the narrator states, 'Para nuestros fines inmediatos, que consisten en seguir contando esta historia con el mayor vigor posible, mejor dejemos que Henry continúe atado a sus creencias' [For our immediate ends, which are to keep telling this story with the utmost effect, we had better let Henry remain attached to his beliefs] (60). Readers are thereby reminded that the author has decided to characterise Henry as stubborn in order to create what he thinks is the best story. Luigi Cazzato (1995, 28) maintains that the author appearing in the text 'makes it difficult for the reader to place him or herself in (or identify with) the world of fiction'. Whereas the mimetic novel suggests that there is a reality simply recreated on the page, the author-in-the-text requires readers to take a step back and consider how the illusion of reality is formed.

Metafictional novels, writes Patricia Waugh (1995, 43), 'tend to be constructed on the principle of a fundamental and sustained opposition: the construction of a fictional illusion (as in traditional realism) and the laying bare of that illusion'. As well as emphasising the creative skill required to write a novel, the foregrounding of fictionality in these texts is a reaction against realism, which, Linda Hutcheon (1984, 43) argues, 'too often [...] became identified with truth, with the universal or with good in general'. Waugh (1995, 44) adds that realism is incompatible with the questioning of grand narratives and certainties in contemporary society. She explains, 'the materialist, positivist and empiricist world-view on which realistic fiction is premised no longer exists' (Waugh, 1995, 44). As Carmen Bustillo (1995, 35) explores, dissatisfaction with the world, a desire for change, difficulties and failure are common features of contemporary Latin American narrative. All the characters in the novels studied here are filled with doubts, disillusioned with the nation, socialism, capitalism, religion and art, incompatible with the certainty and security implied in realist narratives. Consequently, in these metafictional narratives, the conventions of realism are foregrounded, or 'paraded' in Waugh's (1995, 47) terms, in order to demonstrate how inappropriate they are for readers and writers today.

In many ways, *Transilvania unplugged* (Sánchez Rugeles, 2011a) can be read as a document of socio-historical reality, albeit one that paints a very different picture of Venezuela from the official patriotism, portraying disaffection with the country, a lack of national belonging and the perceived shortcomings of the political regime. However, these realistic elements are balanced with a recognition of the fictional, creative and stylised nature of the novel. A reading of *Transilvania unplugged* as a kind of detective fiction is instructive here, given what Stephen Wilkinson (2006, 17) calls the 'explicitly metafictional trend' in the genre. *Transilvania unplugged* begins with 'Mulţumiri' (Thanks) in which Sánchez Rugeles asserts that what we read is inspired by true events (7). This paratextual framing conditions readers' reactions to the text, provoking us to question constantly what is real and what is the product of Sánchez Rugeles's imagination. Paradoxically, after asserting the truthful basis of the text, Sánchez Rugeles reminds readers repeatedly of the fictional nature of the novel. One of the opening sentences, 'Nunca imaginaron que Transilvania sería su perdición' [They never imagined that Transylvania would be their downfall] (13), is typical of detective fiction. It follows the narrative conventions of establishing intrigue and enticing readers to become involved in the mystery. In detective fiction, it is very common to find the characters talking about how the crime to be solved would only ever happen in fiction, not in real life (Hutcheon, 1984, 31). Over and again in *Transilvania unplugged* the characters refer to the literary nature of José Antonio's adventure. We are told, 'José Antonio historiaba una Rumania espectacular: intrigas, traiciones, héroes' [José Antonio was depicting a spectacular Romania: intrigues, betrayal, heroes] (48). Emilio suggests José's story is more a fiction than the truthful account that José maintains it is. Another notable example comes towards the end of the novel, when Emilio turns to a Romanian journalist, Lazar Carabineau, for help to find José Antonio, who has gone missing. After hearing Emilio's account of events, Carabineau exclaims, 'Es una historia extraña, casi literaria. Las coincidencias que surgen en este relato no parecen humanas' [It's a strange story, almost literary. The coincidences that appear in this story don't seem possible] (262). Every time that the characters question the veracity of events recounted, it obliges readers to do the same. Considering what to do with his experience in Romania, José Antonio implies that a novel ought to be believable: '¿Una novela?—se increpó—. Si relato las cosas que me han pasado en los últimos días, esta historia no la creería nadie' ['A novel?', he rebuked. 'If I write the things that have happened to me in the last few days no one would believe that story'] (161). The novel thus questions whether literature should be realistic when reality can be so implausible.

In addition, readers are made to identify with José Antonio as the 'detective' figure. Hutcheon (1984, 72) argues that reading detective fiction is 'an act of interpretation, of following clues to the answer of a given problem', which serves to focus readers on how the story has been constructed. The narrative conventions of detective fiction create certain reader expectations for logic and order, which the reader needs in order to follow the case as they read (Hutcheon, 1984, 72). By contrast, as Michael Holquist (1971, 155) argues, the metaphysical detective story gives us 'not familiarity but strangeness, a strangeness which more often than not is the result of jumbling the well-known patterns of classic detective stories'. *Transilvania unplugged* fits this description of metaphysical detective fiction defying the conventions of classic detective stories. In *Transilvania unplugged*, the criminal is not who we think he is, the detective does not end up solving the crime, and his ultimate downfall results from an unexpected source. In this respect, it is instructive to consider how the motives behind classic detective fiction differ from those apparent in *Transilvania unplugged*. Detective fiction, in its hardboiled, North American form, emerged in the context of urbanisation and industrialisation, as well as what Ernest Mandel (1984, 35) calls 'social corruption'. The conventions of the genre became a way for readers to find order and comfort in these distressing new circumstances. Wilkinson (2006, 17) explains, 'The figure of the detective may be perceived as subjecting the city to a controlling and individualising gaze which ultimately reassures the reader and neutralises the fear of the unknown'. The detective's ability to see the bigger picture, to find reason in seemingly random events, is seen to represent readers' desire better to understand society and other people's motivations. By contrast, *Transilvania unplugged* breaks these conventions of order, as José Antonio loses the plot completely, becoming increasingly confused and eventually abandoning any hope of understanding. Of course, Sánchez Rugeles is not the first to break these conventions, but rather follows many notable examples, above all the work of Borges, in whose short story 'La muerte y la brújula' [Death and the Compass] the search for order turns the detective into a victim. In the case of *Transilvania unplugged*, Sánchez Rugeles uses this removal of reassurance to leave readers feeling disconcerted, lost, or out of their comfort zone. Resisting narrative expectations in this way leads to what Paul Dixon (1985) refers to as 'deautomatisation', breaking readers out of their usual patterns of reading. Convincing readers that they cannot solve the main problem at the heart of the text, Dixon (1985, 20) argues, makes readers focus instead on the book as a creation and recognise 'the illusion, artifice and imitation' inherent within it. By using some of the tropes of the 'intensely self-aware' (Hutcheon, 1984, 72) genre of detective fiction, Sánchez Rugeles draws attention to the fictive and stylised nature of his work, thereby reaffirming his belief in the novel as a creative endeavour. At the same time, by not giving the answers that readers expect, or leaving questions unanswered altogether, the process of reading echoes the experience of those who have left Venezuela since the start of the Bolivarian Revolution, who may find themselves in very different situations to what they are used to and feel disorientated by their new realities.

Like detective fiction, elements of fantasy both highlight the creative skills of the authors and challenge established beliefs. Hutcheon (1984, 32) suggests that fantasy 'force[s] the reader to create a fictive imaginative world separate from the empirical one in which he lives'. Authors can only rely on their literary skills to make these worlds believable. Elda Stanco (2013a, 148) praises Juan Carlos Chirinos for his ability to create in *El niño malo cuenta hasta cien y se retira* (2010) 'oneiric excursions to lands of puzzling fantasies, enfolding chimeras and fictitious realities'. Most of the novel is set in a fantastical 'no-place' known only as El Pueblo. In this supposed reality, the protagonist D.Jota witnesses inexplicable events involving the mysterious grandmother:

> La abuela se acerca al alce y éste huye; pero ella lo detiene con un chillido, como de murciélago. El alce baja su cornamenta hasta el suelo y, ante la mirada incrédula y ambiciosa de D.Jota, comienza a hundirse en el suelo hasta que sólo pueden distinguirse las puntas de sus cuernos. (59)

> [The grandmother approaches the elk and it runs away; but she detains it with a shriek, like that of a bat. The elk lowers its antlers to the ground and, before D.Jota's incredulous and ambitious gaze, starts to sink into the ground until only the tips of its antlers are visible.]

Fantasy writing facilitates creative thinking by making readers imagine settings or actions impossible in the real world. Hutcheon (1984, 77) argues that having to create this fictional world for themselves in their imagination provides readers 'the freedom – or the "escape" – of an ordered vision, perhaps a kind of "vital" consolation for living in a world whose order one usually perceives and experiences only as chaos'. In the middle of the novel, D.Jota has a dream in which his attempts at intercourse with Fanny are repeatedly thwarted, and end in his arrest for public indecency (135–146). All the events in this dream sequence are plausible and set in recognisable locations in Caracas, including the Plaza Bolivar and the Central University of Venezuela campus. The dream juxtaposes the uncanny, otherworldly quality of the rest of the novel, thereby drawing attention to how the 'reality' of the novel has been crafted by Chirinos. At the same time, the distinction between the realistic dream and the fantastic reality encourages readers to consider the blurred borders between reality and fiction in our own lives and the societies we live in.

Because metafiction 'explicitly and overtly lays bare its condition of artifice', Patricia Waugh (1995, 42) argues, it 'explores the problematic relationship between fiction and life'. This is a key concern of *Todas las lunas* (Kozak Rovero, 2013), in which the lines between fiction and history, defined by the characters as an objective account of true facts, are blurred. Fernanda – the oldest member of the group and a mother figure to the rest – is a professional historian and believes firmly in the distinction between fact and fiction. In a letter to Véroncia, Fernanda writes, 'Sigo investigando sobre la historia – certezas, no ficciones como las que ven ustedes en el pasado – de Estefanía y de nuestros cada vez más lejanos antecesores' [I'm still researching the history – truths, not fictions like you all see in the past – of Estefanía and our ever more distant relatives] (146). For Fernanda, the distinction between fiction and history lies in the incorporation of testimonies capturing the lived experience of those involved in the events recounted. She explains, 'Yo quiero que este libro nuestro sea tomado como testimonio de unas existencias temerarias pero muy reales. Para que fuese creíble tenía que escucharse la voz de cada quien' [I want this book of ours to be taken as evidence of some reckless but very real lives. For it to be believable, each person's voice had to be heard] (258). Fernanda values authenticity and truth, in the form of testimony, above more aesthetic criteria. While Fernanda insists that as a historian she is interested in real facts (259), Véronica problematises the idea of any knowable historical truth. Véronica refers to 'aquellas maldades a las que Fernanda siempre ha llamado historia y Robin y yo, literatura' [those wicked deeds that Fernanda has always called history and Robin and I literature] (85), claiming that what has been propagated as history has been fabricated through narrative. Véronica's arguments recall those of Hayden White (1975), who maintains that history is not objective, as historians must construct a narrative from events, using literary structures or archetypal plots. The same events can be plotted as a tragedy, comedy, romance, epic or satire, depending on the way in which the teller wants them to be interpreted. Caught between Fernanda and Véronica's competing stances, readers are faced with the impossibility of knowing what really happened and what has been made up. Despite Fernanda's affirmation that 'quienes lean esta historia deben saber que nuestras vidas han sido punto por punto como las cartas, memorias, diarios, crónicas' [whoever reads this story must know that our lives have been point for point as the letters, memoirs, diaries and *crónicas* say] (266), narrative conventions can lead to accounts of real-life events being read as fiction. Véronica recounts that Robin's non-fiction accounts are read as fantasy stories, despite his wishes (19). Véronica suggests that their reality is too implausible to be read as truth, especially when published by a famous author. In this way, she acknowledges the impossibility of an author controlling the reception of his or her texts, as audiences will take whatever they want from the text to suit their needs, regardless of authorial intentions. At the same time, she questions verisimilitude in literature: if real life is so unbelievable, why should literature not be fantastical? When the group persuade Robin to write about Loren, they suggest that he make up a story and encourage him to put no limits on his imagination. Robin recounts, 'Me dijeron que era ficción y la ficción es libre' [They told me that it was fiction and fiction is free] (210). Although only a brief observation, the comment is loaded with meaning. It implies that the very nature of fiction is unbounded imaginative creation and as such it should not be contained by external concerns. Nonetheless, having to fabricate a story throws Robin into turmoil (216). Robin is aware that even if he identifies this piece of writing as fiction it will still influence the way that his readers view him, his 'family' and their reality.

The examples so far all demonstrate how fiction involves making a reality, turning words into characters, settings and actions for readers to believe in and follow. This is evident in the etymology of the word fiction; from the Latin *fingere*, 'fiction' implies 'a kind of aesthetic "forming", "fashioning" or "shaping"' (Widdowson, 1999, 101–102). Beyond forming a story, as the metafictional texts analysed in this chapter explore, fiction has the power to shape readers' ideas and perceptions of the real world. This power is evident throughout *Transilvania unplugged* (Sánchez Rugeles, 2011a), to give just one example. Apart from a brief search on Wikipedia, all Emilio knew about Romania before he travelled there was 'la Rumania trágica, urdido por literatos románticos' [the tragic Romania, plotted by literary romantics] (14). Consequently, he is surprised by the disjuncture between the fiction and the real Romania: 'Emilio imaginaba algo más sórdido, inhóspito, un desierto salvaje poblado de vampiros u osamentas de turcos' [Emilio had imagined something more sordid, inhospitable, a wild desert peopled by vampires or Turkish skeletons] (22). Emilio's Romanian friend Alex Nicea explains to him that Bram Stoker never went to Romania and yet the Transylvania known by the West was invented by him (129). Nonetheless, Alex adds, Romanians have exploited the Dracula myth, partly for the economic benefits of increased tourism, but also because this shared mythology links them to the West culturally (129). Sánchez Rugeles also references how fiction has been instrumental in creating stereotypes of Latin Americans. The statement 'Caía la noche y, más que mágica, la realidad le resultaba superflua' [Night was falling and, more than magical, reality seemed to him superfluous] (179) alludes to the argument that, since the Boom of the 1960s and 1970s, North American and European audiences have expected Latin American writers to employ magical realism, which carries with it stereotypes of Latin Americans as exotic and, at worst, primitive (see Fuguet and Gómez, 1996; Nichols and Robbins, 2015, 59). Despite the potential for writing to promulgate stereotypes, writing is also seen as the antidote to stereotypes and misrepresentations. The Romanian Carol Dutu – the alter ego of Luzny Hervasy, whom Emilio has befriended unwittingly – urges Emilio to escape Romania and to write the truth that he learned there, 'que Rumania nunca podrá ser parte de Occidente, que somos un pueblo triste, acomplejado y solitario' [that Romania will never be part of the West, that we are a sad, solitary people with an inferiority complex] (242).

Given how literature can shape the way that readers view the world, Patricia Waugh (1995, 47) warns that the conventions of realism 'endorse and sustain power structures'. By presenting something as true, writers can make readers believe it, including the idea that established power relations are natural or to the benefit of those subordinated within such structures. Metafiction offers 'resistance within the form of the novel itself', drawing attention to the devices used not only in fiction, but in forming any narrative (Waugh, 1995, 47), including journalism and official history. By highlighting the way that events are plotted in fiction and to what effect, metafiction encourages readers to consider how the same process takes place for factual discourses. According to Jeffrey Cedeño (2007, 35):

> Ciegos ante los términos reduccionistas que estructuran la crisis política [...] muchos venezolanos cruzan indistintamente realidades y ficciones – paranoias apocalípticas, utopías triunfalistas, compromisos revolucionarios, resistencias reaccionarias, claras indiferencias.
>
> [Blind before the reductive terms that structure the political crisis, many Venezuelans mix up truths and fictions indeterminably – apocalyptic paranoia, triumphalist Utopias, revolutionary commitments, reactionary resistances, clear indifferences.]

This blurring of the boundary between truth and fiction was at the heart of the increasingly violent and destructive polarisation of Venezuelan society. As Fernando Coronil (2005, 93) explains, each side believed vehemently that their truth was *the* truth, often with insufficient knowledge and understanding of the complex social, political and economic processes at work in Venezuela. When people were encouraged to question the borders between truth and reality, it was still within ideologically polarised frameworks. One of the main aims of the Plan Revolucionario de Lectura [Revolutionary Plan for Reading], the reading programme introduced by the Bolivarian government in 2009, for example, was to 'desarrollar en las comunidades una lectura crítica de la realidad' [develop a critical reading of reality among communities] (Ministerio del Poder Popular para la Cultura, 2009, 15). In practice, this 'critical reading' encouraged readers to dismantle the myths of capitalism and imperialism in favour of socialism and a Latin American, Caribbean identity (Ministerio del Poder Popular para la Cultura, 2009, 15). By contrast, the metafictional texts analysed in this chapter encourage a critical reading of reality that is antithetic to the Bolivarian government. *El niño malo cuenta hasta cien y se retira* (Chirinos, 2010) presents the charismatic storyteller as a political leader, shedding light on how Chávez's rhetorical skills allowed him to cement his power, while *Bajo las hojas* (Centeno, 2010) and *Rating* (Barrera Tyszka, 2011) explore explicitly the ways in which writing was used and abused by the Bolivarian government to fashion a reality that fits their needs; *Bajo las hojas* through a fantastical allegory and *Rating* through a study of the *telenovela*.

Through the character of Svevo ('el cuentacuentos' [the storyteller]) in *El niño malo cuenta hasta cien y se retira*, Chirinos (2010) explores how 'truth' is created through storytelling, and the power that this ability bestows upon the storyteller. Although most of the novel takes place in the mysterious 'El Pueblo', far from Venezuela, parallels can still be drawn between Svevo and Hugo Chávez as the 'oral president' (Barrera Linares, 2006b), who ruled through speech more than through legal documents (Dabove, 2011). *El niño malo* shows clearly how in storytelling the borders between truth and fiction are blurred. According to A.N. Doane (1991, 79), 'The intention of the traditional oral performer is to "tell the truth" as he and his audience have always understood it: within the resources of his language, that leaves him free to invent considerable detail and to connect the performance to his present audience'. Svevo at first thinks he cannot tell stories because nothing worth telling has happened to him (111), but Eugenio encourages him to tell other people's stories as his own (116). Buoyed by the realisation that it is acceptable to invent details to create a believable story, Svevo lets his imagination run wild. He becomes so confident in the truth of his stories that when a group of students accuse him of having stolen one of his tales from a pirate film, he swears, 'Qué me lleven los demonios de los mares si lo que digo no es verdad' [May the sea demons take me if what I say is not true] (121). As Doane (1991, 81) explains, 'truth' in oral performances does not necessarily mean an objectively provable fact, but rather a statement that the audience will believe to be true because it fits with their already established stance. Svevo's stories are valid because they relate to the way that his listeners understand life. A good example of this is Svevo's story (56–57) about how Derdriu and a *duende* invent the things on Earth, from animals to aeroplanes. He recounts:

> '¿Y si lanzamos al hombre a la luna?', preguntó la abuela y el duende, ayudado por su ingenio, inventó lo del Apolo XI y toda esa historia de

la caminata por la luna. Al final, la televisión nos mostró esas imágenes, que, todos lo sabemos, son inventos de los 'americanos' para engañar a los rusos ... (57)

['And what if we sent man to the moon?' asked the grandmother and the *duende*, aided by her ingenuity, invented the Apollo XI thing and that whole story about walking on the moon. In the end, the television showed us those images, which, we all know, were invented by the 'Americans' to trick the Russians ...]

Svevo's story is confused, suggesting both that Derdriu and the *duende* sent man to the moon and that the moon landings were an American scam. Although this is a common conspiracy theory, the reference to 'americanos' in this speech echoes *chavista* rhetoric against U.S. imperialism. The quotation marks around 'americanos' reinforce the argument that the United States has no right to monopolise a term that refers to people from Canada to Chile. The audience does not notice the contradictions in Svevo's narrative, as they are involved in the story, the 'we all know' obliging them to agree. Juan Pablo Dabove (2011, 120), argues that 'the people' to which Chávez always referred did not exist outside of his speech, suggesting that 'the moment of synthesis, in which "the people" is born, is the voice of Chávez, his digressive and totalising answers'. Svevo demonstrates this totalising rhetoric, bringing diverse strands into his stories to keep everyone happy. Moreover, Svevo is convincing because he involves his audience in the performance. Franz Bäuml (1984, 36) observes in oral storytelling a 'dynamic means of structuring texts that directs the traditional audience in its participation in the structuring of the performative situation, for composition and reception are simultaneous in the oral text'. As he tells a story, Svevo gauges what his audience wants to hear and adapts his narrative accordingly. A similar trait was observable in Chávez's communication, with Luís Pedro España (2009) suggesting that the president used language to create perceptions of participation among his followers. Svevo's performance is also physically impressive: 'Cuando Svevo comenzaba a contar historias, su rostro cambiaba y parecía el mismísimo duende recordando sus tratos con la abuela' [When Svevo began to tell stories, his face would change and he would resemble the *duende* himself remembering his dealings with the grandmother] (56). In her fascinating study of Chávez's political communication, mimetisation and the politics of identity-building, Elena Block (2016, 3–4) describes Chávez as a 'spell-binding storyteller' who used this skill to create an 'emotional bond' with voters. Dabove (2011, 109) similarly compares Chávez to Caliban, a barbarian who used words, the preserve of the elite, against them. The parallels between Svevo and Chávez are heightened by the fact that Svevo rises to a position of political power through his storytelling talents. This man who 'apenas sí había aprendido a leer y escribir' [had barely learned to read and write] (111) is able first to earn a handsome living wowing tourists and waitresses in the dockside bar (117) before becoming the political leader of his native El Pueblo. We are told, 'Si alguna vez se les hubiera ocurrido tener un alcalde, nadie hubiera dudado en dar el puesto a Svevo, quien ya lo era sin necesidad de elecciones' [If it had ever occurred to them to have a mayor, nobody would have doubted in giving the job to Svevo, who already did it without needing elections] (85). By exposing how Svevo shapes ideas of history and belonging for the people of El Pueblo through his rhetorical skills, *El niño malo* sheds light on how Chávez's rhetoric, 'dirigida a maravillar' [designed to wow] (Coronil, 2005, 96), could have the same effect on Venezuelan voters.

Having grown up among the radical Left of 1960s and 1970s Venezuela, Israel Centeno became a fierce critic of Chávez and his government, who Centeno perceived as having betrayed the revolutionary ideals of those movements. Following his 2002 novel, *El complot* [The Conspiracy], in which a fictional guerrilla attempts to assassinate the president, Centeno received death threats and ultimately fled the country, becoming a writer-in-residence at City of Asylum, Pittsburgh. Since then, a major theme of his prolific literary output has been the exploitation of writing by those in power to sustain their power through creating their own truth. His 2010 novel *Bajo las hojas* is a prime example of this. The story of a struggling Venezuelan writer who is hired by the government, Centeno's epic and fantastical novel exposes the fabrication behind what is perceived as real in contemporary Venezuela, asserting that those who control writing control history. When Julio, in desperate need of work, is offered a position writing for the government, he is immediately sceptical, stating, 'Vaya, un trabajo literario para el alto gobierno. ¿Qué? ¿Van a reescribir el Código del Presidente o a inventarse un nuevo magnicidio? ¿Van a redactar una nueva Constitución?' [Wow, a literary job for the upper echelons of government. What? Are they going to rewrite the Presidential Code or invent a new assassination? Are they going to write another Constitution?] (23). This snide comment belies his disdain for the government's attitude towards writing and his belief that the only writing that they really care about is the documents that guarantee their power. It references various real-life ways in which the government used writing to maintain or increase its power, from the rewriting of the Constitution shortly after Chávez became president, through which the country officially became the Bolivarian Republic of Venezuela. The mention of assassination attempts also suggests that Chávez's repeated references to attempts on his life by opposition forces and especially by the CIA were a way to cement sympathy from voters and encourage distrust of opposition forces. Julio takes the job out of necessity, but remains suspicious. It is later revealed that Julio has been recruited to a mysterious group of 'relatores' [narrators]. The *relatores*, who at certain points take over the narration of the novel, explain, 'Era un trabajo difícil, porque él no era el relator, formaba parte de un equipo de varios relatores que pre-digerían las situaciones, era un grupo élite, ubicuo' [It was a difficult job, because he wasn't the only narrator, he was part of a team of various narrators who pre-directed situations, it was an elite, ubiquitous group] (260). The *relatores* conform to the Bolivarian idea of writing as a collective endeavour, yet them being an elite group contradicts the government's claims to wage war on the elites.

Even before he gets involved with the *relatores*, Julio is well aware of the power of writing to change history, as is his friend Rubén Tenorio, who asserts that:

> Mucha gente ha sido asesinada y sus crímenes han quedado impunes, porque aquellos que han puesto en palabra escrita sus historias movieron una coma, introdujeron un personaje oblicuo, restaron algunos adjetivos y elaboraron alguna coartada. [... L]os que escriben la historia no necesariamente escriben la verdad de los hechos, ellos escriben la fuerza de una ilusión y la ordenan de tal manera que seduce aún más que la verdad. (155–156)

> [Many people have been killed and the crimes have gone unpunished, because those who wrote down their stories moved a comma, introduced an oblique character, left out a few adjectives and came up with an alibi. Those who write the story don't necessarily write the truth of the events, they write an illusion and order it in such a way that it is more seductive than the truth.]

Raising the question of the 'emplotment' of information to form a narrative (White, 1975), Rubén maintains that what really happened does not matter, only the official version of the story, especially when those in power have the resources to make the official version far more appealing to people. His reference to unpunished crimes in this context must surely have hit a nerve with readers aware of the 91 per cent rate of unpunished crimes reported by the NGO Venezuelan Observatory of Violence in 2009 and the claims by the observatory's director Roberto Briceño-León that Chávez barely mentioned problems of insecurity because he did not want voters to associate them with his leadership (Vilella, 2010). *Bajo las hojas* suggests that the authorities, in the form of the *relatores*, have the power not only to cover up crimes, but to alter completely what is perceived as true, to make the innocent guilty and to make doubters believe: 'Luego viene el otro texto y el relato nuevo, y los agredidos se convierten en agresores, el relato te hace dudar, cambiar el discurso, bajar la cabeza, aceptar, y no es tan difícil' [Then comes the other text and the new story, and the victims become the aggressors, the story makes you doubt, change your speech, keep your head down, accept, and it's not so difficult] (258). The reality behind the fantasy of the all-seeing, all-powerful 'Inteligencia Movil' [Mobile Intelligence] who write the scripts to individual lives in the novel is evident in the novel's exploration of the power of writing – in the form of legal documents, propaganda and lobbies – in global politics. Praising Julio's indefatigable efforts since he was recruited to the *relatores*, Rubén Tenorio exclaims that, through writing books, war propaganda, pamphlets for global lobbies, and scripting confessions and witness testimonies, Julio:

Ha actuado en el ejército, ha creado organizaciones ficticias y alzamientos militares inexistentes, ha llamado a insurrecciones imposibles, y construye personajes que se mueven por la calle y capitalizan el descontento, personajes que ineluctablemente decepcionarán y sembrarán de desconcierto a aquellos que aún se empeñan, cada vez menos, pero se empeñan en buscar salidas y dejarán de empeñarse porque si no hay esperanza, el empeño es vano. (259–260)

[He's acted in the army, he's created fictitious organisations and non-existent military uprisings, he's called for impossible insurrections, and he creates characters who move through the streets and foster discontent, characters who will inevitably lose faith and will sow confusion among those who still insist, less and less, but still insist on searching for a way out and will stop insisting because if there is no hope, the effort is in vain.]

Those in the position to write legal documents and official histories hold the power to fabricate a reality that will not be questioned, a reality that enables them to maintain such a position. Centeno suggests that this writing is designed to crush hope, as hope is the only power the opposition have left. This passage alludes to the conspiracies spread by these stories, such as satanic cults intent on overthrowing the government, which are designed to win sympathy and hence cement public support (260). Such conspiracies are common in contemporary Venezuelan politics, from the CIA having caused Chávez's cancer to the opposition hiding all the toilet roll supplies to destabilise the government. Centeno warns readers not to believe such stories spread by *chavistas*, stating explicitly that 'el poder autoritario necesita distorsionar la expresión libre de la sociedad' [the authoritarian power needs to distort the free expression of society] (306). Although Chávez is not named, there can be no doubt that he and his Bolivarian government are the subject of this novel. The narratorial voice, offering the point of view of Julio's former comrades who now form part of the group of *relatores*, affirms, 'Siempre quisimos hacer la historia, era un sueño revolucionario. Ahora, al menos, la intervenimos' [We always wanted to make history, it was a revolutionary dream. Now, at least, we are intervening in it] (312). The word 'intervenir' is used in Venezuela frequently to refer to the government seizing private properties. The *relatores* therefore imply that history no longer belongs to individuals but is the property of the government.

The explicit claims throughout *Bajo las hojas* that writing is being used to mould perceptions of reality and history in order to maintain power and control, are reinforced by the metafictional style of the novel. Cazzato (1995, 33) argues that, 'in an age where the power of language tends to overlap with Power in all instances, hard metafiction employs all of its demystifying potential to expose the functioning of both, through the exposing of its own functioning'. In *Bajo las hojas*, the mysterious collective narrators, who seem to be controlling everything, explain repeatedly how they are manipulating the narration to make it more believable. They exemplify Cazzato's (1995, 31) notion of the 'author–narrator' who 'acknowledges to the reader his presence and power of manipulation [...] challenging the separateness of fiction and reality'. The *relatores* state, for example, 'Ahora, en beneficio de la historia que contamos, es preciso verlo sonreír' [Now, to benefit the story that we are telling, it is necessary to see him smile] (91). Such metafiction reveals how narrative can create an illusion of truth, encouraging readers to question what they take for granted as reality. It must be asked, however, to what extent Centeno's book is able to combat this blurring of truth and fiction. Bourdieu (1993, 96) argues, 'in accordance with the law that one only ever preaches to the converted, a critic can only "influence" his readers in as far as they extend him this power because they are structurally attuned to him in their view of the social world, their tastes and their whole habitus'. Centeno's readers are likely to share similar views as him, as well as a similar level of education. *Bajo las hojas* is a dense and challenging novel, replete with erudite references and constant changes in perspective and narratorial voice that require an engaged and educated reader. Would such a reader not already be aware that history is not objective, that narrative techniques are employed by those in power to create the illusion of truth? Nonetheless, for Centeno at least, writing is a protest against the manipulation of the truth for political ends that is so prevalent in Venezuela. Centeno (2009) maintained, 'Se escribe, pienso yo, porque hay algunas cosas que nos gustaría que fuesen de algún modo y hay otras que nos gustaría que no fuesen del modo que realmente son. Cada historia bien lograda subvierte, altera y resignifica y origina consecuencias' [One writes, I think, because there are things that we would like to be a certain way and there are others that we would like to be different from what they really are. Each successful story subverts, alters, resignifies and has consequences]. Unlike his character Julio, who by the end of *Bajo las hojas* has become so disillusioned and full of self-loathing for his part in the government's manipulation of the truth through writing that he decides not to write again (394), Israel Centeno refuses to give up. Although he could never match the resources of those in power, for as long as he perceives injustice in Venezuelan politics and society he will feel compelled to write about it.

In *Rating* (2010), Alberto Barrera Tyszka offers another example of how what is given to us as reality – in this case 'reality' television – is manipulated and falsified. This creation of reality, following the rules for writing a *telenovela*, is shown to be exploited by the Bolivarian government as a way to maintain and increase their power. The *telenovela* is both one of the most watched television genres worldwide and 'a key cultural ingredient to Venezuela's daily diet' (Acosta-Alzuru, 2011, 245). As Carolina Acosta-Alzuru (2003, 193) highlights, 'Huge audiences that transcend nation, class, culture and gender differences sit daily in front of their television sets' to follow the latest saga. Despite this, few books have been published in Venezuela focusing on *telenovelas* (Acosta-Alzuru, 2011, 245), and not many more that even touch upon the subject. Barrera Tyszka's novel provides a rare insight into the genre, exposing the inner workings of the *telenovela* industry for the first time, through the story of a *telenovela*-style reality show featuring homeless people as contestants.

'La realidad también es un espectáculo' [Reality is also a show] (18), veteran scriptwriter Manuel Izquierdo tells his unwilling apprentice Pablo Manzanares at the beginning of *Rating*. The novel blurs the boundaries between fiction and reality, presenting the behind-the-scenes of *telenovelas* as just as dramatic as what is presented to viewers. At one point, Manuel reimagines his conversations with his boss, Vice President of Special Projects, Rafael Quevedo, as a *telenovela* script:

DE REPENTE, QUEVEDO ENTRA A CUADRO.
QUEVEDO (ALGO INCÓMODO): Perdona el retraso … ¡El tráfico hoy está terrible!
IZQUIERDO (DISIMULA, MIENTE). No te preocupes … Yo acabo de llegar …
QUEVEDO: ¡Perfecto! (MIRA FUERA DE CUADRO, HACIA LAS MESAS) ¿Nos sentamos? (VOLTEA HACIA IZQUIERDO CON CIERTA INTENCIÓN) Tenemos cosas importantes que conversar …
AUDIO: ACORDE. (71)

[QUEVEDO ENTERS THE SHOT SUDDENLY.
QUEVEDO (SOMEWHAT UNCOMFORTABLE): Sorry I'm late … The traffic is terrible today!
IZQUIERDO (PRETENDING, LYING): Don't worry… I just arrived …
QUEVEDO: Perfect! (LOOKS OUT OF SHOT, TOWARDS THE TABLES) Shall we sit? (HE TURNS TOWARDS IZQUIERDO WITH INTENT) We have important things to talk about …
AUDIO: CHORD]

This scene highlights how, in television, sounds, stage directions and camera angles are used to shape viewers' responses, prompting readers to look for similar devices in supposedly factual broadcasting. At the same time, it suggests that people are always acting in real life, adapting their movements and tone of voice to achieve the required response from their interlocutor.

'La realidad también es un espectáculo' also refers to Quevedo's plan to make a *telenovela* out of real life. *Rating* is remarkably prescient; before 'scripted reality' series such as the *Real Housewives of…* or *Jersey Shore* became a widely accepted global television phenomenon, the Venezuelan television executives of *Rating* present as real life a programme that follows a script crafted following the rules of *telenovelas*. Manuel informs Pablo that they will 'intervenir' in the storyline, and although Pablo notes that none of the dictionary definitions of 'intervene' seems relevant to reality television (18), it soon becomes clear that the two will alter details of the contestants' life stories to make them more appealing to viewers. Manuel explains, 'Tenemos que convertir la mierda de esa gente en una historia de amor, un relato de éxito' [We have to convert these people's shit into a love story, a success story] (19). The homeless contestants are moulded to fit one of the stock characters of *telenovelas* – the macho, the innocent virgin, the *femme fatale* – and even given acting lessons. All the while, the viewers are expected to believe that what they are watching is real. The novel therefore encourages readers to question to what extent what is presented to them as true has in fact been fabricated.

Through narration of the writing process, *Rating* examines at length the rules of *telenovelas*, their purpose, and how this reflects the Venezuelan people. Towards the beginning of the novel, Barrera Tyszka establishes the importance of *telenovelas* in the definition of Venezuelan identity, particularly by those outside of Venezuela. Manuel notes, 'Nuestras telenovelas se veían en Europa, en Asia, incluso en algunos países del mundo árabe. Cuando un venezolano estaba de viaje, en el extranjero nos reconocían por el acento: "usted habla igual que en las telenovelas", decían' [Our *telenovelas* were seen in Europe, in Asia, even in some part of the Arab world. When a Venezuelan went travelling, people abroad would recognise us for our accent: 'You speak just like in the *telenovelas*', they'd say] (30). This traditional *telenovela* that Manuel Izquierdo describes throughout the novel, the kind that he has been writing over the course of his 20-year career, always stars a young and beautiful heterosexual couple – usually a poor woman and a rich man – who must overcome obstacles, such as amnesia and evil twins, to reach a happy ending in marriage. This model presents 'unidimensional characters that offer a Manichean view of social roles, that is, the villain is pure evil, the heroine is sweet, virtuous and naïve' (Acosta-Alzuru, 2003, 194). In *Venezuela es una telenovela*, Acosta-Alzuru (2007, 25–27) argues that Venezuelan politics in the Bolivarian period mirror this melodramatic *telenovela* structure, with both the government and the opposition presenting themselves as entirely good and their opponents as entirely evil. Venezuela is the beautiful heroine caught in a series of intrigues and high passions. Political rhetoric can therefore be seen to be plotted in a way that people are familiar with from *telenovelas*, to appeal to similar passions. Acosta-Alzuru (2007, 25) adds that, in *telenovelas*, there is often a character who changes the fate of the others, and that it is common for characters from humble backgrounds to reach the top. For this reason, she suggests, Venezuelans would have found Chávez's rise to power and promises to change the fate of the country familiar and believable. Another similarity between *telenovelas* and Bolivarian politics, as highlighted by *Rating*, is their use of language. Manuel asserts, 'La telenovela no es un tema, no es una historia; sólo es un lenguaje' [The *telenovela* isn't a theme, it's not a story; it's only a language] (198). He recalls that there are certain words, such as *arpía* [harpy], that he would write every single day in his scripts and yet would never use or even hear in the real world (197). This discussion of *telenovela* language calls to mind the very distinctive language of Bolivarian rhetoric, which should already be clear by now from the examples in this book. In particular, we can think of the repeated use of certain archaic words, above all, 'escuálidos' [squalid] and 'oligarcas' [oligarchs], both used to signify members of the opposition, no matter their socio-economic level. Similarly, we are told that 'la *telenovela* es el arte de la repetición' [the *telenovela* is the art of repetition] (124), where the same plots, even the same conversations, are repeated over and over within the same series. This repetition is another characteristic of Bolivarian rhetoric, in which the same messages and slogans are given again and again.

Despite these similarities, *telenovelas* themselves fail to engage with contemporary issues. With a few notable exceptions, such as Leonardo Padrón's series *Cosita Rica*, 'Venezuelan telenovelas have skirted the country's political context' (Acosta-Alzuru, 2011, 268). In *Rating*, Manuel recounts that he only once had the chance to try something different:

> Fue un primer esfuerzo por crear historias distintas, donde podían aparecer los problemas reales de la audiencia. Intentábamos incluir temas como las injusticias del sistema judicial, el hacinamiento carcelario, la corrupción de la clase política, en vez de repetir el típico cuento rosa de la empleada doméstica que se enamora del hijo de una familia millonaria. (161)

> [It was a first attempt to make different stories, where the audience's real problems could be seen. We tried to include topics like the injustices of the judicial system, the overcrowding in prisons, the corruption of the political class, instead of repeating the typical love story of the maid who falls in love with the son of a millionaire family.]

Manuel explains that the programme had some success, but the channel insisted that it was due to the novelty factor, the success would not be repeated, there was no way to sell the programme abroad, and therefore they ought to return to the 'abc clásico' (161). Manuel tries to teach Pablo this traditional model, which governs their writing choices for the *telenovela*-cum-reality show around which the novel revolves. We are told repeatedly that this format works, that it is a hit in the ratings, because what viewers want, what viewers need, is escapism. Both Manuel and his boss, Vice-President of Special Projects Rafael Quevedo, as well as the many earlier scriptwriters to whom Manuel frequently refers, such as the Cuban legend Gerardo Lima, emphasise the viewers' need for something to aspire to. Gerardo taught Manuel when he began writing, 'El público tiene una vida de mierda, triste, aburrida, sin éxito y sin excesos de ningún tipo. La gente se sienta frente al televisor para olvidar su propia mediocridad' [The audience has a shitty life, sad, boring, unsuccessful, and without any kind of excesses. People sit in front of the television to forget their own mediocracy] (161). While the middle class was growing in Venezuela at this time (the 1980s), many people remained living in difficult conditions, hoping for better. For this reason, Gerardo maintained, in *telenovelas*, everyone had to be rich, beautiful and elegant, and luxury had to be visible everywhere (162). *Telenovelas* have to build a fantasy world, hiding away the poverty and scarcity in which many people live:

Los pobres, en el ideal creativo de Lima, jugaban un papel secundario. Si no eran una amenaza delictiva, les tocaba ser entonces sirvientes simpáticos y ciegamente fieles a sus amos: una cocinera chismosa, un chofer tartamudo, un jardinero negro que practica una brujería extraña únicamente cuando debe salvar a la 'niña Isabel' o a la 'señorita María Fernanda' de un peligro terrible. (162)

[The poor, in Lima's creative ideal, played a secondary role. If they weren't a criminal threat, they got to be servants, kind and blindly loyal to their employers: a gossipy cook, a stuttering chauffeur, a black gardener who practises a strange witchcraft only when he needs to save 'little Isabel' or 'Miss María Fernanda' from terrible danger.]

Evident in these descriptions of the generic conventions of *telenovelas* is the conjunction of race and class in Venezuela, where poor people of colour are doubly marginalised (Cannon, 2008). Gerardo displays an equally disparaging view of his typical viewer as 'una mujer que sólo estudió hasta tercer grado de primaria' [a woman who only studied up to the third year of primary school], suggesting that *telenovelas* need to be simple and repetitive for them to understand. Gerardo, Manuel and others involved in the creation of *telenovelas* are highly aware of, and indeed governed by, the profound social inequality that persists in Venezuela. Rather than trying to improve this situation, television executives exploit it for commercial gain. Although little research on the production of *telenovelas* has been carried out, Barrera Tsyzka's portrayal of *telenovela* executives matches the findings from Acosta-Alzuru's pioneering work. The veteran Venezuelan *telenovela* actor Javier Vidal, for example, maintained in an interview with Acosta-Alzuru that, because the majority of the audience are relatively poor and uneducated, 'the message has to be very rudimentary, very primary, lots of repetition and reiteration' (Acosta-Alzuru, 2003, 211). Advocates for the Bolivarian Revolution, Mario Sanoja Obediente and Iraida Vargas Arenas, criticise this attitude of *telenovela* producers in *La revolución bolivariana: historia, cultura y socialismo* [The Bolivarian Revolution: History, Culture and Socialism] (2008). They claim that *telenovelas* are exploitative and directed towards working classes 'con la finalidad de inducirles comportamientos de sometimiento al poder del imperio y la oligarquía político-empresarial venezolano' [in order to induce in them the habit of submitting to the power of the empire and the Venezuelan politico-entrepreneurial oligarchy] (Sanoja Obediente and Vargas Arenas, 2008, 137). *Rating* takes a very different stance, suggesting that the government allows and encourages such escapism to distract from its own failings. The novel implies that this escapism is a particularly Venezuelan trait, stemming from the poverty and low standard of living of a large section of the audience despite the country's wealth. While trying to generate enthusiasm for his project, which will give homeless people the chance to win a house, Quevedo exclaims '¡No hay nada más venezolano que ese sueño, además! ¡Siempre nos hemos creído ricos, siempre estamos pensando que alguien nos quitó la fortuna que era nuestra! ¡Ésa es nuestra historia! ¡Tenemos petróleo y estamos jodidos!' [There is nothing more Venezuelan than this dream too! We've always believed we're rich, we're always thinking that someone stole the fortune which belonged to us! That's our history! We've got oil and we're fucked!] (39). Quevedo's comments reflect the enduring belief in Venezuela that oil will be the key to wealth and happiness for all Venezuelans, as explored perceptively by Fernando Coronil in *The Magical State: Nature, Money and Modernity in Venezuela* (1997) and Miguel Tinker Salas in *The Enduring Legacy: Oil, Culture, and Society in Venezuela* (2009). Using oil revenue to populist ends – funding short-term benefits which win public support – rather than investing in the future has been an enduring problem in Venezuela. As early as 1936, Arturo Uslar Pietri famously wrote an editorial for the newspaper *Ahora*, in which he emphasised the need to 'sembrar el petróleo', that is, to use oil revenue to create a more sustainable economy.

Quevedo's cynical aim to exploit the need for escapism feeds into a wider criticism of the government that permeates the novel. The premise behind the reality show that Quevedo produces is a competition to win a house open to those who were made homeless by the floods. Although never named as such, these floods appear to be the Vargas tragedy of 1999, the first major challenge faced by Chávez as president. Using the floods as a background allows Barrera Tyszka to include in his novel fictional testimonies from a handful of the reported 100,000 Venezuelans affected by the tragedy. These testimonies highlight the lack of infrastructure in Venezuela and the inability of the government to deal with the crisis, as well as the favouritism shown to those who support the regime. Quevedo explains that his idea of using flood victims as contestants came from watching the rain through his window. He tells Manuel and Pablo:

> No ha parado de llover en los últimos días. Los desastres se multiplican. Hay barrios enteros afectados, zonas del país sin luz. El gobierno responsabiliza de todo al fenómeno del Niño y al calentamiento global, pero lo cierto es que cada día que pasa aumentan los derrumbes, dejando a más familias damnificadas, sin techo, sin lugar adonde ir, sin nada. (116)

> [It hasn't stopped raining in the last few days. The disasters are multiplying. There are whole neighbourhoods affected, parts of the country with no electricity. The government blames everything on El Niño and global warming, but what's certain is that with every day that passes there are more landslides, leaving more families flooded, homeless, with nowhere to go, with nothing.]

What is striking here is how the government takes no responsibility for the damage caused. While they cannot control the weather, the infrastructural and housing problems that plague Venezuela clearly exacerbate the situation.

During the audition process for the television programme, one hopeful testifies to the favouritism that he had witnessed in the government's conduct towards the flood victims, suggesting that those closest to the government were put in a Marriott hotel while he ended up in an army tent (160). It is hard to know how much to believe these claims, as, on one hand, such rumours frequently circulated in opposition media and online, while on the other hand, the contestant is trying to impress the producers to win a place on the television show.

Barrera Tsyzka portrays the government as eager to latch on to Quevedo's programme and use it as a chance to show that they are doing something to help the victims. In the build-up to the programme, Quevedo asserts that 'el programa formaría parte de la emergencia nacional que encabeza el gobierno' [the programme will be part of the national emergency effort led by the government] (117). The Bolivarian government as portrayed in *Rating* exemplifies anarchist Rafael Uzcátegui's notion of 'la revolución como espectáculo' [the revolution as a show], as set out in his 2010 book of the same name, in which he argued that the Bolivarian Revolution was maintained via spectacle (see also España, 2009). In *Rating*, the government does very little to help the flood victims, leaving thousands stranded in camps with very poor conditions, yet they are eager to present an image of themselves as caring for the plight of these citizens. Uzcátegui (2010, 228–229) claims that supporters of the Bolivarian Revolution are linked not by marked improvements to their quality of life, but through the images broadcast by the government, adding, 'De allí, la vocación por los largos discursos, o la inauguración permanente de urbanizaciones de viviendas, granjas agrícolas y fábricas gestionadas por sus trabajadores que desaparecen cuando se marchan las cámaras de televisión' [Hence the taste for long speeches, or the permanent inauguration of housing developments, farms and factories run by their works, which disappear as soon as the television cameras leave]. Once Quevedo's programme is on air and attracting an audience, it becomes an unmissable opportunity for propaganda: 'Ya había toda una mesa de negociaciones para que, de pronto, el próximo domingo en la noche, el propio presidente de la República llamara por teléfono a la casa y hablara con los concursantes. Eso lo propuso el propio presidente' [There was now a whole negotiation going on, so that, soon, the following Sunday evening, the president of the Republic himself would call the house and talk to the contestants. The president had suggested it himself] (261). Readers familiar with Chávez's overwhelming media presence would have no trouble believing that he would volunteer to appear on such a programme. The most notable example of his use of the media both to create a bond with voters and to distract people from the many problems faced by the country is his own weekly television programme, *Alo, Presidente*, the first talk show in Latin America to be presented and produced by a president (Block and Negrine, 2017, 188). Journalist Rory Carroll (2013, 51), who once appeared on *Aló, Presidente*, described the programme as:

An unscripted, freewheeling affair, it started at 11 a.m. and could last until sunset, during which Chávez might announce a new agricultural policy, nationalise an industry, hire ministers, fire ministers, assail the U.S., mobilise troops, rap, recite poetry, blow kisses, interview guests, salute Fidel Castro, ride a bicycle, a horse, a helicopter. It was rule by television, and you never knew what might happen.

This making a spectacle out of politics is not simply the government exploiting the media for its own gains. Television executives similarly seek to benefit from the government's desire for spectacle, adapting their output in exchange for favours or support. As the title suggests, the novel portrays television executives' obsession with ratings, the measure of audience share, which dictates everything the networks do: 'El rating es la droga que mueve al canal' [The rating is the drug that moves the channel] (94). Throughout the novel, the extent of their desperation to increase their rating share is made painfully clear, so it is not hard to believe that networks would promulgate Bolivarian ideology if they thought it would draw an audience. Quevedo states at the outset, 'La izquierda también está de moda. Esto podría ser un programa muy revolucionario, ¿no?' [The left is fashionable too. This could be a very revolutionary programme, no?] (19). In this way, Barrera Tyszka once again brings to the page echoes of actual practice within the television industry. One remarkable real-life example of this is the meeting in 2004 between Chávez and Gustavo Cisneros, which was mediated by Jimmy Carter. Cisneros is head of Grupo Cisneros, one of the largest privately held media entertainment organisations in the world. Uzcátegui (2010, 84) recounts that following the meeting, Venevisión, Cisneros's channel, changed from openly favouring one end of the political spectrum to publicising the other. Suspiciously, after this, Chávez did not renew their main competitor RCTV's licence. In *Rating*, we are given examples of the television producers adopting the language of the revolution, such as using 'Porque todos somos un solo país' [Because we are all one country] as a slogan for the new programme (141). However, it is made explicit throughout the novel that the executives are merely playing at socialism. Their show of solidarity is just a front. Far from wanting to help people in need, the network executives want to exploit their suffering to draw in viewers. Quevedo is particularly forceful on this point:

> Necesitamos historias fuertes entre ellos: amor, violencia, sexo. No los vamos a juntar para enseñarlos a leer y a escribir, para que canten el himno nacional y se conviertan en buenos ciudadanos. Eso no le interesa a nadie. Si los carajos no se pelean o no se enamoran, si no se hacen daño o no cogen, la audiencia no va a voltear a vernos. Ése es el reto. Que nos miren y que ya no puedan despegarse de nuestra pantalla. (19–20)
>
> [We need strong stories between them: love, violence, sex. We're not going to bring them together to teach them to read and write, so that they can

sing the national anthem and become good citizens. Nobody cares about that. If the bastards don't fight or fall in love, if they don't hurt each other or screw, the audience won't watch us again. That is the challenge. That they watch and they can't tear themselves away from our screen.]

While Quevedo borrows the revolutionary message of national unity to promote his programme, his contempt towards the lower classes is obvious. He advises Pablo that the contestants 'tienen que seguir confundiendo las erres con las eles. No tienen que perder su mierdita original, ¿entiendes?' [have to keep mixing up their Rs and their Ls. They can't lose their original filth, understand?] (185). Quevedo shows no sympathy for people's poverty or lack of education, but instead sees these disadvantages as sources of entertainment. He has a stereotypical image of poverty, and by sticking with this in his programme he will only reinforce that image for viewers.

As well as the use of television for propaganda, Uzcátegui (2010, 228) lists the imitation of Fidel Castro and the Cuban Revolution among his reasons for calling the Bolivarian Revolution a spectacle. Throughout *Rating*, parallels are drawn between the repetition of Cuban revolutionary rhetoric by the Bolivarian government and the constant recycling of Cuban *novelas*. Manuel recalls how his mentor Gerardo Lima '[n]ació en Cuba y, en los primeros años de la revolución, huyó de la isla según reza la leyenda, llevándose varias maletas hinchados de libretos. Ése fue su equipaje, los grandes éxitos de la radionovela cubana' [was born in Cuba and, in the first years of the revolution, fled the island, so the legend goes, carrying various suitcases stuffed with scripts. That was his luggage, the greatest hits of the Cuban *radionovela*] (123). Manuel notes that many of the *telenovelas* that he wrote for over the years began life as Cuban *radionovelas* or *telenovelas*. To give just one example, 'Yo escribí *Marisela*, que fue una versión nueva de *Ana María*, que a su vez era la versión de *Sombra de ayer*, folletín televisivo escrito por Estefanía Monge, leyenda cubana de la escritura de melodrama' [I wrote *Marisela*, which was a new version of *Ana María*, which in turn was a version of *Shadow of Yesterday*, a soap opera written by Estefanía Monge, Cuban legend of melodrama] (99). As a result of this constant recycling, 'El país consumía melodramas con conflictos extemporáneos y muchas veces ajenos, escritos con una moralina insufrible, dialogados con un lenguaje pomposo, que nadie usaba' [The country consumed melodramas with out-of-date plots and foreign accents, written with an insufferable moralising, with dialogue in a pompous language that nobody used] (100). While the influence of Cuban *novelas* on Venezuelan ones is a fact, Barrera Tyszka's repeated insistence on this matter draws attention to the recycling of language and themes from 1970s Cuba in Bolivarian rhetoric. Just like the *radionovelas*, Castro's revolutionary socialist language and Cold War preoccupations are out of date and alien to many contemporary Venezuelans. Edgar Mejía Galeana (2015, 429) suggests that, in *Rating*, the Bolivarian Revolution is presented as a 'monstrous' adaptation of the Cuban model. He picks up on the word 'intervenir', noting its meaning as suspension of freedom, which takes on further significance when we find out that, for the television show, the flood victims will be confined to a house under 24-hour surveillance. Mejía Galeana (2015, 429) claims 'la novela no puede ser más explícita en cuanto a esa voluntad biopolítica de confinamiento e intervención de los cuerpos de indigentes, esa humanidad desechable' [the novel could not be more explicit about this biopolitical will to confine and supress the bodies of the poor, this disposable humanity]. The programme reveals that promises of housing, as well as providing for other needs, such as food, are an effective means of control. As well as linking this biopolitics to Cuba, Mejía Galeana (2015, 430) notes the hint within *Rating* that this biopolitics has roots in the dictatorship of Marcos Pérez Jiménez (1948–1958), as the house in which the contestants will be confined dates from that era. The allusion to Pérez Jiménez encourages readers to question the official image of the Bolivarian Revolution as a new and radical form of politics for Venezuela.[1]

Under a regime which called itself a socialist revolution but was neither truly socialist nor truly revolutionary, Fernando Coronil (2005, 91) argued:

> La vida cotidiana venezolana se ha convertido en una decodificación permanente del espectáculo público: se practica diariamente el arte de leer entre líneas, de ver detrás de la fachada, de identificar conspiraciones, de descubrir los disimulos del poder y las transfiguraciones de lo que aparece como la verdad.

> [Daily life in Venezuela has become a permanent decoding of the public spectacle: every day, one practises the art of reading between the lines, seeing behind the façade, identifying conspiracies, discovering the tricks of power and the transfigurations of that which appears as truth.]

Metafiction, as 'fiction against its disguised contriving function' (Cazzato, 1995, 28), is a response to the blurred lines between truth and fiction in such a context. By asking readers 'to detect fiction rather than identify with it' (Cazzato, 1995, 29), metafiction both reminds readers that what they are reading has been skilfully crafted by the author and encourages them to continue to detect fiction outside of the novel, in 'reality' television, official histories, news reports and political rhetoric.

---

[1] Michael Derham draws many parallels between the Bolivarian Revolution and the Pérez Jiménez dictatorship in his book *Politics in Venezuela: Explaining Hugo Chávez* (2010).

Conclusion

This book began life with a simple question: what does it mean to be a writer from Venezuela in the context of the Bolivarian Revolution? From reading novels written since Hugo Chávez came to power in 1999, it was clear that questions about why to write, how, and who for were at the forefront of their writers' minds. I therefore set out to analyse the Venezuelan literary field, asking what values were attributed to literature by both the Bolivarian regime and by authors, and how these values had developed through Venezuelan literary history. I use values as a portmanteau to include ideas about the uses of literature (why write, why read) and about literary quality. This book responds to calls by Emilia Bermúdez and Natalia Sánchez (2009) and Ana Afanador et al. (2011) for better understanding of Bolivarian cultural policy, given that both Hugo Chávez and Francisco Sesto have stated that culture is an integral part of the revolutionary 'Process'. It builds on studies of Bolivarian cultural policy by Venezuelan scholars, particularly Gisela Kozak Rovero (2007b; 2008; 2015a) and Manuel Silva-Ferrer (2014), offering an analysis of how the context of Bolivarian cultural policy has had an impact on the content and form of narrative produced outside of the state system. In response to recent definitions of Latin American literature as 'global' (Hoyos, 2015) or 'post-national' (González 2012; Robbins and González, 2014), and building on comments by Miguel Gomes (2012), I argue that the national has an enduring significance for Venezuelan writers, even those operating outside of the state system. Beyond Gomes's assertion that Venezuelan social and political concerns shape the content of narrative, including narrative set outside the country's borders, I maintain that there are structural reasons why we must take the national context into account. For a number of reasons, including the legacy of the Boom, the state funding of literature under Punto Fijo and the relatively low levels of migration from Venezuela, Venezuelan literature has until very recently been markedly absent from the international literary market, particularly when it comes to translation. This means that changes to the state publishing system on which most writers relied have been very deeply felt. It is therefore unsurprising that so much recent fiction responds to the changes in the way that reading and writing were viewed by the state.

The development of Venezuelan literature during the Punto Fijo period (1958–1999) set the stage for the extreme polarisation of the literary field with the emergence of the Bolivarian Revolution (1999 onwards). In this period, disillusionment from political commitment following the failure of the radical leftist movements of the 1960s and 1970s, together with a system of state funding which freed writers from the constraints of the market, meant that literature became increasingly introspective and experimental. The leading voices of this generation, including Salvador Garmendia (1928–2001), Renato Rodríguez (1927–2011) and Adriano González León (1931–2008), continue to inspire Venezuelan writers to create complex, self-reflexive narratives. Miguel Gomes (2010, 833) argues that the fact that writers under Chávez can be compared with Garmendia means little changed between the 1970s and the Bolivarian Revolution in terms of social improvement or trust in politics, despite the repeated claims to radical change in *chavista* slogans.

Bolivarian cultural policy is in many ways a reaction against the foreign influences, the focus on the individual and the limit to an elite audience that characterised the literary field by the end of Punto Fijo. Despite little engagement with the literary field initially, the Bolivarian government made itself present in all stages of literary production, from training writers, through publishing, to distribution and promotion, forming a Ministry for Culture in 2005. Through the Plataforma del Libro y la Lectura, launched in 2007, it both appropriated pre-existing literary institutions and founded new ones, in particular El perro y la rana publishing house. The Plataforma unites the institutions at every stage of literary production in a shared ideology of nationalism, socialism and democratisation. The use of state literary institutions to inculcate 'revolutionary' values and maintain support for the Bolivarian government has been condemned by certain writers and critics. In response, the early 2010s saw the rise of small private publishers and the use of websites and social media to discuss literature, which led to a sense of an alternative community, based on a shared appreciation of literature, being built in opposition to the state-run cultural system. Writers also reached out to audiences outside of national borders, especially as more and more writers moved abroad and began to publish in their new countries. Notably, while freedom from the constraints of the market has traditionally often appeared in definitions of literary autonomy, in the context of state-sponsored literary production in Venezuela, recourse to the private and international markets became a way for some authors to gain more creative freedom, as well as potentially offering them the distinction that the state system could not. However, writing for the market is not without its challenges, especially when Venezuelan literature is not a proven commodity.

While *Chulapos Mambo* (Méndez Guédez, 2011) and *Bajo las hojas* (Centeno, 2010) condemn the connections between a successful or unsuccessful writing career and Bolivarian politics, others, especially *La fama, o es venérea, o no es fama* (Castañeda, 2012), demonstrate different challenges faced by authors who try their luck in the private international literary market. The novels present 'writer–critics' who attest to the significance of well-written literature for them, in response to the perceived threat of a loss of literary quality in the utilitarian approach to literature shown by the Bolivarian government. In their explorations of literary quality, the writer–critics show concern not only about subject matter, but the way a story is crafted, its structure, feeling, and how it will affect readers. *El niño malo cuenta hasta cien y se retira* (Chirinos, 2010), *Todas las lunas* (Kozak Rovero, 2013) and *Rating* (Barrera Tyszka, 2011) all express how reading and writing make their protagonists feel and help them to understand themselves better. These are stories of sadness and failure, but also love and personal connections, which foreground the individual and the familial. In a context of official nationalism and socialism, where the individual is subjugated to the collective and individual experimentation is dismissed as an 'elitist' pursuit which must be 'eliminated' in the name of the 'proletariat', the subjective turn which Raquel Rivas Rojas (2010) observes in writing from the Pérez Jiménez dictatorship (1948–1958) can today once again provide an escape from oppressive grand narratives. Ana Teresa Torres (2006, 923) affirms the need for private and intimate narratives in the face of demands for narratives about national concerns. The texts analysed here emphasise individual processes (Rivas Rojas, 2010, 11) as a means of distancing themselves from the Bolivarian Revolution. *Círculo croata* (Zupcic, 2012) and *Transilvania unplugged* (Sánchez Rugeles, 2011a) also challenge the idea of nation-building literature, as well as the common theme in literature across the world of travel as a means to 'find yourself'. Their writer–protagonists, both second-generation immigrants, rummage through their family histories in search of a story to tell and of answers to their questions about national belonging. As well as fictional writers, real-life writers appear as characters, with Alfredo Bryce Echenique and Mario Vargas Llosa in *Chulapos Mambo* (Méndez Guédez, 2011), Eugenio Montejo in *El niño malo cuenta hasta cien y se retira* (Chirinos, 2010) and Salvador Prasel and William Faulkner in *Círculo croata* (Zupcic, 2012). In contrast to the mass participation promoted in Bolivarian cultural policy, these novels put emphasis on literary talent and respect for literary tradition, placing their own work as a continuation thereof. Linking their own writing to that of an author they admire through quotation, allusion or reference allows the authors to explore issues of importance to them: Méndez Guédez criticises the Bolivarian habit of dismissing writers like himself as elites and putting political concerns over the literary, Chirinos asserts the value of literature and explores issues of being a writer abroad, and Zupcic inserts Venezuela into wider literary tradition. The authors of these novels also display their beliefs about literary quality through their stylistic choices. They engage with popular genres, not to make their books more accessible, but to suit the political or aesthetic aims of their writing. Through elements of the gothic in *Bajo las hojas*, comedy in *Chulapos Mambo* and detective fiction, as well as global popular media, in *Transilvania unplugged*, Centeno, Méndez Guédez and Sánchez Rugeles simultaneously tie their novels into international literary trends and comment on the specific socio-political realities of Venezuela. Through *El niño malo*, meanwhile, Chirinos argues against keeping indigenous culture separate from European cultural references. Experimentation with genre also draws attention to the fictional nature of the novels. Metafiction is both a reaction against the delegitimisation of the author as an individual talent, and a message to readers to detect fiction outside of the novel: in 'reality' television, official histories, news reports and political rhetoric.

Of course, contemporary Venezuelan cultural policy and literary developments do not take place in a void. To understand the novels in this corpus, the wider Latin American context provides instructive points for comparison, particularly the effects on literature of the Cuban Revolution, the factors leading to 'the Boom', and the literary developments such as the 'new novel' and the McOndo generation. Similarly, these books not only speak to or about Venezuela but have wider implications for the study of literature in general. Specifically, they shed light on the uses of metafiction and intertextuality in contemporary literature. I disagree with Joseph Hillis Miller's (2002, 4) claim that 'calling literature "self-reflexive" is a way of calling it powerless'. Far from making them sterile and boring, self-reflexivity gives these novels agency, allowing their authors not only to challenge the ideas about literary value found in Bolivarian cultural policy, but to stand up to a political regime to which they are opposed. In this way, the novels demonstrate 'the freedom-inducing potential of metafiction' (Hutcheon, 1984, 161).

Finally, I hope to have inspired readers to seek out the novels analysed here and continue to explore other aspects of Venezuelan literature, in an effort to counter the relative absence of contemporary Venezuelan narrative in Latin American Studies. As Héctor Hoyos (2015, 205–206) argues, 'it is structural to transnational literary institutions that semi-peripheral works do not receive as much concentrated critical attention "in real time" as central texts do'. This is even more the case with Venezuela, given the factors discussed in this book, such as the absence of Venezuela from the Boom and the traditionally low levels of migration from Venezuela to centres of academic study. Writer Dayana Fraile (2012b) has claimed that the lack of international attention to Venezuelan literature has led Venezuelans to doubt the quality of the work they produce: 'El síndrome del patito feo insufla en sus víctimas la sólida creencia de que la poca o nula atención que recibe la literatura venezolana en la escena internacional se debe a la falta de calidad de su corpus' [The ugly duckling syndrome fills its victims with the solid belief that the little or non-existent attention that Venezuelan literature receives on the international scene is due to the lack of quality of its corpus]. Following Hoyos's (2015, 208) claim that 'to theorize contemporary Latin American literature – to theorize *along with* it – [...] restores an actuality that is lost to belated translation, weak cultural institutions, neglect, and market forces', this book is an attempt to counter these structural issues and bring contemporary Venezuelan fiction to wider critical attention.

Bibliography

Corpus

Barrera Tyszka, Alberto. (2011). *Rating*. Barcelona: Anagrama.
Castañeda, Armando Luigi. (2012). *La fama, o es venérea, o no es fama*. New York: Sudaquia.
Centeno, Israel. (2010). *Bajo las hojas*. Caracas: Alfaguara.
Chirinos, Juan Carlos. (2010). *El niño malo cuenta hasta cien y se retira*. Madrid: Ediciones Escalera.
Kozak Rovero, Gisela. (2013). *Todas las lunas*. New York: Sudaquia.
Méndez Guédez, Juan Carlos. (2011). *Chulapos Mambo*. Madrid: Casa de Cartón.
Sánchez Rugeles, Eduardo J. (2011a). *Transilvania unplugged*. Caracas: Alfaguara.
Zupcic, Slavko. (2012). *Barbie/Círculo croata*. New York: Sudaquia.

References

ACCSI [Acción Ciudadana Contra el SIDA]. (2013). 'Crímenes de odio por orientación sexual, identidad de género y expresión de género' (accessed 26 February 2019).
Acosta-Alzuru, Carolina. (2003). 'Tackling the Issues: Meaning Making in a Telenovela', *Popular Communication*, 1(4), 193–215.
———. (2007). *Venezuela es una telenovela*. Caracas: Alfa.
———. (2011). 'Venezuela's Telenovela: Polarization and Political Discourse in *Cosita Rica*', in David Smilde and Daniel Hellinger (eds.), *Venezuela's Bolivarian Democracy: Participation, Politics and Culture under Chávez*. Durham, NC: Duke University Press, pp. 244–270.
Afanador, Ana, Melany Centeno, Kelvin Malave, Cesar Pastaran and Amando Soriano. (2011). 'Observatorio Venezolano de Cultura y Desarrollo: una necesidad en tiempos de cambio', II Seminário Internacional Políticas Culturais, 21–23 September 2011, Fundação Casa de Rui Barbosa, Brazil.
Alario, Antonietta. (2006). 'Política e ideología en la narrativa venezolana de la última década', in Carmen Díaz Orozco (ed.), *Laberintos del poder*. Mérida: Universidad de los Andes, pp. 31–42.

Alberca, Manuel. (2007). *El pacto ambiguo: de la novela autobiográfica a la autoficción*. Madrid: Biblioteca Nueva.
Allen, Graham. (2000). *Intertextuality*. New York: Routledge.
Almela, Harry. (ed.) (2004). *Cartas a la batalla: desde la razón a la desilusión*. Caracas: Alfadil.
Anderson, Benedict. (2006). *Imagined Communities: Reflections on the Origin and Spread of Nationalism*. 2nd ed. London: Verso.
Avilez, Maritza. (2007). *La segunda oportunidad*. Caracas: El perro y la rana.
Bakhtin, Mikhail. (1984). *Rabelais and his World*. Trans. Hélène Iswolsky. Bloomington: Indiana University Press.
Balza, José. (1977). *D: Ejercicio narrativo*. Caracas: Monte Ávila.
Barragán, Luis. (2005). '"D" de José Balza o el extravío del rock venezolano', *Espéculo. Revista de estudios literarios*. https://webs.ucm.es/info/especulo/numero30/jbalza.html (accessed 26 February 2019).
Barrera Linares, Luis. (2005). 'Garmendia: capitán en puerto literario seguro', in Salvador Garmendia, *El Capitán Kid*. Caracas: Otero, pp. 3–8.
———. (2006a). 'Llegaron los ochenta: confluencia y diversidad en la narrativa finisecular', in Carlos Pacheco, Luis Barrera Linares and Beatriz González Stephan (eds.), *Nación y literatura: itinerarios de la palabra escrita en la cultura venezolana*. Caracas: Equinoccio/Fundación Bigott, pp. 801–817.
———. (2006b). 'Palabras en guerra: enfrentamientos discursivos de principios de siglo', in Carlos Pacheco, Luis Barrera Linares and Beatriz González Stephan (eds.), *Nación y literatura: itinerarios de la palabra escrita en la cultura venezolana*. Caracas: Equinoccio/Fundación Bigott, pp. 873–888.
———. (2012). 'Renato Rodríguez, topo de la narrativa venezolana'. http://barreralinares.blogspot.co.uk/2006/11/renato-rodrguez-topo-de-la-narrativa.html?m=1 (accessed 26 February 2019).
Barrera Tsyzka, Alberto. (2001). *También el corazón es un descuido*. Mexico: Plaza y Janés.
———. (2006). *La enfermedad*. Barcelona: Anagrama.
———. (2009). *Crímenes*. Barcelona: Anagrama.
———. (2011). *Rating*. Barcelona: Anagrama.
———. (2015). *Patria o muerte*. Barcelona: Tusquets Editores.
Barrera Tyszka, Alberto and Cristina Marcano. (2004). *Hugo Chávez, sin uniforme: una historia personal*. Caracas: Debate.
Barricco, Alessandro. (2006). *I Barbari: Saggio sulla mutazione*. Rome: Fandango libri.
Barrios, Belkis. (2011). 'Literatura venezolana de la primera década del siglo XXI: la narrativa de Eduardo Sánchez Rugeles', MA thesis, University of British Columbia.
Bartels, Kathleen. (2008). 'Building Female Cultural Identity: Sor Juana in Contemporary Juvenile Literature', *Cuadernos de Música, Artes Visuales y Artes Escénicas*, 4(1–2), 263–290.
Bäuml, Franz H. (1984). 'Medieval Texts and the Two Theories of Oral-Formulaic Composition: A Proposal for a Third Theory', *New Literary History*, 16, 31–39.
Becerra Jiménez, Richard. (2010). 'La revolución bolivariana encabeza reivindicación de los pueblos indígenas', INPSASEL [El Instituto Nacional de Prevención,

Salud y Seguridad Laborales]. https://web.archive.org/web/20111025010150/http://www.inpsasel.gob.ve/moo_news/Prensa_513.html (accessed 26 February 2019).
Beezley, William and Linda Curcio-Nagy. (2012). *Latin American Popular Culture Since Independence: An Introduction*. 2nd ed. Lanham, MD: Rowman & Littlefield.
Bencomo, Anadeli. (2006). 'El premio Rómulo Gallegos: avatares de una trayectoria', in Carlos Pacheco, Luis Barrera Linares and Beatriz González Stephan (eds.), *Nación y literatura: itinerarios de la palabra escrita en la cultura venezolana*. Caracas: Equinoccio/Fundación Bigott, pp. 763–780.
———. (2007). 'La lógica de los premios literarios: políticas culturales, prestigios literarios y disciplinas de lectura en la época de la literatura transnacional', *Estudios* 14(28), 13–29.
Bermúdez, Emilia and Natalia Sánchez. (2009). 'Política, cultura, políticas culturales y consumo cultural en Venezuela', *Cuaderno Venezolano de Sociología*, 8(3), 541–576.
———. (2013). *Política, cultura y consumo cultural en Venezuela*. Saarbrücken: Dictus Publishing.
Bhabha, Homi (ed.) (1990). *Nation and Narration*. London: Routledge.
Blanton, Casey. (2002). *Travel Writing: The Self and the World*. New York: Routledge.
Blaustein, Daniel. (2011). *Procedimientos miméticos y antimiméticos en obras del 'post-boom'*. Hildesheim: Georg Olms Verlag.
Block, Elena. (2016). *Political Communication and Leadership: Mimetisation, Hugo Chávez and the Construction of Power and Identity*. London: Routledge.
Block, Elena and Ralph Negrine. (2017). 'The Populist Communication Style: Toward a Critical Framework', *International Journal of Communication*, 11, 178–197.
Bloom, Harold. (1997). *The Anxiety of Influence*. 2nd ed. Oxford: Oxford University Press.
———. (2000). *How to Read and Why*. London: Fourth Estate.
Bolaño, Roberto. (2001). 'La paciencia de Bolaño', *Tal Cual*. https://web.archive.org/web/20010720073730/http://www.talcualdigital.com/ediciones/2001/07/09/p23s1.htm (accessed 26 February 2019).
Bourdieu, Pierre. (1993). *The Field of Cultural Production: Essays on Art and Literature*. Cambridge: Polity Press.
Brading, Ryan. (2013). *Populism in Venezuela*. New York: Routledge.
Britto Garcia, Luis. (1999). 'La vitrina rota: narrativa y crisis en la Venezuela contemporánea', in Karl Kohut (ed.), *Literatura venezolana hoy: historia nacional y presente urbano*. Frankfurt: Verveurt, pp. 37–53.
Brockmeier, Jens. (2015). *Beyond the Archive: Memory, Narrative, and the Autobiographical Process*. Oxford: Oxford University Press.
Brodsky, Louis Daniel. (1987). 'William Faulkner's "Impressions" of "Danzas Venezuela": The Original Manuscript', *Studies in Bibliography*, 40, 226–228.
Brown, J. Andrew. (2015). 'Googling McOndo: Papered Multimedia and the Aesthetics of Reading with the Internet', in Matthew Bush and Tania Gentic (eds.), *Technology, Literature, and Digital Culture in Latin America: Mediatized Sensibilities in a Globalized Era*. New York: Routledge, pp. 78–90.

Brown, Katie. (2013). 'Juan Carlos Méndez Guédez Q + A @ Universidad Complutense, Madrid'. https://venezuelanliterature.co.uk/2013/01/27/mendez-guedez-qa/ (accessed 26 February 2019).
——. (2014a). 'Blue Label/Etiqueta Azul de Eduardo Sánchez Rugeles: una historia que cruza fronteras', Anales de literatura hispanoamericana, 42, 15–26.
——. (2014b). 'Interview with Sudaquia Editores Founder Asdrúbal Hernández'. https://venezuelanliterature.co.uk/2013/01/27/mendez-guedez-qa/ (accessed 26 February 2019).
——. (2018). '"There Can Be No Revolution without Culture": Reading and Writing in the Bolivarian Revolution', Bulletin of Latin American Research. Early View. https://onlinelibrary.wiley.com/doi/abs/10.1111/blar.12785 (accessed 5 February 2018).
Bryce Echenqiue, Alfredo. (1970). Un mundo para Julius. Barcelona: Seix Barral.
——. (1977). Tantas veces Pedro. Lima: Libre 1.
Bustillo, Carmen. (1995). El ente de papel. Caracas: Vadell.
——. (1997). La aventura metaficcional. Caracas: Equinoccio.
Buxton, Julia. (2011). 'Venezuela's Bolivarian Democracy', in David Smilde and Daniel Hellinger (eds.), Venezuela's Bolivarian Democracy. Durham, NC: Duke University Press, pp. ix–xxii.
Cannon, Barry. (2008). 'Class/Race Polarisation in Venezuela and the Electoral Success of Hugo Chávez: A Break with the Past or the Song Remains the Same?', Third World Quarterly, 29(4), 731–748.
——. (2009). Hugo Chávez and the Bolivarian Revolution: Populism and Democracy in a Globalised Age. Manchester: Manchester University Press.
Carreño, Víctor. (2013). 'Apuntes para una narrativa de la diáspora venezolana: enfoques, tendencias y problemas', INTI, 77/78, 93–104.
Carroll, Rory. (2013). 'And You Thought Boris Was a Show-off'', Shortlist Magazine (March), 50–52.
Casa Bello. (2013a). 'Formación literaria'. https://web.archive.org/web/20131230072800/http://casabello.gob.ve/formacion-literaria/ (accessed 26 February 2019).
——. (2013b). 'La Comunidad y su Escritura'. https://web.archive.org/web/20131230073123/http://casabello.gob.ve/formacion-literaria/la-comunidad-y-su-escritura/ (accessed 26 February 2019).
——. (2013c). 'Talleres'. https://web.archive.org/web/20130818211059/http://casabello.gob.ve/formacion-literaria/talleres/ (accessed 26 February 2019).
Casanova, Pascale. (2004). World Republic of Letters. Trans. M.B. Debevoise. Cambridge, MA: Harvard University Press.
Casas, Ana (ed.) (2012). La autoficción: reflexiones teóricas. Madrid: Arco Libris.
——. (2014). El yo fabulado: nuevas aproximaciones críticas a la autoficción. Madrid: Iberoamericana.
Casique, Iraida. (2006). 'Modelos de intelectualidad marginal en la narrativa de los sesenta y setenta', in Carlos Pacheco, Luis Barrera Linares and Beatriz González Stephan (eds.), Nación y literatura: itinerarios de la palabra escrita en la cultura venezolana. Caracas: Equinoccio/Fundación Bigott, pp. 605–623.
Castañeda, Armando Luigi. (1994). Mujer desnuda mirando a un enano negro arrodillado. Caracas: Fundarte.

———. (1997). *La crisis de la modernidad*. Caracas: Memorias de Altagracia.
———. (1998). *Historia de la burra y la motocicleta*. Venezuela: Fondo Editorial de la Secretaria de Cultura de Aragua.
———. (2007). *Guía de Barcelona para sociópatas*. Xalapa: Universidad Veracruzana.
———. (2012). *La fama, o es venérea, o no es fama*. New York: Sudaquia.
———. (2015). 'Una entrevista I/III'. Blog post. http://luigicastaneda.blogspot.com/2015/05/nombre-armando-luigi-castaneda-pais-de.html (accessed 26 February 2019).
Castillo E., María Auxiliadora. (2011). 'Transformación de la cultura lectora en Venezuela: políticas y praxis', *Anuario GRHIAL*, 5, 125–168.
Castillo Zapata, Rafael. (1999). 'Último ensayo venezolano: apuntes de fin de siglo', in Karl Kohut (ed.), *Literatura venezolana hoy: historia nacional y presente urbano*. Frankfurt: Verveurt, pp. 77–83.
Castro, Fidel. (1961). 'Palabras a los intelectuales'. http://www.cuba.cu/gobierno/discursos/1961/esp/f300661e.html (accessed 26 February 2019).
Cazzato, Luigi. (1995). 'Hard Metafiction and the Return of the Author–Subject: The Decline of Postmodernism?', in Jane Dowson and Stephen Earnshaw (eds.), *Postmodern Subjects/Postmodern Texts*. Amsterdam: Rodopi, pp. 25–41.
Cedeño, Jeffrey. (2007). 'Venezuela en el siglo XXI: "Nuevos hombres, nuevos ideales, nuevos procedimientos"', *Guaraguao*, 11(24), 23–49.
CELARG. (2013). 'Seminarios y Talleres de Creación Celarg, septiembre–diciembre de 2013'. https://web.archive.org/web/20140529171347/http://www.celarg.org.ve/Espanol/talleres%20de%20creacion%20celarg_2013.html (accessed 26 February 2019).
CENAL. (2013). 'Estudio del comportamiento lector, acceso al libro y la lectura en Venezuela 2012'. https://queleerblog.files.wordpress.com/2013/04/estudio-del-comportamiento-lector-y-acceso-a-la-lectura.pdf (accessed 26 February 2019).
Centeno, Israel. (1992). *Calletania*. Caracas: Monte Ávila.
———. (2002). *El Complot*. Caracas: Alfa.
———. (2009). 'Reflexión sobre la lectura y la escritura', *Exploradores del abismo*. http://exploradoresdelabismo.tumblr.com/post/95168221/reflexion-sobre-la-lectura-y-la-escritura-israel (accessed 8 April 2015). No longer available.
———. (2010). *Bajo las hojas*. Caracas: Alfaguara.
———. (2013). 'Cuando el libro solo sirve para apuntalar una mesa coja', *El País*. 13 March. https://elpais.com/cultura/2013/03/12/actualidad/1363114154_095559.html (accessed 26 February 2019).
———. (2015a). *La Marianne*. New York: Sudaquia.
———. (2015b). 'The Books'. https://israelcen3.wixsite.com/israelcenteno/books (accessed 26 February 2019).
CERLALC [Centro Regional para al Fomento del Libro en América Latina y el Caribe]. (2012). *El libro en cifras*. Bogotá: CERLALC-UNESCO.
Chacón, Inma. (2009). 'Gisela Kozak Rovero: la reinvención de Caracas', *Arbor*, 185(A1), 31–53.
Chambers, Ross. (1990). 'Irony and the Canon', *Profession*, 90, 18–24.
Chirinos, Juan Carlos. (2010). *El niño malo cuenta hasta cien y se retira*. Madrid: Ediciones Escalera.
———. (2011). *Nochebosque*. Madrid: Casa de Cartón.

——. (2012a). 'Por qué no hablo de la revolución'. Blog post. http://juancarloschirinos.blogspot.co.uk/2012/03/por-que-no-hablo-de-la-revolucion.html (accessed 27 October 2012). No longer available.

——. (2012b). 'Mañas de las élites'. Blog post. http://juancarloschirinos.blogspot.co.uk/2012/10/manas-de-la-elite.html (accessed 27 October 2012). No longer available.

——. (2013a). *Gemelas*. Madrid: Casa de Cartón.

——. (2013b). 'Irse, volver y regresar', in Silda Cordoliani (ed.), *Pasaje de ida: 15 escritores venezolanos en el exterior*. Caracas: Alfa, pp. 49–54.

——. (2014). (Juance) '@KatieBrown161 No puedo imaginar un mejor fin para mis novelas: Difundir el amor por la poesía de Eugenio Montejo: ¡un lujo! ¡Gracias!'. 4 November 2014, 12:35 a.m. Tweet.

——. (2015). Personal communication.

——. (2017). *Venezuela: biografía de un suicidio*. Madrid: La Huerta Grande.

——. (2018). Personal communication.

Chirinos Castellanos, Laura. (2014). 'Aproximación hermenéutica a las migraciones literarias de "Transilvania unplugged" y "Liubliana"', *Arjé*, 8(14), 155–172.

Cioran, Emil M. (2010). *A Short History of Decay*. London: Penguin.

Cloyd, Jerry S. and Alan P. Bates. (1964). 'George Homans in Footnotes: The Fate of Ideas in Scholarly Communication', *Sociological Inquiry*, 34(2), 115–128.

Cohn, Deborah. (2004). 'William Faulkner's Ibero-American Novel Project: The Politics of Translation and the Cold War', *Vanderbilt e-Journal of Luso-Hispanic Studies*. http://ejournals.library.vanderbilt.edu/index.php/lusohispanic/article/view/3187/1379 (accessed 26 February 2019).

Colectivos de trabajadores y trabajadoras del ministerio del poder popular para la cultura. (2012). 'Logros y retos culturales de la Revolución bolivariana. Encuentros regionales cultura y socialismo. Borrador para el debate'. http://www.cendis.gob.ve/descargas/Logros%20y%20Retos.pdf (accessed 13 October 2014). No longer available.

Colmenares Gil, Carlos. (2012). 'The Ghosts of the City', Welcome address at *Palabras Errantes* event, 'Voices from the Venezuelan City', Passing Clouds, Dalston, London, 22 October 2012. http://www.palabraserrantes.com/carlos-colmenares-gil-the-ghosts-of-the-city/ (accessed 26 February 2019).

Comisión Permanente de Educación, Cultura, Deportes y Recreación de la Asamblea Nacional. (2005). 'Ley Orgánica de la Cultura'.

Congreso de la República de Venezuela. (1975). 'Gaceta oficial de la República de Venezuela. Número 1.768 Extraordinario. Ley del Consejo Nacional de la Cultura'. https://docs.venezuela.justia.com/federales/leyes/ley-del-consejo-nacional-de-la-cultura.pdf (accessed 26 February 2019).

Conroy, Jane. (2003). 'Introduction', in Jane Conroy (ed.), *Cross-Cultural Travel*, Papers from the Royal Irish Academy International Symposium on Literature and Travel Cross-Cultural Travel, National University of Ireland, Galway, November 2002. New York: Peter Lang, pp. xiii–xxii.

Cordoliani, Silda. (2011). 'O todo se está escribiendo o ya ha sido escrito', Text read at the presentation of *Bajo las hojas*. https://500ejemplares.wordpress.com/2011/02/25/o-todo-se-esta-escribiendo-o-ya-ha-sido-escrito/ (accessed 26 February 2019).

——. (2013). 'Del país a la distancia', in *Pasaje de ida: 15 escritores venezolanos en el exterior*. Caracas: Alfa, pp. 7–9.
Coronil, Fernando. (1997). *The Magical State: Nature, Money, and Modernity in Venezuela*. Chicago: University of Chicago Press.
——. (2005). 'Estado y nación durante el golpe contra Hugo Chávez', *Anuario de Estudios Americanos*, 62(1), 87–112.
Corral, William H. (2013). 'General Introduction', in William H. Corral, Juan E. de Castro and Nicholas Birns (eds.), *The Contemporary Spanish American Novel: Bolaño and After*. New York: Bloomsbury, pp. 1–18.
Craig-Odders, Renée W. (2006). 'Introduction', in Renée W. Craig-Odders, Jackie Collins and Glen S. Close (eds.), *Hispanic and Luso-Brazilian Detective Fiction: Essays on the Género Negro Tradition*. Jefferson, NC: McFarland and Co., pp. 1–15.
Currie, Mark. (1995). 'Introduction', in Mark Currie (ed.), *Metafiction*. London: Longman, pp. 1–18.
Dabove, Juan Pablo. (2011). 'Hugo Chávez and Maisanta: Orality, Literacy and the Construction of Legitimacy Outside the Law', *Vanderbilt e-Journal of Luso-Hispanic Studies*, 7. https://ejournals.library.vanderbilt.edu/index.php/lusohispanic/article/view/3269 (accessed 26 February 2019).
Davies, David. (2007). *Aesthetics and Literature*. London: Continuum.
De Castro, Juan E. and Nicholas Birns. (2010). *Vargas Llosa and Latin American Politics*. New York: Palgrave Macmillan.
De Stefano, Victoria. (2002). *Lluvia*. Caracas: Oscar Todtmann.
Deleuze, Giles and Félix Guattari. (1975). *Kafka pour une littérature mineure*. Paris: Éditions de Minuit.
Derham, Michael. (2010). *Politics in Venezuela: Explaining Hugo Chávez*. Berne: Peter Lang.
Diaconu, Diana. (2017). 'La autoficción: simulacro de teoría o desfiguraciones de un género', *La Palabra*, 30, 35–52.
Dinneen, Mark. (2001). *Culture and Customs of Venezuela*. Westport, CT: Greenwood Press.
Dix, Hywel. (2017). *The Late-Career Novelist*. London: Bloomsbury.
Dixon, Paul B. (1985). *Reversible Readings: Ambiguity in Four Modern Latin American Novels*. Tuscaloosa: University of Alabama Press.
Doane, Alger N. (1991). 'Oral Texts, Intertexts and Intratexts: Editing Old English', in J. Clayton and E. Rothstein (eds.), *Influence and Intertextuality in Literary History*. Madison: University of Wisconsin Press, pp. 75–113.
Donoso, José. (1972). *Historia personal del 'Boom'*. Barcelona: Anagrama.
Doubrovsky, Serge. (1977). *Fils*. Paris: Éditions Galilée.
Duncan, James and Derek Gregory. (1999). 'Introduction', in James Duncan and Derek Gregory (eds.), *Writes of Passage: Reading Travel Writing*. London: Routledge, pp. 1–13.
The Economist. (2008). 'Propaganda, Not Policy: Hugo Chávez Has Not Ended Illiteracy'. https://www.economist.com/the-americas/2008/02/28/propaganda-not-policy (accessed 26 February 2019).
Ediciones Puntocero. (2010). 'Dossier de prensa 2009'. https://edicionespuntocero.files.wordpress.com/2010/11/dossier-puntocero-01.pdf (accessed 26 February 2019).

EFE. (2010). 'J. Carlos Chirinos presenta su novela de amor y humor, con retranca venezolana'. http://escaletra.blogspot.co.uk/2010/04/el-nino-malo-se-pasea-por-efe.html (accessed 26 February 2019).
El País. (2009). 'Perú sanciona a Bryce Echenique por plagio de diversos artículos', *El País*. 9 January. https://elpais.com/cultura/2009/01/09/actualidad/1231455605_850215.html (accessed 26 February 2019).
El Periódico de Catalunya. (1999). 'Los hijos hartos del Boom', *El Periódico de Catalunya*. 7 May, pp. 142–143.
Emanuelsson, Dick. (2010). '"Ahora rompemos con la dictadura de Hollywood": Hugo Chávez (1)', *Vimeo*. https://vimeo.com/18034180 (accessed 26 February 2019).
España, Luis Pedro. (2009). *Detrás de la pobreza: diez años después*. Caracas: UCAB [Universidad Católica Andrés Bello].
Falcón, Dubraska. (2011). 'Sesto dio balance cultural sin números: el ministro de Cultura compareció frente a la Asamblea Nacional'. http://sosmuseosve.blogspot.com/2011/02/sesto-dio-balance-cultural-sin-numeros.html (accessed 26 February 2019).
Falcón, Dubraska and Angel Ricardo Gómez. (2011). 'Se acabaron los "ratones" en Lectura', *El Universal*. 8 February. https://web.archive.org/web/20130313085813/http://www.eluniversal.com/2011/02/08/til_art_se-acabaron-los-rat_2185143.shtml (accessed 26 February 2019).
Fermín, Daniel. (2011). '95% de los libros del mundo no llegan al país', *El Universal*. 8 February. https://web.archive.org/web/20170318154057/http://www.eluniversal.com/2011/02/08/til_art_95-de-los-libros-de_2185546.shtml (accessed 26 February 2019).
———. (2012). 'La literatura debe hacer reír', *El Universal*. 27 February. https://web.archive.org/web/20120702192605/http://www.eluniversal.com/arte-y-entretenimiento/120227/eduardo-sanchez-rugeles-la-literatura-debe-hacer-reir (accessed 26 February 2019).
———. (2013a). 'Para volver a leer', *El Universal*. 4 January. http://www.eluniversal.com/arte-y-entretenimiento/130104/para-volver-a-leer (accessed 5 February 2018). No longer available.
———. (2013b). 'Editoriales no consiguen papel', *El Universal*. 23 May. https://web.archive.org/web/20130607154718/http://www.eluniversal.com/arte-y-entretenimiento/130523/editoriales-no-consiguen-papel (accessed 26 February 2019).
Fernandes, Sujatha. (2017). *Curated Stories: The Uses and Misuses of Storytelling*. Oxford: Oxford University Press.
Ficción Breve. (2015). 'La séptima edición del Premio de la Crítica abre su convocatoria'. http://ficcionbreve.org/la-septima-edicion-del-premio-de-la-critica-abre-su-convocatoria/ (accessed 26 February 2019).
Fraile, Dayana. (2012a). 'Sobre la escasa difusión de la literatura venezolana en el exterior'. http://dayanafraile.blogspot.com/2012/04/sobre-la-escasa-difusion-de-la.html (accessed 26 February 2019).
———. (2012b). 'Apuntes sobre el síndrome del patito feo y la escena literaria venezolana'. http://www.dayanafraile.blogspot.co.uk/2012/04/apuntes-sobre-el-sindrome-del-patito.html (accessed 26 February 2019).

Franco, Jean. (1994). *An Introduction to Spanish American Literature*. Cambridge: Cambridge University Press.
——. (2002). *The Decline and Fall of the Lettered City: Latin America in the Cold War*. Cambridge, MA: Harvard University Press.
Frow, John. (2006). *Genre*. London: Routledge.
Fuentes, Carlos. (1969). *La nueva novela hispanoamericana*. Mexico: J. Moritz.
Fuguet, Alberto and Sergio Gómez. (1996). *McOndo*. Barcelona: Mondadori.
Gallegos, Rómulo. (1929). *Doña Bárbara*. Barcelona: Araluce.
García Canclini, Néstor. (1995). *Hybrid cultures: strategies for entering and leaving modernity*. Trans. C.L. Chiappari and S.L. López. Minneapolis: University of Minnesota Press.
García Julio, Ana. (2012). Personal communication.
Garmendia, Salvador. (2006). 'Los sesenta: la disolución del compromiso', in Carlos Pacheco, Luis Barrera Linares and Beatriz González Stephan (eds.), *Nación y literatura: itinerarios de la palabra escrita en la cultura venezolana*. Caracas: Equinoccio/Fundación Bigott, pp. 593–603.
Gaspar Károsy, Catalina. (2005). 'De saberes y miradas: metaficción y narrativa venezolana contemporánea', *Letralia*. https://letralia.com/128/ensayo01.htm (accessed 26 February 2019).
Genette, Gérard. (1997). *Palimpsests: Literature in the Second Degree*. Trans. C. Newman and C. Doubinksy. Lincoln: University of Nebraska Press.
Gomes, Miguel. (1997). 'Venezuela', in Verity Smith (ed.), *Encyclopedia of Latin American Literature*. Chicago: Fitzroy Dearborn, pp. 838–841.
——. (2010). 'Modernidad y abyección en la nueva narrativa venezolana', *Revista Iberoamericana*, 76(232–233), 821–836.
——. (2012). 'La persistencia de la nación: el país como signo en la nueva narrativa venezolana', *Revista de Estudios Hispánicos*, 46(1), 115–133.
Gomes Porras, Mauricio. (2017). 'Pocaterra, el último relámpago', *El Nacional*. 7 December. http://www.el-nacional.com/noticias/columnista/pocaterra-ultimo-relampago_214388 (accessed 26 February 2019).
González, Aníbal. (2012). 'Introducción', *Revista de Estudios Hispánicos*, 46(1), 51–53.
González Iñárritu, Alejandro. (Producer and director). (2003). *21 Grams* [motion picture]. United States: Focus Pictures.
González León, Adriano. (1968). *País portátil*. Barcelona: Seix Barral.
Gott, Richard. (2000). *In the Shadow of the Liberator: Hugo Chávez and the Transformation of Venezuela*. London: Verso.
Guerra, Rubi. (2007). 'Introducción', in *21 por XXI: antología del cuento venezolano del siglo XXI*. Caracas: Ediciones B.
——. (2012). *La tarea del testigo*. Caracas: Lugar Común.
Guerrero, Gustavo. (2005). 'Réquiem por un galardón', *El País*. 15 July. https://elpais.com/diario/2005/07/15/cultura/1121378402_850215.html (accessed 26 February 2019).
——. (2013a). 'Todos los rostros de Venezuela', in Silda Cordoliani (ed.), *Pasaje de ida: 15 escritores venezolanos en el exterior*. Caracas: Alfa, pp. 11–22.
——. (2013b). '¿Qué literatura tras Chávez?' *El País*. 13 March. https://elpais.com/cultura/2013/03/08/actualidad/1362767093_120316.html (accessed 26 February 2019).

Guevera, Ernesto. (1965). 'El socialismo y el hombre en Cuba', https://www.marxists.org/espanol/guevara/65-socyh.htm (accessed 26 February 2019).
Hendrickson, Janet. (2014). 'The Reader as Translator: Rewriting the Past in Contemporary Latin American Fiction', in Timothy R. Robbins and José Eduardo González (eds.), *New Trends in Contemporary Latin American Narrative: Post-National Literatures and the Canon*. New York: Palgrave Macmillan, pp. 169–189.
Hernández G., Ana María. (2010). 'A la Cultura Urbana le pasaron cerrojo', *El Universal*. http://www.eluniversal.com/2010/07/21/til_art_a-la-cultura-urbana_1979121.shtml (accessed 5 February 2018). No longer available.
Hillis Miller, Joseph. (2002). *On Literature*. London: Routledge.
Holquist, Michael. (1971). 'Whodunit and Other Questions: Metaphysical Detective Stories in Post-War Fiction', *New Literary History*, 3(1), 135–156.
Hoyos, Héctor. (2015). *Beyond Bolaño: The Global Latin American Novel*. New York: Columbia University Press.
Hughes, William. (2013). *Historical Dictionary of Gothic Literature*. Lanham, MD: Scarecrow Press.
Hutcheon, Linda. (1984). *Narcissistic Narrative: The Metafictional Paradox*. New York: Routledge.
———. (1995). *Irony's Edge: The Theory and Politics of Irony*. London: Routledge.
Iampolski, Mikhail. (1998). *The Memory of Tiresias: Intertextuality and Film*. Berkeley: University of California Press.
Kantaris, Geoffrey and Rory O'Bryen. (2013). 'The Fragile Contemporaneity of the Popular', *Latin American Popular Culture: Politics, Media, Affect*. Woodbridge: Tamesis, pp. 1–42.
Kobbe, Montague and Adolfo Calero. (2009). 'Words in Revolution', *The Latin American Review of Books*. 1 October. http://www.latamrob.com/words-in-revolution/ (accessed 26 February 2019).
Kozak Rovero, Gisela. (2005). *Pecados de la capital*. Caracas: Monte Ávila.
———. (2007a). *Latidos de Caracas*. Caracas: Alfaguara.
———. (2007b). 'Políticas culturales y hegemonía en la revolución bolivariana: "ética y estética socialistas"', *Estudios*, 14(28), 101–121.
———. (2008). *Venezuela, el país que siempre nace*. Caracas: Alfa.
———. (2011). *En rojo*. Caracas: Alfa.
———. (2013). *Todas las lunas*. New York: Sudaquia.
———. (2014). *Ni tan chéveres ni tan iguales*. Caracas: Puntocero.
———. (2015a). 'Revolución Bolivariana: políticas culturales en la Venezuela Socialista de Hugo Chávez (1999–2013)', *Cuadernos de literatura*, 15(37), 38–56.
———. (2015b). Personal communication.
———. (ed.) (2017). *Siete sellos: crónicas de la Venezuela revolucionaria*. Madrid: Kalathos.
Kozloff, Nicolas. (2008). *Revolution! South America and the Rise of the New Left*. New York: Palgrave Macmillan.
Kranjenbrink, Marieke and Kate M. Quinn. (2009). 'Introduction', *Investigating Identities: Questions of Identity in Contemporary International Crime Fiction*. New York: Rodopi, pp. 1–10.

Kristal, Efraín (ed.) (2005). *The Cambridge Companion to the Latin American Novel*. Cambridge: Cambridge University Press.
Kritsky, Gene, Dan Mader and Jessee J. Smith. (2013). 'Surreal Entomology: The Insect Imagery of Salvador Dalí', *American Entomologist*, 59(1), 28–37.
Kumaraswami, Par. (2007). 'Cultural Policy, Literature and Readership in Revolutionary Cuba: The View from the 21st Century', *Bulletin of Latin American Research*, 26(1), 69–87.
———. (2012). 'Peripheral Visions? Literary Canon Formation in Revolutionary Cuba', in *Rethinking the Cuban Revolution Nationally and Regionally: Politics, Culture and Identity*. Oxford: Wiley-Blackwell, pp. 91–109.
Laberinto. (2012). 'Carta de apoyo a Alfredo Bryce Echenique'. 16 October. https://sclaberinto.blogspot.com/2012/10/carta-de-apoyo-alfredo-bryce-echenique.html (accessed 26 February 2019).
Lecarme, J. (1994). 'L'autofiction: un mauvais genre?' RITM, 6, 227–249.
Letralia. (2008). 'Falleció el poeta Eugenio Montejo'. 2 June. https://letralia.com/188/0605montejo.htm (accessed 26 February 2019).
Levine, Suzanne Jill. (2005). 'The Latin American Novel in English Translation', in Efraín Kristal (ed.), *The Cambridge Companion to the Latin American Novel*. Cambridge: Cambridge University Press, pp. 297–317.
Linares, Albinson. (2012). 'Barrera Tyszka: "El éxito y el fracaso son lo mismo, siempre vienen juntos"', *Prodavinci*. 6 May. http://historico.prodavinci.com/2012/05/06/artes/barrera-tyszka-el-exito-y-el-fracaso-son-lo-mismo-siempre-vienen-juntos/ (accessed 26 February 2019).
Lionetti, Julieta. (2012). 'Venezuela's Book Import Controls Threaten Cultural Isolation', *Publishing Perspectives*. 22 February. http://publishingperspectives.com/2012/02/venezuelas-book-import-controls-threaten-cultural-isolation/ (accessed 26 February 2019).
Liscano, Juan. (1984). *Panorama de la literatura venezolana actual*. Caracas: Alfadil.
Lockhart, Darrell B. (2004). *Latin American Mystery Writers: An A-to-Z Guide*. Westport, CT: Greenwood Press.
Lodge, David. (1995). 'The Novel Now', in Mark Currie (ed.), *Metafiction*. London: Longman, pp. 145–160.
López Ortega, Antonio. (1999). 'Fin de siglo: extremidades de la cultura venezolana', in Karl Kohut (ed.), *Literatura venezolana hoy: historia nacional y presente urbano*. Frankfurt: Verveurt, pp. 67–76.
———. (2006). 'Las voces secretas (notas para un lector desprevenido)', in Antonio López Ortega (ed.), *Las voces secretas: el nuevo cuento venezolano*. Caracas: Alfaguara, pp. 11–19.
———. (2012). 'Cuatro pérdidas', *Prodavinci*. 22 June. http://historico.prodavinci.com/blogs/cuatro-perdidas-por-antonio-lopez-ortega/ (accessed 26 February 2019).
Lovera, Roberto. (2012). '"Todas las lunas" de Gisela Kozak', *Código Venezuela*. http://www.codigovenezuela.com/2012/03/opinion/roberto-lovera-de-sola/todas-las-lunas-de-gisela-kozak-por-roberto-lovera-de-sola (accessed 1 March 2015). No longer available.

Lozada, Mariel. (2016). 'Venezuela brilló en el Premio Latinoamericano de Diseño Editorial', *Efecto Cocuyo*. 24 April. http://efectococuyo.com/efectococuyo/venezuela-brillo-en-el-premio-latinoamericano-de-diseno-editorial/ (accessed 26 February 2019).
Ludmer, Josefina. (1994). 'El coloquio de Yale: máquinas de leer "fin de siglo"', in Carlos Alonso and Josefina Ludmer (eds.), *Las culturas de fin de siglo en América Latina*. Buenos Aires: Virtebo, pp. 7–24.
Macht de Vera, Elvira. (1979). *La crítica social en tres novelas venezolanas: vidas oscuras, En este país ... Cubagua*. Caracas: Universidad Central de Venezuela.
Maldonado, Jason. (2010). 'Bajo las hojas'. Blog post. 18 November. http://palabrasyescombros.blogspot.com/2010/11/bajo-las-hojas.html (accessed 26 February 2019).
Mandel, Ernest. (1984). *Delightful Murder: A Social History of the Crime Story*. Minneapolis: University of Minnesota Press.
Mansutti Rodríguez, Alexander. (2011). 'Culturas indígenas y revolución bolivariana', *Revista venezolana de ciencia política*, 39, 45–62.
Marcus, Laura. (2003). 'Detection and Literary Fiction', in M. Priestman (ed.), *The Cambridge Companion to Crime Fiction*, Cambridge: Cambridge University Press.
Márquez Rodríguez, Alexis. (1999). 'La función de la editorial Monte Ávila en el proceso de la literatura venezolana', in Karl Kohut (ed.), *Literatura venezolana hoy: historia nacional y presente urbano*. Frankfurt: Verveurt, pp. 85–94.
Martínez, Marta Eugenia. (2006). '¿Y entonces? ¿Qué es lo que pasa con la narrativa venezolana?', in Carmen Díaz Orozco (ed.), *Laberintos del poder*. Mérida: Universidad de los Andes, pp. 19–29.
Martínez Bachrich, Roberto. (2013). '"Todas las lunas" o el triunfo de lo irreal', *Prodavinci*. 2 March. http://historico.prodavinci.com/2013/03/02/arte/todas-las-lunas-o-el-triunfo-de-lo-irreal-por-roberto-martinez-bachrich/ (accessed 26 February 2019).
Mata, Humberto. (2007). *Pie de página*. Caracas: El perro y la rana.
Mejía Galeana, Edgar. (2015). 'Avatares de la subjetividad intelectual venezolana y del Estado comunal bolivariano en "Rating" (2011) de Alberto Barrera Tyszka', *Revista Canadiense de Estudios Hispánicos*, 39(2): 415–437.
Méndez, María Gabriela. (2013). 'Un mundo perdido', *Revista Arcadia*. 18 July. https://www.revistaarcadia.com/impresa/reportaje/articulo/un-mundo-perdido/32469 (accessed 26 February 2019).
Méndez Guédez, Juan Carlos. (1997). *Retrato de Abel con isla volcánica al fondo*. Caracas: Troya.
——. (2009). *Tal vez la lluvia*. Barcelona: DVD.
——. (2011). *Chulapos Mambo*. Madrid: Casa de Cartón.
——. (2013a). *Arena negra*. Madrid: Casa de Cartón.
——. (2013b). 'Pretextos del plátano frito', in Silda Cordoliani (ed.), *Pasaje de ida: 15 escritores venezolanos en el exterior*. Caracas: Alfa, pp. 33–39.
——. (2015). *Y recuerda que te espero*. Caracas: Editorial Madera Fina.
——. (2017). *La ola detenida*. Madrid: HarperCollins Ibérica.
Michelutti, Lucia. (2016). '"We Are All Chávez": Charisma as an Embodied Experience', *Latin American Perspectives*, 44(1) 232–250.

Minh-ha, Trinh T. (1994). 'Other than Myself/My Other Self', in George Robertson, Melinda Mash, Lisa Tickner, Jon Bird, Barry Curtis and Tim Putman (eds.), *Travellers' Tales: Narratives of Home and Displacement*. London: Routledge, pp. 9–26.
Ministerio de Comunicación e Información. (2005). 'Misión Cultura'. http://www.minci.gob.ve/wp-content/uploads/downloads/2013/02/misioncultura.pdf (accessed 26 February 2019).
Ministerio del Poder Popular para la Cultura. (2009). 'Procesos del Libro y Plan Revolucionario de Lectura en Venezuela'. http://koha.cenamec.gob.ve/cgi-bin/koha/opac-retrieve-file.pl?id=45a154c24f641f32278b44afde696be6 (accessed 26 February 2019).
Monsiváis, Carlos. (1973). 'Ustedes que jamás han sido asesinados', *Revista de la universidad de México*, 27(7) (March), 1–11.
Montañez Cortez, John. (2013). 'Diez preguntas al escritor Israel Centeno (Caracas, 1958)'. http://www.cervantesmilehighcity.com/2013/02/diez-preguntas-al-escritor-israel.html (accessed 26 February 2019).
Monte Ávila. (2014). 'Quiénes somos: Monte Ávila Editores en el siglo XXI'. https://web.archive.org/web/20140804233934/http://www.monteavila.gob.ve:80/2014/quienes.php (accessed 26 February 2019).
Montejo, Eugenio. (1978). *Terredad*. Caracas: Monte Ávila.
Montilla, Oriana. (2015). 'Lugar Común: balsa para la literatura venezolana', *El Estimulo*. http://elestimulo.com/climax/lugar-comun-una-balsa-para-la-literatura-venezolana-2/ (accessed 26 February 2019).
Munday, Jeremy. (2009). *The Routledge Companion to Translation Studies*. London: Routledge.
Negroni, María. (2009). *Galería fantástica*. Sinaloa: Siglo XXI Editores.
Nichols, Elizabeth Gackstetter and Timothy R. Robbins. (2015). *Pop Culture in Latin America and the Caribbean*. Santa Barbara, CA: ABC-CLIO.
Norberg, Johan. (2010). 'Mario Vargas Llosa: "La idea de que el liberalismo está muerto en América Latina es exagerada"', *La ilustración liberal*. https://www.clublibertaddigital.com/ilustracion-liberal/45-46/mario-vargas-llosa-la-idea-de-que-el-liberalismo-esta-muerto-en-america-latina-es-exagerada-joh.html (accessed 26 February 2019).
Nuño, Ana. (2014). 'An Introduction to New Venezuelan Writing', *Words without Borders*. https://www.wordswithoutborders.org/article/an-introduction-to-new-venezuelan-writing (accessed 26 February 2019).
Olivar, José Norberto. (2008). *Un vampiro en Maracaibo*. Caracas: Alfaguara.
Olivares, Francisco. (2014). 'Best and brightest for export', *El Universal*. 13 September. https://web.archive.org/web/20160207133010/http://www.eluniversal.com/nacional-y-politica/140913/best-and-brightest-for-export (accessed 26 February 2019).
Orwell, George. (1949). *Nineteen Eighty-Four*. London: Secker & Warburg.
Paullier, Juan. (2011). 'Venezuela: una feria del libro en revolución', *BBC Mundo*. 26 March. https://www.bbc.com/mundo/noticias/2011/03/110325_venezuela_feria_libro_filven_revolucion_ideologia_jp.shtml (accessed 26 February 2019).
Payares, Gabriel. (2012). 'Guillermo Parra: "La tradición literaria venezolana no tiene nada que envidiarle a la de nadie"', *Prodavinci*. 14 September. http://

historico.prodavinci.com/2012/09/14/actualidad/guillermo-parra-la-tradicion-literaria-venezolana-no-tiene-nada-que-envidiarle-a-la-de-nadie/ (accessed 26 February 2019).

———. (2013). 'Ese azul que no es el nuestro: un vistazo al modo venezolano de imaginar(se)', *INTI*, 77/78, 169–175.

Pew Research Center. (2013). 'The Global Divide on Homosexuality'. http://www.pewglobal.org/2013/06/04/the-global-divide-on-homosexuality/ (accessed 26 February 2019).

Plataforma del Libro y la Lectura del Ministerio del Poder Popular para la Cultura. (2007). 'Manifiesto sobre la gestión cultural a favor del libro y la lectura'. http://secretariadoculturalcarabobo.blogspot.com/2007/07/manifiesto-sobre-la-gestin-cultural.html (accessed 26 February 2019).

Ponce, Merwin. (2016). 'Polarización política divide familias venezolanas', *Alternos*. 22 August. http://alternos.la/2016/08/22/polarizacion-politica-divide-familias-venezolanas/ (accessed 26 February 2019).

Porras, María Carmen. (2006). 'Tres revistas literarias de los años sesenta y el problema de la cultura nacional', in Carlos Pacheco, Luis Barrera Linares and Beatriz González Stephan (eds.), *Nación y literatura: itinerarios de la palabra escrita en la cultura venezolana*. Caracas: Equinoccio/Fundación Bigott, pp. 625–639.

Portes, Alejandro and Rubén G. Rumbaut. (2001). *Legacies: The Story of the Immigrant Second Generation*. New York: Russell Sage Foundation.

Portuondo, José Antonio. (1963). *Estética y revolución*. Havana: Ediciones Unión.

Posada-Carbó, Eduardo. (1998). 'Fiction as History: The *bananeras* and Gabriel García Márquez's *One Hundred Years of Solitude*', *Journal of Latin American Studies*, 30, 391–414.

Prasel, Salvador. (1975). *Máxima culpa*. Caracas: Monte Ávila.

Prensa-CONAC. (2005). 'Certamen Mayor de las Artes y las Letras en su Capítulo Literatura', *Aporrea*. 17 May. https://www.aporrea.org/actualidad/n16615.html (accessed 26 February 2019).

Primera, Maye. (2009). 'Chávez lanza su revolución cultural', *El País*. 14 May. https://elpais.com/diario/2009/05/14/internacional/1242252001_850215.html (accessed 26 February 2019).

Prodavinci. (2010). 'Fundación para la Cultura Urbana sigue viva'. 5 August. http://historico.prodavinci.com/2010/08/05/prodavinci/fundacion-para-la-cultura-urbana-sigue/ (accessed 26 February 2019).

———. (2012). '5 libros imprescindibles para Juan Carlos Méndez Guédez'. 3 May. http://historico.prodavinci.com/blogs/5-libros-imprescindibles-para-juan-carlos-mendez-guedez/ (accessed 26 February 2019).

PSUV [Partido Socialista Unido de Venezuela]. (2008). 'PSUV lanza el disco "Música para la batalla"'. http://www.psuv.org.ve/temas/noticias/PSUV-lanza-el-disco-Musica-para-la-batalla/#.XHkdt4j7SHt (accessed 26 February 2019).

Punter, David and Glennis Byron. (2003). *The Gothic*. Oxford: Blackwell.

Qué Leer. (2013a). 'Jezabel, en sentido estricto, no es novela negra'. 4 June. https://web.archive.org/web/20150406123653/http://queleer.com.ve/2013/06/04/jezabel-en-sentido-estricto-no-es-una-novela-negra/ (accessed 26 February 2019).

———. (2013b). 'Libros del Fuego, nueva editorial venezolana'. 10 December. https://web.archive.org/web/20150406095856/http://queleer.com.ve/2013/12/10/libros-del-fuego-nueva-editorial-venezolana/ (accessed 26 February 2019).

———. (2015). 'Oscar Todtmann editores sigue apostando a la literatura venezolana'. 2 July. https://web.archive.org/web/20160528201709/https://queleer.com.ve/2015/07/02/oscar-todtmann-editores-sigue-apostando-a-la-literatura-venezolana/ (accessed 26 February 2019).

Quinn, Kate M. (2009). 'Cases of Identity Concealed and Revealed in Chilean Detective Fiction', in Marieke Kranjenbrink and Kate M. Quinn (eds.), *Investigating Identities: Questions of Identity in Contemporary International Crime Fiction*. New York: Rodopi, 295–310.

Quintana, Emilio. (2010). '¿Un Nobel racista, machista y neoliberal?', *La ilustración liberal*. https://www.clublibertaddigital.com/ilustracion-liberal/45-46/un-nobel-racista-machista-y-neoliberal-emilio-quintana.html (accessed 26 February 2019).

Rama, Ángel. (1982). *La novela en América Latina: panoramas 1920–1980*. Santiago: Ediciones Universidad Alberto Hurtado.

Ramírez Requena, Ricardo. (2012). 'Sobre cómo leer a Liubliana', *Libro del día*. 12 June. https://librodeldia.wordpress.com/2012/06/12/sobre-como-leer-a-liubliana-de-eduardo-sanchez-rugeles/ (accessed 26 February 2019).

Reisz, Susana. (2016). 'Formas de autoficción y su lectura', *Lexis*, 15(1), 73–98.

Riffaterre, Michael. (1990). 'Compulsory Reader Response: The Textual Drive', in Michael Worton and Judith Still (eds.), *Intertextuality: Theories and Practices*. Manchester: Manchester University Press, pp. 56–78.

Rivas, Luz Marina. (2011). '¿Irse o quedarse? La migración venezolana en la narrativa del siglo XXI', Paper presented at Jornadas de Investigación Humanística y Educativa, San Cristóbal. https://www.academia.edu/3860554/Irse_o_quedarse._La_migraci%C3%B3n_venezolana_en_la_narrativa_del_siglo_XXI (accessed 26 February 2019).

Rivas Rojas, Raquel. (2010). *Narrar en dictadura: renovación estética y fábulas de identidad en la Venezuela perezjimenista*. Caracas: El perro y la rana.

———. (2011). 'Ficciones de exilio o los fantasmas de la pertenencia en la literatura venezolana', seminar, King's College London, 23 November 2011.

———. (2012). 'Ficciones de exilio o los fantasmas de la pertenencia en la literatura del desarraigo venezolano', in Araceli Tinajero (ed.), *Exilio y cosmopolitismo en el arte y la literatura hispánica*. Madrid: Verbum, pp. 189–206.

———. (2014). 'Ficciones diaspóricas: identidad y participación en los blogs de tres desterradas venezolanas', *Cuadernos de literatura*, 28(35), 226–246.

Robbins, Timothy R. and José Eduardo González (2014). '*Posnacionalistas*: Tradition and New Writing in Latin America', in *New Trends in Contemporary Latin American Narrative: Post-National Literatures and the Canon*. New York: Palgrave Macmillan, pp. 1–13.

Roberts, Kenneth. (2004). 'Social Polarization and the Populist Resurgence in Venezuela', in Steve Ellner and Daniel Hellinger (eds.), *Venezuelan Politics in the Chávez Era: Class, Polarization, and Conflict*. Boulder, CO: Lynne Rienner, pp. 55–72.

Roberts, Nick. (2009). *Poetry and Loss: The Work of Eugenio Montejo*. Woodbridge: Tamesis.
Roche Rodríguez, Michelle. (2013). 'Carlos Pacheco: los festivales literarios nos humanizan y nos ayudan a dialogar', *El Nacional*. 12 April. http://www.el-nacional.com/noticias/historico/carlos-pacheco-los-festivales-literarios-nos-humanizan-nos-ayudan-dialogar_165801 (accessed 26 February 2019).
Rodríguez, Renato. (1963). *Al sur del Equanil*. Caracas: Monte Ávila.
Romero, Juan Manuel. (2013). 'Chulapos Mambo', *Letras*, 55(89), 145–148.
Rose, Jacqueline. (1996). *States of Fantasy*. Oxford: Oxford University Press.
Saavedra, Naida. (2012). 'Forja de una identidad amalgamada: El europeo y el colombiano en la literatura venezolana contemporánea', unpublished doctoral thesis, Florida State University.
Sainz Borgo, Karina. (2014). 'Exile Hangouts: Cuatro escritores venezolanos sobre la diáspora', *Prodavinci*. 15 January. http://historico.prodavinci.com/blogs/exile-hangouts-cuatro-escritores-venezolanos-sobre-la-diaspora-por-karina-sainz-borgo/ (accessed 26 February 2019).
Sánchez Aparicio, V. (2012). 'Chulapos Mambo: mixtura y risa', *El Nacional*. 13 April. http://www.el-nacional.com/noticias/historico/chulapos-mambo-mixtura-risa_170581 (accessed 26 February 2019).
Sánchez Rugeles, Eduardo J. (2010). *Blue Label/Etiqueta Azul*. Caracas: CEC.
——. (2011a). *Transilvania unplugged*. Caracas: Alfaguara.
——. (2011b). 'Transilvania, Unplugged'. 7 April. https://web.archive.org/web/20120127143357/http://sanchezrugeles.wordpress.com/2011/04/17/transilvania-unplugged/ (accessed 26 February 2019).
——. (2011c). *Los desterrados*. Caracas: Ediciones B.
——. (2012). *Liubliana*. Mexico City: Fondo Editoriales Estado de México.
——. (2013). *Jezabel: versión original sin censura*. Caracas: Ediciones B (Kindle ed.).
——. (2014). *Julián*. Caracas: Ediciones B.
——. (2015). '*Transilvania unplugged*, prólogo a la segunda edición'. http://sanchezrugeles.com/viewpost.php?id=810 (accessed 26 February 2019).
Sanoja Obediente, Mario and Iraida Vargas Arenas. (2008). *La revolución bolivariana: historia, cultura y socialismo*. Caracas: Monte Ávila.
Saraceni, Gina A. (2000). 'La lengua del desarraigo: identidad y memoria en las novelas de Roberto Raschella', *Estudios*, 8(16), 199–220.
Sarup, Madan. (1994). 'Home and Identity', in George Robertson, Melinda Mash, Lisa Tickner, Jon Bird, Barry Curtis and Tim Putnam (eds.), *Travellers' Tales: Narratives of Home and Displacement*. London: Routledge, pp. 89–101.
Schulberg, Budd. (1950). *The Disenchanted*. New York: Random House.
——. (2013). *On the Waterfront*. London: Allison & Busby.
Serrano, Carmen. (2010). 'El vampiro en el espejo: elementos góticos en *Yo el Supremo*', *Revista Iberoamericana*, 76(232–233), 899–912.
Sesto, Francisco. (2006). *¿Por qué soy chavista? Razones de una Revolución*. Caracas: Ocean Sur.
Shaw, Donald L. (1998). *The Post-Boom in Spanish American Fiction*. New York: State University of New York Press.
Silva-Ferrer, Manuel. (2014). *El cuerpo dócil de la cultura: poder, cultura y comunicación en la Venezuela de Chávez*. Madrid: Iberoamericana.

Simpson, Amelia S. (1990). *Detective Fiction from Latin America*. Plainsboro, NJ: Associated University Presses.
Sklodowska, Elzbieta. (2003). 'Latin American Literatures', in Philip Swanson (ed.), *The Companion to Latin American Studies*. London: Arnold, pp. 87–106.
Smilde, David. (2011). 'Participation, Politics, and Culture: Emerging Fragments of Venezuela's Bolivarian Democracy', in David Smilde and Daniel Hellinger (eds.), *Venezuela's Bolivarian Democracy*. Durham, NC: Duke University Press, pp. 1–27.
Smilde, David and Daniel Hellinger (eds.) (2011). *Venezuela's Bolivarian Democracy*. Durham, NC: Duke University Press.
Sommer, Doris. (1991). *Foundational Fictions: The National Romances of Latin America*. Berkeley: University of California Press.
Stam, Robert. (1985). *Reflexivity in Film and Literature: From Don Quixote to Jean-Luc Godard*. Ann Arbor, MI: UMI Research Press.
Stanco, Elda. (2013a). 'Juan Carlos Chirinos', in William H. Corral, Juan E. de Castro and Nicholas Birns (eds.), *The Contemporary Spanish American Novel: Bolaño and After*. New York: Bloomsbury, pp. 147–149.
———. (2013b). 'Juan Carlos Méndez Guédez', in William H. Corral, Juan E. de Castro and Nicholas Birns (eds.), *The Contemporary Spanish American Novel: Bolaño and After*. New York: Bloomsbury, pp. 164–167.
Storey, John. (2003). *Inventing Popular Culture*. London: Blackwell.
Súarez, Jésus. (2014). 'Caminos de la novela venezolana actual'. http://undiasea.blogspot.com/2014/10/caminos-de-la-novela-venezolana-actual_18.html (accessed 26 February 2019).
Swanson, Philip. (1995). *The New Novel in Latin America: Politics and Popular Culture after the Boom*. Manchester: Manchester University Press.
Tinker Salas, Miguel. (2009). *The Enduring Legacy: Oil, Culture, and Society in Venezuela*. Durham, NC: Duke University Press.
Tischler, Henry. (2007). *Introduction to Sociology*. 9th ed. Belmont, CA: Wadsworth/Thomson Learning.
Torres, Ana Teresa. (1999). 'Literatura y país: reflexiones sobre sus relaciones', in Karl Kohut (ed.), *Literatura venezolana hoy: historia nacional y presente urbano*. Frankfurt: Verveurt, pp. 55–65.
———. (2006). 'Cuando la literatura venezolana entró en el siglo XXI', in Carlos Pacheco, Luis Barrera Linares and Beatriz González Stephan (eds.), *Nación y literatura: itinerarios de la palabra escrita en la cultura venezolana*. Caracas: Equinoccio/Fundación Bigott, pp. 911–925.
Torres, Ana Teresa and Héctor Torres (eds.) (2006). *De la urbe para el orbe*. Caracas: Alfadil.
———. (2008). *Quince que cuentan*. Caracas: Fundación para la Cultura Urbana.
———. (2010). *Tiempos de ciudad*. Caracas: Fundación para la Cultura Urbana.
Torres, Héctor. (2014). 'Gisela Kozak: Ser feliz es el único oficio que vale la pena', *Ficción Breve*. 15 June. http://ficcionbreve.org/gisela-kozak-ser-feliz-es-el-unico-oficio-que-vale-la-pena/ (accessed 26 February 2019).
———. (2015). Personal communication.
Trelles Paz, Diego. (ed.) (2012). *The Future Is Not Ours*.

Uslar Pietri, Arturo. (1936). 'Sembrar el petróleo'. Originally published in *Ahora*. http://webdelprofesor.ula.ve/economia/ajhurtado/lecturasobligatorias/sembrar%20el%20petroleo.pdf (accessed 26 February 2019).

Uzcátegui, Rafael. (2010). *La revolución como espectáculo: una crítica anarquista al gobierno bolivariano*. Caracas: El Libertario.

Valera Mora, Víctor. (2015). *Amanecí de bala y otros poemas*. Caracas: El perro y la rana.

Valery, Yolanda. (2009a). 'Venezuela: "sobran" y "faltan" libros', *BBC Mundo*. 18 May. https://www.bbc.com/mundo/america_latina/2009/05/090518_1905_venezuela_edicion_jg.shtml (accessed 26 February 2019).

———. (2009b). 'Boliburguesía: nueva clase venezolana', *BBC Mundo*. 2 December. https://www.bbc.com/mundo/economia/2009/12/091202_1045_venezuela_boliburguesia_wbm.shtml (accessed 26 February 2019).

Valladares-Ruiz, Patricia. (2013). 'Desplazamiento y disenso político en la narrativa de Eduardo Sánchez Rugeles', *INTI*, 77/78, 115–136.

Vargas Llosa, Mario. (1967). 'La literatura es fuego'. Acceptance speech for the Rómulo Gallegos Prize. http://www.literaterra.com/mario_vargas_llosa/la_literatura_es_fuego/ (accessed 26 February 2019).

———. (1977). *La tía Julia y el escribidor*. Barcelona: Seix Barral.

———. (2012). *Civilización del espectáculo*. Madrid: Alfaguara.

Vásquez Lezama, Paula. (2014). *Le chavisme: un militarisme compassionnel*. Paris: Maison des sciences de l'homme.

Velásquez, Ronny. (1993). *Mitos de creación de la Cuenca del Orinoco*. Caracas: FUNDEF.

Vidal, Laura. (2010). 'Venezuela: Cierra Fundación para la Cultura Urbana', *Global Voices*. 30 July. https://es.globalvoices.org/2010/07/30/venezuela-cierra-fundacion-para-la-cultura-urbana/ (accessed 26 February 2019).

———. (2012). 'The Authors Behind the Venezuelan Literary Boom', *Global Voices*. 16 October. https://globalvoices.org/2012/10/16/the-authors-behind-the-venezuelan-literary-boom/# (accessed 26 February 2019).

Vilella, Paula. (2010). 'Venezuela, el país de los crímenes sin resolver', *El Mundo*. 3 March. https://www.elmundo.es/america/2010/03/03/noticias/1267626916.html (accessed 26 February 2019).

Volpi, Jorge, Eloy Urroz, Ignacio Padilla, Ricardo Chávez Castañeda and Miguel Ángel Palou. (1996). 'Manifiesto Crack'. https://web.archive.org/web/20060212083118/http://www.lai.at/wissenschaft/lehrgang/semester/ss2005/fs/files/crack.pdf (accessed 26 February 2019).

Volpini, María Anaya. (2011). 'Entrevista a Juan Carlos Méndez', *Culturamas*. 22 November. https://www.culturamas.es/blog/2011/11/22/entrevista-a-juan-carlos-mendez/ (accessed 26 February 2019).

Waugh, Patricia. (1995). 'What Is Metafiction and Why Are They Saying Such Awful Things about It?', in Mark Currie (ed.), *Metafiction*. London: Longman, pp. 39–54.

White, Hayden. (1975). *Metahistory: The Historical Imagination in Nineteenth-Century Europe*. Baltimore, MA: Johns Hopkins University Press.

Widdowson, Peter. (1999). *Literature*. London: Routledge.

Wilkinson, Stephen. (2006). *Detective Fiction in Cuban Society and Culture*. Berne: Peter Lang.
Wisotzki, Rúben. (2006). *El pueblo es la cultura: conversación con Farruco Sesto, Ministro de la Cultura*. Caracas: El perro y la rana.
Worthington, Marjorie. (2017). 'Fiction in the "Post-Truth" Era: The Ironic Effects of Autofiction', *Critique: Studies in Contemporary Fiction*, 58(5), 471–483.
Worton, Michael and Judith Still. (1990). *Intertextuality: Theories and Practices*. Manchester: Manchester University Press.
Zupcic, Slavko. (1989). *Dragi Sol*. Caracas: Fundarte.
——. (2005). *Máquinas que cantan*. Caracas: CONAC.
——. (2006). *Tres novelas*. Mérida: El otro y el mismo.
——. (2012). *Barbie/Círculo croata*. New York: Sudaquia.
——. (2014). *Médicos, taxistas, escritores*. New York: Sudaquia.
——. (2015). Personal communication.

Index

affect 87–89, 92–93, 103
Alfa 18
Alfaguara 17, 29, 32, 76
Anagrama 17, 33, 76
author–narrator 35–36, 43, 71–80, 97, 110, 149, 161
autobiography 40, 72, 84, 93
autofiction 35, 57, 71–79, 149
   definitions of 39–40
Avilez, Maritza
   La segunda oportunidad 51, 131

Balza, José 3, 18, 113, 119, 123, 128
Barrera Tyszka, Alberto 15, 17, 32, 38
   La enfermedad 4, 17
   Rating 25, 32–33, 35–36, 43, 61, 67–69, 81, 93–95, 104, 148, 156, 161–170, 173
belonging 6, 7, 84, 85, 88–89, 95–96, 101, 118–119, 150, 158, 173
Ber, Krina 20
Biblioteca Ayacucho 8, 58
boliburguesia 45, 55, 142
Bolivarian Revolution 1, 5–7, 10–16, 22–26, 43–44, 48–55, 58–60, 61–63, 69–70, 81–84, 88, 90, 95, 104, 105, 111, 118, 127, 130, 135–137, 142, 146–147, 148, 167, 169–170, 171–174
bookshops 19–20, 22
Boom, the 1–3, 9, 23–24, 37, 46–47, 107–108, 124–125, 155, 171, 174

Borges, Jorge Luis 2, 25, 108–109, 152
Bourdieu, Pierre 39, 42, 61, 64–65, 68, 71, 74, 79–80, 110, 125, 161
Bryce Echenique, Alfredo 37, 41, 44, 109–112, 125, 173

Cada día un libro 13, 49–51, 68, 102
Cadenas, Rafael 18, 55, 70
Casanova, Pascale
   closed literary space 83–84, 105, 126
   world literary space 1–4, 58, 79, 105, 109, 124–125
Castañeda, Armando Luigi 34, 39
   La fama, o es venérea, o no es fama 25, 34–35, 43, 61, 71–80, 149, 172
Centeno, Israel 14, 15, 16–17, 23, 26, 28, 57, 62, 70
   Bajo las hojas 25, 28–29, 35, 42–43, 44, 45, 57–60, 127, 132–134, 147, 148, 149, 156, 158–161, 172, 173
   El complot 28, 158
Chávez Frías, Hugo 1, 6, 13–14, 25, 31, 32, 33, 43, 54, 81–82, 84, 111, 116, 129, 136, 142, 146, 159, 160, 163, 166, 171, 172
   Aló, Presidente 129, 167–168
   rhetorical style 156–158
   rise to power 5, 11

Chirinos, Juan Carlos 15, 23, 26, 38, 125
  El niño malo cuenta hasta cien y se retira 25, 26–27, 36, 43, 44, 81, 86–87, 104, 105, 113–120, 123, 127, 144–147, 148, 152–153, 156–158, 173, 174
  Nochebosque 26, 114
Chocrón, Sonia 20
Cioran, Emil 100, 139
comedy 42, 44, 112, 127, 129, 135–139, 147, 173
Consejo Nacional de Cultura (CONAC) 8, 49–50, 58
Cortázar, Julio 108
crime 159
crime fiction 17, 29, 31, 35, 73, 128, 129, 139–142, 150–152
criticgraphic mode 77
Croatia 27–28, 36, 44, 97–99, 120–124
Cuban Revolution 14, 15–16, 46, 52–53, 63–64, 130–131, 169, 174
  Congreso de Educación y Cultura 14, 55
  Palabras a los intelectuales 55, 130
  Portuondo, José Antonio 14, 63, 131
cultural capital 20, 43, 62, 70, 80, 102, 128
cultural policy 1, 6, 11–13, 15–16, 23, 24, 30, 39, 42–44, 45–48, 52–54, 59, 64, 68, 79, 81–82, 105–106, 131, 146, 171–174
currency controls 17, 19n6, 58, 106

de la Cruz, Sor Juana Inés 88
de Stefano, Victoria 20, 25, 70
democracy 9, 62
democratisation of culture 13, 48–50, 130, 172
desarraigo 96–104
detective fiction *see* crime fiction
Díaz Sánchez, Ramón 7, 124
distinction 43, 57, 61–80, 98, 172
Donoso, José 3n1, 23–24, 47, 124
doppelgängers 133–134

Ediciones B 17, 31, 32, 139
Editorial Madera Fina 18
El Estilete 18
El perro y la rana 13, 14, 25, 49–50, 88, 131, 172
emplotment 153, 159
Equinoccio 18, 19, 34
exports 3–4, 58, 106

fan reading 87, 90
fantasy 26, 29, 42, 60, 129, 132–134, 152–153, 159
fathers 96–99
Faulkner, William 41, 44, 120, 124–126, 173
Ficción Breve 20
Fitzgerald, F. Scott 69
Fraile, Dayana 2–3, 19
  ugly duckling syndrome 4, 108, 174
Fuentes, Carlos 2, 37, 47, 50n1, 63, 108, 129
Fundación para la Cultura Urbana 21–22

Gallegos, Rómulo 7, 85, 113n1
García Arreaza, Enza 16
García Márquez, Gabriel 2, 47, 50n1, 56, 62, 108
García París, Lucas 18
Garmendia, Salvador 8–9
global Latin American novel 1–2, 4–6, 171
Gomes, Miguel 18
González León, Adriano 10, 172
gothic 29, 44, 127, 132–134
Guerra, Rubi 1, 18, 25

history 7, 13, 84, 88, 141, 144, 148, 153–155, 158–161

Ibero-American novel Project 124
identity 5, 6, 7, 9, 12, 13, 23–24, 27, 28, 32, 36, 40, 43, 46, 81–84, 87–90, 95–104, 106, 114, 119–120, 130–131, 136, 138, 140–141, 145, 156, 157, 163

indigenous traditions 144–146
Instituto Nacional de Cultura y Bellas Artes (INCIBA) 8, 57–58
intertextuality 37, 105–126, 174
    definitions of 40–42
introspection 3, 10, 71–73, 82, 85, 90–95, 172
invisibility 1, 4, 58
irony 30, 35, 38, 48, 60, 74, 76, 106, 137

Kalathos 19
Kozak Rovero, Gisela 6, 14, 15, 18, 20, 26, 33, 38, 70, 171
    Siete sellos 92
    Todas las lunas 5, 25, 33–34, 36, 43, 61, 66–67, 81, 87–93, 153–154, 173

language 96, 100–101, 103, 119
Law of Culture 11, 83, 106, 129
Léctor Cómplice 18, 41n15
Libros del Fuego 19
literary isolation 14, 43, 105–107
literary markets 2–4, 9, 11, 16–18, 22, 43, 46, 55, 58–59, 61, 65, 69–80, 113, 128, 171–172, 174
literary prizes 4, 20–21
    Premio de la crítica de la novela 20, 31, 32
    Premio Herralde 4, 32
    Rómulo Gallegos Prize 8, 43, 61, 62–63, 111
literary quality 2, 15, 35, 36, 39, 43, 61, 64, 67, 70–71, 74, 80, 102, 111, 128, 171, 173
Lope de Vega 67, 90
Lozada, Carolina 16
Lugar Común 18–19, 30

Maduro, Nicolás 25, 92
magical realism 3, 155
Martínez Bachrich, Roberto 16
mass participation 48, 53, 60, 65, 98, 173
master status 97, 100
Mata, Humberto 25

McKey, Willy 16
Méndez Guédez, Juan Carlos 15, 18, 23, 25, 26, 29–30, 38, 39, 96, 125
    Chulapos Mambo 25, 30, 35, 42, 43, 45–57, 60, 105–112, 127, 132, 135–139, 149, 172–173
    Y recuerda que te espero 18, 29
Meneses, Guillermo 3, 7, 85, 113
Mercerón, Juan 19
metafiction 25, 35–39, 44, 81, 110–111, 148–150, 153–156, 160–161, 170, 174
migration 22–23, 88–89, 95–96, 103–104, 133, 143, 171, 173
    second-generation immigrants 96, 100, 173
Ministry of Popular Power for Culture 11–12, 49–50, 83, 172
Misión Cultura 6, 25, 84
Monte Ávila Editores 8, 19, 43, 58, 61–62, 70, 128
Montejo, Eugenio 18, 27, 36, 41, 44, 105, 113–120, 123, 126, 173
Morenza, Mario 18

nationalism 5–6, 10, 12–13, 17, 43, 81–85, 95, 100, 104, 118, 131, 136, 172–173
    nation-building literature 7, 82
new novel, the 42, 128–129, 147

objectivity 72–73
Olivar, Norberto José 25
oral text *see* storytelling
Oropeza, José Napoleón 20
Oscar Todtmann Editores 18

Palacio, Andrés Mariño 7, 85
Pasajes de ida 30, 117, 118
Payares, Gabriel 16, 21
Pérez Jímenez dictatorship (1948–1958) 7–10, 38, 43, 81, 85, 95, 113n1, 170, 173
Pino, Camilo 18
Platform for Books and Reading 12, 41, 43, 52, 81, 83–84, 101, 104, 131, 172

Pocaterra, José Rafael 64–65
polarisation 10, 13–14, 43, 44, 56–57, 61, 66, 129, 132, 155, 172
politically committed literature 8–10, 14, 15
popular culture 5, 6, 7, 44, 127–147
populism 8, 13, 28, 48, 82, 166
post-national Latin American literature *see* global Latin American literature
Prasel, Salvador 28, 36, 41, 44, 97, 99, 105, 120–126, 173
  Máxima culpa 121–122
Prodavinci 20, 33
Punto Fijo period (1958–1998) 8–12, 15, 18, 38, 57–58, 61–63, 82–83, 85, 95, 104, 113, 127–128, 130, 135, 136, 147, 171–172
Puntocero 18

Ramos Sucre, José Antonio 4, 25
Revolutionary Plan for Reading 13, 22, 79, 84, 155
Rodríguez, Renato 3, 10, 85, 113, 115, 172
  Al sur del Equanil 38, 95
Romania 31–32, 64, 97, 100, 102–103, 139–142, 141, 154–155

Sánchez Rugeles, Eduardo 16, 17, 20, 26, 30–31, 38, 39, 84
  Blue Label/Etiqueta Azul 30–31
  Jezabel 31, 139
  Transilvania unplugged 5, 25, 31–32, 36, 43, 44, 61, 64–66, 81, 95–97, 100–104, 127, 139–144, 147, 150–152, 154–155, 173
Santaella, Fedosy 17, 20
Schulberg, Budd 69
Sesto, Francisco 8, 9–10, 11, 12, 14, 16, 24, 26, 48, 55, 63, 69–70, 83, 129–130, 148, 171
socialism 12–13, 15, 22, 41, 44, 49, 53, 61, 84, 131, 150, 156, 168, 172–173
  Partido Socialista Unido de Venezuela (PSUV) 55, 136

socialist realism 63, 131
  twenty-first-century socialism 140–142
Spain 26, 27, 29, 34, 35, 76, 79, 114, 117, 119
storytelling 6, 15, 27, 36, 84, 116, 129, 132
  oral storytelling 142, 144–145, 156–158
subjective turn 43, 81, 85, 173
Sudaqía Editores 23, 28, 34, 35
Suniaga, Francisco 17, 18
Surrealism 10, 36, 86, 146

telenovelas 6, 32–33, 68, 94, 103, 156, 161–165, 169
Terán, Ana Enriqueta 113–114
Torres, Ana Teresa 14, 15, 16, 18, 20, 21, 70
Torres, Héctor 17, 18, 20, 21
translation 1–4, 47, 171, 174
travel 29, 86, 100–104, 118, 139, 173

Uslar Pietri, Arturo 7, 31, 63, 124, 66

Valera Mora, Víctor 87–88
Valle, Gustavo 20, 96
vampires 25, 133–134, 154
Vargas Llosa, Mario 2, 14, 24, 37, 41, 44, 47, 62, 108, 109, 111–112, 128–129, 173
Vegas, Federico 18

websites 20
writer–critic 38–39, 43, 61, 80, 173
writing workshops 13, 52–53, 60, 97–98

Ye'kuana 145

Zupcic, Slavko 15, 27, 58
  Círculo croata 25, 27–28, 36, 43, 44, 81, 95–99, 104, 105, 120–126, 173
  Dragi Sol 27, 36
  Máquinas que cantan 36, 120–121